Making Decisions about Children

Understanding Children's Worlds

General Editor Judy Dunn

The study of children's development can have a profound influence on how children are brought up, cared for and educated. The central aim of this series is to encourage developmental psychologists to set out the findings and the implications of their research for others – teachers, doctors, social workers, students – who are responsible for caring for and teaching children and their families. It aims not to offer simple prescriptive advice to other professionals, but to make important innovative research accessible to them.

How Children Think and Learn
David Wood

Children and Emotion
Paul L. Harris

Making Decisions about Children
Psychological Questions and Answers
H. Rudolph Schaffer

Making Decisions about Children

Psychological Questions and Answers

H. Rudolph Schaffer

Basil Blackwell

First published 1990

Basil Blackwell Ltd
108 Cowley Road, Oxford, OX4 1JF, UK

Basil Blackwell, Inc.
3 Cambridge Center
Cambridge, Massachusetts 02142, USA

British Library Cataloguing in Publication Data

A CIP catalogue record for this book is available from the British Library.

Library of Congress Cataloging in Publication Data

Schaffer, H. Rudolph.
   Making decisions about children: psychological questions and answers/H. Rudolph Schaffer.
     p.   cm – (Understanding children's worlds)
   Includes bibliographical references.
   ISBN 0–631–17166–5 ISBN 0–631–17167–3 (pbk.)
   1. Child development. 2. Child development – Research. 3. Child psychology. I. Title. II. Series.
HQ767. 9. N295 1990
305.23′1–dc20   89-29753
                                                     CIP

Typeset in 10½ on 12 pt Sabon
by Graphicraft Typesetters Ltd., Hong Kong
Printed in Great Britain by
T.J. Press Ltd, Padstow, Cornwall

Contents

Series editor's preface

Decisions about how children's interests in matters of custody, adoption, fostering can best be served, or about when to intervene in troubled families are taken daily by social workers, lawyers, doctors and nurses. The questions at the heart of the difficult choices that they have to make – practical decisions that may have enormous impact on children's lives – are issues on which a great deal of developmental research effort is expended. But how can busy practitioners possibly keep informed about the nature and quality of the knowledge gained from such research? What *have* we learnt in recent years about the significance of children's early social experiences, about the impact of divorce, separation or adoption? Should children in divorce cases be in the custody of mothers rather than fathers? Do women make better parents than men? If mothers go to work does it harm their children? Should we avoid group care for babies? Does it matter more if babies are separated from their mothers in the early rather than later months of their lives? What weight should we put on the results of the research? Where the findings conflict, whom should we believe?

The gap between research findings and the information that is available to practitioners is striking in many domains, but nowhere more poignant than in matters concerning children's lives and happiness. The bridge that Rudolph Schaffer's book provides between research and practice is of great importance, and its timeliness in this period of changing family lives is striking. Each of the issues that he examines has clear significance for those taking decisions about children, and on many of these widely divergent opinions are firmly held (in some cases not only by the public but by the researchers too). Rudolph Schaffer provides a judicious account of the background of research on each topic, guiding us through complex, tangled issues with clarity, and also gives us sample studies from which readers can gain a vivid sense of both the revelations and the limitations of the research. Throughout the book he shows us how important it is to be aware of our assumptions and preconceptions about children's development, and to understand how these are influencing children's lives. That the recent research on young children's social and emotional development can and should alter many of these preconceptions is clear from the evidence he presents within a framework of balanced and perceptive commentary. To clarify the implications of developmental research for children's lives, as this volume does, is a central aim of the series *Understanding Children's Worlds* in which it appears.

Judy Dunn

Preface

The idea for this book came to me during a court case. I had been asked to appear as a professional witness in a dispute involving a 10-month-old girl, who had been born to an unmarried mother and fostered within the first few days by a childless couple. That couple now wanted to adopt the girl; the biological mother, however, had changed her mind and asked for the child's return. A judge had been given the task of settling the dispute.

The case brought up a number of issues. Is there such a thing as a blood bond? Can a child's relationship with a non-biological parent ever be as 'natural' as with the biological parent? When do children first form attachments to people? Is there a safe period in infancy when a child can still be moved from one person to another without harm? What are the effects on a young child of severing an established relationship, and are there long-term consequences of such an experience? There is now a considerable literature available that is relevant to these questions, and what impressed me were the valiant efforts made by the lawyers representing the two parties to master that work – indeed, they were surrounded by academic journals, textbooks, reprints and monographs which they had waded through in order to find some definitive answers. The fact that some of that work was old and now outdated, its conclusions contradicted by more recent, methodologically sounder research to which the lawyer happened not to have access, brought home to me the difficulty professional people have in arriving at decisions about children based on up-to-date knowledge – knowledge about child development which may be highly relevant to the particular case and useful in deciding between alternative courses. A brief statement about what we know with respect to some of the questions that arise in making decisions about children was clearly needed – hence the idea to write this book.

The book attempts to bridge the gap between research and practice. It is addressed to those practitioners who find themselves with the responsibility of weighing up alternative courses of action as they affect young children and their families – practitioners such as social workers, lawyers, paediatricians, nurses, psychiatrists and anyone else wanting access to an information base provided by research in order to use such information to derive guidelines for action. Quite a lot of potentially useful knowledge has gradually been accumulating over the last few decades, and though there are still great gaps, enough is now known to bring the most relevant aspects together and make them more accessible to professional workers.

Thus, the intention of the book is to present the current state of knowledge with respect to a number of specific issues that are of concern to those charged with making decisions about children. We shall focus primarily on issues involving children's social development in the early years: the role of parents, the nature of primary bonds, the function of the family, the effects of maternal employment and of divorce, children's vulnerability in the face of stress, the long-term significance of early behaviour problems, and so forth. Not that this is the only area where psychological research can inform practice: one can, for example, envisage a similar exercise with regard to intellectual development in childhood. However, that would appeal to a rather different readership (a mainly educationally oriented one), whereas here our interest lies in the young child in the family and in the factors to be taken into account when considering such questions as custody, fostering and adoption, removal from home, shared care, group care, early intervention and the implications of such experiences as family discord and separation.

The aim is therefore to apply the results of research on psychological development during the early years to problems and practical issues concerning young children and their families. We shall do so by, first, considering the relationship of research to practice – a relationship that is unfortunately only too often misunderstood by both research workers and practitioners. In particular, if the intention is to help practitioners to make use of research it is essential that they appreciate the nature of this enterprise and know something of both its advantages and its limitations. In the main body of the book we shall then discuss a number of specific issues and consider them in the light of evidence obtained from a variety of investigations. Summaries of relevant studies are provided, together with some comments on research in this area generally and also on the implications for practice which emerge from the findings obtained. Finally, we shall look at some of the general themes and conclusions that have emerged from the knowledge now accumulated and consider what they tell us about the nature of human development.

Part 1

On using research

Increasingly, professional people from many different disciplines are required to make decisions about children. The line that separates the responsibility of parents for their children's upbringing from that of agencies outside the family has for a long time gradually been shifting. Decisions that were once made entirely within the family are more and more being made by others – decisions about children's welfare, their health, their education, their moral training, even (under certain circumstances) where they are to live and who their caretakers are to be. Consider that much discussed topic, child abuse – a phenomenon probably as old as the family itself and just as prevalent in previous centuries as now, if not more so (de Mause, 1974). What is different now is the extent to which society is prepared to step in and take responsibility for what was previously considered to be purely a family matter. In ancient Rome, for instance, children were deemed to be the property of the father, to do with as he wished, and if it were his wish to abuse and injure his children it was no one's business but his own. This situation prevails no more; the fate of children is no longer exclusively in the hands of their parents; society feels responsible for children's welfare and is prepared to intervene in family affairs if that welfare appears to be seriously threatened.

How far the shift from parental responsibility to community responsibility should proceed is a matter of much debate but not one that will be pursued here. Our concern is with what has happened, not with what ought to happen. Accordingly we need to recognize that a great many professional people – lawyers, doctors, social workers and others – are nowadays called upon, to a considerable

and apparently increasing extent, to make decisions about children –
decisions such as the child's removal from home, the allocation of
custodial rights to one parent rather than the other, the child's
placement for adoption or fostering, the choice of particular child-
rearing practices and settings, and so forth. For the children and
families concerned such decisions may well have vast implications;
for the decision-makers the responsibility can be awesome.

Sources of decision-making

When one examines individual incidents of decision-making and
attempts to unravel the factors responsible for the course of action
adopted, it soon becomes evident that we are confronted with a
highly complex, frequently obscure and far from rational process. It
may be comforting to think of it as a thoughtful, deliberate, intellectually guided exercise, in which our general knowledge of human
nature is systematically applied to the specific needs and characteristics of the individual case. In fact, the influences shaping particular
decisions are by no means always rational or even within conscious
awareness. They include, for instance, the prevailing moral climate
and whatever values, stereotypes and dogmas that climate has given
rise to, the psychological characteristics of the decision-makers and
their own personal history, various political and ideological considerations, administrative and financial pressures, and so forth. Such
influences constitute a set of assumptions that determine the course
of action taken, yet they may not be overtly acknowledged and so
do not enable one to make explicit the actual reasons for that
decision.

Take as an example the often very difficult question of custody
awards in divorce cases. Until quite recently it was automatically
assumed that an adulterous parent was unfit to have responsibility
for children, that such an individual was likely to have an undesirable influence by virtue of his or her amoral behaviour and that it
was therefore in the child's best interests not to be brought up by
such a person. Custody decisions were thus often made on the basis
of parental adultery – irrespective of the child's actual relationships
with the parents, these being brushed aside in the face of unques-
tioned moral assumptions about the 'right' environment for children. This situation no longer prevails; our attitudes to adultery
have changed and we do not now judge parental competence by

marital fidelity. Yet there are other firmly entrenched beliefs that continue to have an equally powerful influence on action taken, even though they may be just as irrational and lacking in evidence – beliefs such as that the mother is the 'natural' parent in some sense that the father is not, and that she would normally be the fitter person to care for the children. Once again empirical knowledge about the nature of parenting plays little part in arriving at a decision; instead, various preconceptions are used as guidelines, overriding the requirements of particular cases.

Sometimes the course taken is defended as a matter of 'common sense', suggesting thereby that every right-minded person is bound to subscribe to the conclusions reached. However, common sense as a guide to action needs to be treated with caution: too often it turns out to be a vague and fallible instrument, no more than a cloak for personal opinion or dogma – a global, unanalysable gut feeling difficult to challenge and reason with because propositions are defended simply as 'self-evident'. The bringing up of children in particular is frequently asserted to be nothing but common sense, yet utterly different practices and mutually contradictory philosophies of child rearing are all passed off in this way. This is evident not only in the contrasting convictions that different individuals possess as to what is right and what is wrong for children; it is also seen in the considerable variations that exist in this respect from one period of time to another (Hardyment, 1983; Kessen, 1965). That there are fashions in rearing methods is very evident – fashions in whether permissiveness or strictness is emphasized, whether the mothers of young children should be urged to stay at home or go out to work, whether it is right under certain circumstances to remove children from home or whether they should be kept with their own parents at all costs, whether fathers can be regarded as equally competent in child care as mothers, and so on. Each position has had its defendants; so often, however, the debate between them has been conducted simply by means of bald assertion. Appeals to empirical evidence, especially that derived from scientifically conducted research, do not figure in such discussions.

Let us make a distinction between opinion and research as sources of knowledge about the nature and conditions of human development. In one case conclusions are arrived at primarily on the basis of subjective factors (personal experience, beliefs, assumptions and preconceptions); in the other they derive from objectively carried out procedures, systematically executed and publicly available. Such a distinction is especially worth bearing in mind when evaluating the advice of 'experts' – authority figures who, in the manner of Dr Spock, may exercise an enormous influence on the practices of parents and professional workers alike. To some extent we are, of course, all bound to rely on authority figures, and their role is an honoured and well established one. What is essential, however, is that we do not simply take for granted their wisdom but examine closely the sources of their knowledge. Only too often it will then become clear that their pronouncements are derived from no firmer a base than a mixture of personal opinion, guesswork, folklore, work with clinical cases and the experience of rearing their own children. No doubt the resulting advice can sometimes be shrewd and helpful; there is also no doubt that at times it verges on the fantastic. To advocate, for instance, that parents should be prevented by law from administering physical punishment to their children as in this way we shall be able to stamp out child abuse, and merely to assert, without producing any empirical evidence at all, that the connection between abuse and punishment is self-evident (Freeman, 1988), is of no use whatsoever to those attempting to tackle this problem. Action on behalf of children requires a firmer foundation.

Nor is it of use merely to proclaim that one must adopt whatever courses are 'in the best interests of the child'. This has become one of the most unhelpful and abused phrases resorted to in order to justify all kinds of decision-making (Goldstein et al., 1973). On the one hand everyone is bound to agree with it; on the other hand it is utterly vague in that it begs the question of what actually is the child's best interests. Should parents stay together despite conflict or is it better for them to separate? Must mothers stay at home or can they go out to work? Is it preferable for a child to be looked after in an affectionate but conventional household or in a less warm but traditional family setting? Each alternative has been defended as being in the child's best interest – more often than not, however, simply on the basis of dogma and opinion.

What is required in all these instances is a much more painstaking analysis, based on empirical examination and the use of procedures that exclude as far as possible preconception and prejudice. Whatever our private inclinations may be about issues such as divorce, working mothers and corporal punishment, in our professional capacity we need to be aware of the pitfalls of making decisions merely on that basis. More convincing and reliable guides to action are available from the ever-increasing body of knowledge derived from research about children and their families.

The nature of research

Objective enquiry into the facts of child development and family life has only quite recently come to be recognized as a legitimate source of information for practitioners. To be of use to them, however, it is essential to know not only *what* findings have been obtained but also *how* these findings have been obtained. Some account, that is, must be given of the nature of the research enterprise so that its limitations as well as its advantages can be appreciated.

Let us start with the advantages. These derive from the fact that the research process can be described as being empirical, systematic, controlled, quantitative and public. To expand on each of these characteristics:

1 *Empirical.* Conclusions are based on direct observation of the relevant phenomena; they are not derived from hunch, armchair theorizing or the mere assumption that they are self-evident but from verifiable experience available to all.

2 *Systematic.* The data are collected according to an explicit plan (the research design) which spells out all phases and aspects of the investigation. The plan is rigidly adhered to by all the investigators involved in the study, so that methods of obtaining the required information do not depend on private whim and inclination.

3 *Controlled.* The research is designed in such a way as to enable one to rule out all possible explanations for the findings but one. This may involve adopting a number of special measures, such as double-blind procedures which eliminate the influence of expectations on the part of both subjects and investigators, and the use of control groups whereby individuals exposed to a particular condition (say parental divorce, hospitalization or day care) are compared with other individuals not undergoing that condition but as similar as possible in all other respects.

4 *Quantitative.* However useful data of a descriptive nature may be for many purposes, quantification represents an essential part of most research. In the social sciences our ability to present findings in numerical form may still be limited; nevertheless,

quantifying data means that we can, *inter alia*, make statistical comparison between groups or conditions and so decide with a measure of confidence that they are indeed different, i.e. that one is 'better' or more effective according to some stated criterion than the other.

5   *Public*. All aspects of a research study, its methods as well as its findings, need to be made available to the scrutiny of others. In this way the work can be critically assessed and subsequently replicated by other investigators. If there is failure to obtain the same results the published descriptions of the conduct of the research should then make it possible to find out the reasons for the divergence.

It is features such as these that justify one in characterizing the research process as 'objective' (for more detailed discussions see Grosof and Sardy, 1985; Kerlinger, 1986). Implied thereby is the notion that all investigators of a particular problem using the same research procedures will obtain identical results, and that these are not influenced by any values, beliefs and assumptions held by these individuals. The contrast with 'subjective' procedures such as hunches, guesses and intuition as means of arriving at conclusions is largely a matter of the checks which are built into any properly designed research project but which are missing from subjective procedures. In addition the latter also lack the explicitness and detail that research workers use in spelling out the means which they employ for arriving at particular conclusions. Of course, hunches, guesses and intuition do have an important role in research, and especially so in the early stages of attempting to investigate some phenomenon; at that point 'following one's nose' and 'getting a feel for' the topic may well be justified and indeed essential. Such measures, however, are only precursors; in due course they must lead up to formalized research characterized by the features listed above, which together make it possible to trace the sources of any conclusions reached and, if need be, challenge those conclusions.

Let us now acknowledge, however, that this account presents an idealized picture of research. We shall list some of the limitations of the research process below; here we should first remind ourselves that there is clearly both good and bad research – not everything that finds its way into print is credible. This is, of course, what makes it so important that a full account is available of the way in which each study was conducted, so that one can then assess such aspects as the representativeness of the sample, the adequacy of the instruments used to collect the data, the appropriateness of the procedures employed in analysing the findings and the fit between results and conclusions. In so far as there is no such thing as a perfect study, replication is always desirable, and though it may be an exaggeration to state that no single study can be believed until it has been borne out by other investigators, it has to be acknowledged that work which has not yet been replicated forms a relatively risky base for action.

This makes research a slow affair – frustrating perhaps to practitioners wanting quick answers to immediate problems, but under the circumstances inevitable. Research is intrinsically a slow process, in the social sciences at least, for each study can take only a small bite off the overall problem. To enquire into the effects of maternal employment, for example, is to tackle a topic far too wide-ranging for any one study, for so much depends on a great range of conditions: the age of the child, the length of the mother's daily absence from home, the child's previous experience of out-of-home care, the nature of the substitute care provided, and so on. Indeed, in the course of investigating particular problems it only too often becomes clear that the results are affected by influences that one had not previously taken into account (as happened in the case of maternal employment with respect to factors such as the mother's satisfaction with her role, her motive for working and the child's sex) – influences that may not have been allowed for in the research design and that subsequent studies will therefore need to investigate. In any case, each study is always constrained by the particular methods that have been chosen for its execution – a vital point to bear in mind, for the results obtained are not merely a function of what is 'out there' but also of the nature of the tools used to obtain those results. Two studies investigating the same topic, one using self-report questionnaires and the other observational techniques, may come up with contradictory findings which reflect the influence of each of these methods of data gathering. No wonder the history of research is littered with examples of non-replicated findings!

One other constraint must also be acknowledged. Research findings are specific to particular places and particular times, and what applies to one locality or to one period may not apply to another. Conclusions from work carried out in California are not necessarily valid in Scotland; a study done in the 1930s may not longer be relevant to conditions prevailing 50 years later. Naturally, any one investigation will provide pointers and suggestions, but its conclusions may have to be modified in the light of local and current conditions. This is particularly important because we need to acknowledge that every piece of research takes place in a particular ideological, moral and political context that can influence the results obtained in highly subtle yet all-pervasive ways. Take, for example, the effect of parental divorce on children. The early work on this topic was done at a time when there was still widespread social disapproval of divorce, and as a result there was a general expectation that experiencing such an event is bound to lead to harmful consequences for children. Under these circumstances it is hardly surprising that research workers looked for nothing but pathology and that their inventories and questionnaires were constructed to include only symptoms such as anxiety, aggression, disruption in sex-role development and regressive behaviour. The possibility that there might also be positive consequences was not considered. Only now, at a time when in many countries divorce has become so much more common and acceptable, are investigators willing to concede that, whatever pathological consequences there may be, the occurrence of positive effects (increased tolerance for stress, greater independence, and so forth) should also be allowed for and that studies should be designed accordingly.

Thus, research is by no means immune from value judgements: it has to be conceded that its objectivity is in fact only relative. Take, for example, the kinds of problems that research workers select for investigation. This is not a matter of following some orderly progression designed to map out in a logical manner the course of human nature; instead, research frequently shows a bandwagon effect, in that particular topics become fashionable and are then explored in enormous detail to the neglect of other, perhaps more pressing, problems. In social-science research these fluctuations often reflect highly subjective beliefs about what constitutes human nature and what it is that society ought to be concerned with at that time (it has been said, not altogether light-heartedly, that if Freud were alive today he would be writing about money, not sex). Even the choice of methods used to obtain data is subject to fashion and cannot always be accounted for by rational considerations. Thus, whether to put the emphasis on 'hard', scientific methods used under highly controlled, laboratory-like conditions or whether to rely primarily on tools yielding more qualitative, 'softer' data is a choice often depending less on the intrinsic merits of these approaches and more on the materialistic as opposed to humanistic conception of human nature prevalent at the time and held by individual investigators.

Some limitations

It may be tempting simply to extol the virtues of research and say no more, but if one were to leave it at that practitioners and other potential consumers would have unrealistic expectations and come away disillusioned. We have already seen that research is not as totally objective as ideally one might like it to be: in addition, however, there are other, more specific, limitations.

For one thing, there will always be some questions that cannot be answered by research. Take a question such as 'Is it better to have a bad mother or no mother at all?' Even if one could agree on how to define 'bad' and even if one could assemble two otherwise comparable samples to represent the alternatives, the research worker can only gather the facts as they pertain to the outcome of the two conditions. What he or she cannot do is to pass judgement on what is 'better', that being a matter of values which society as a whole needs to determine. As another example, take the question 'Should adopted children know the identity of their biological parents?' Research can provide answers to problems such as the effect of knowing as opposed to not knowing; similarly, it can assemble data about the wishes of children, biological parents and adoptive parents in this matter. However, whether children have a 'right' to know is a moral issue which society rather than the research community needs to resolve.

There are other questions which, though legitimate issues for research, cannot be answered because as yet we do not have adequate methodological tools to tackle them. In general, finding valid and acceptable techniques for assessing human beings has proved to be an extraordinarily difficult task for social scientists. Thus, research on emotional aspects of behaviour has for long been held back because of the apparently elusive nature of these phenomena, making it difficult to capture let alone quantify them. Even in the area of intelligence, after a burst of enthusiasm for the use of IQ tests extending over several decades, disillusionment has set in as the limitations of such tests have become increasingly apparent. Under these circumstances investigators perforce often rely on such assessment techniques as rating scales or questionnaires that may sometimes be rather crude but that at least make it possible to continue to describe and analyse the phenomena of interest. Yet the very variety of techniques available for assessing any one aspect of human behaviour brings its own problems: as we have already seen, different investigators may come up with different results because they have employed different methodological tools. This is a common story: for example, the controversy about the effects of lead pollution on children's intelligence has turned to a considerable extent on how these effects are measured, i.e. by using either blood or hair or teeth for analysis – different techniques that can provide sharply contrasting conclusions (Harvey, 1984). To take another example: the effects of day care on children's social competence in peer relationships can be assessed either by direct observation of the children or by administering questionnaires to their teachers (or to their parents) or by asking the teachers (or the parents) to make global judgements on rating scales. Each method adds its own distinctive flavour to the results obtained; consequently studies that play safe by using a multi-method approach, whereby the same phenomena are examined by means of several assessment techniques, have a distinct advantage over studies relying on only a single method.

There are still other methodological problems (see Wald, 1976 for a more detailed discussion of practice-relevant research): the difficulty in obtaining large and representative samples, the problems of time and expense in following up children for sufficiently lengthy periods to determine long-term effects, the loss of subjects because the family moves away or no longer wishes to co-operate, and the fact that in real life one cannot randomly assign people to 'treatment' and 'control' conditions. Take the last point: in a comparison of employed with non-employed mothers an investigator might find, say, that the mother–child relationship differs between the two groups, and it is then tempting to conclude that maternal employment is responsible for the difference. However, it may be that the difference existed beforehand, in that certain kinds of women choose to work outside the home and their relationship with the child would therefore be different anyway, irrespective of their absence during the day. If one could randomly assign women to employment and non-employment groups this problem would not arise; but as this is, of course, not possible, one needs to bear in mind the possibility of such pre-existing influences and be duly cautious in interpreting the results of any study that did not properly make allowance for this factor.

These considerations ought not to detract from the ultimate value of research as a means of generating useful knowledge. In comparison with the standards of the physical sciences, work in the social sciences may sometimes appear downright 'messy', yet the limitations we have talked about do not imply that we should decry the role of such work. On the contrary, we need a great deal more research in order progressively to refine our techniques and do justice to the multiple influences that determine human development. The advantages which we have spelled out still apply, though they are less absolute than is sometimes suggested. Subjective and objective approaches, we have to conclude, are not wholly distinct; they differ in degree, and in evaluating any specific research contribution the personal, social and practical context in which the study was carried out ought therefore to be borne in mind.

Research as an ongoing process

There is, of course, no such thing as a wholly definitive study – one that will stand for good and will present conclusions that need never be revised. Research is a matter of continuous updating – not merely in terms of adding completely new bodies of knowledge but also in terms of progressively refining existing knowledge. In asking, for instance, whether young children's separation from their parents brings about adverse psychological consequences, one might initially expect research to produce a clear cut 'yes' or 'no' to that question. It gradually becomes apparent, however, that this would grossly over-simplify matters, in that such an experience is defined by all sorts of conditions, each one of which may differ considerably from one case to the next and affect the outcome accordingly. Further research must therefore be mounted in order to pin-point these influences: the child's age, the circumstances responsible for the child's removal from home, the nature of the child's relationships with the parents, the type of care experienced during the separation period, the length of that period, and so forth. In due course it also becomes apparent that identical experiences can affect children differently, for example some children are more vulnerable than others, and also the nature of symptoms shown may vary from one individual to another. It then becomes necessary to carry out further work to track down the sources of such variability. In addition, it may emerge that whatever pathology is to be found affects some psychological functions but not others (for example, socio-emotional behaviour but not intellectual behaviour), so that further work is required that will use means of assessment appropriately sensitive to these differences. Finally, one cannot assume that these effects will last for ever: the immediate consequences of the experience become absorbed into the course of subsequent life events, to be transformed, minimized or exaggerated. Still further research will then be called for to do justice to these later developments. It is hardly surprising, therefore, that it takes so long for research to assemble a reasonably thorough body of knowledge about any one particular topic.

Almost inevitably, early studies tend to be cruder and less refined than studies that can build on an established tradition of work in that area. An example is to be seen in the trend from 'clinical' to 'systematic' research. Thus, several of the topics that we shall discuss later began life in a clinical context: children, that is, who have been adversely affected by some past experience subsequently seek help for their condition, and clinicians, after treating a number of such children, may then propose a cause-and-effect sequence between that experiences and the presenting pathology. As a means of generating hypotheses about the potential harm of certain experiences, clinical work can be most useful, but its drawback is that only those children who have been adversely affected come to notice, so that one has no knowledge of those left unscathed or affected only in the short term. More systematic work is therefore required to investigate *all* children who had undergone the experience; only by selecting children on the basis of that experience and not on the basis of their subsequent pathology can one make confident statements about causation. Initially, such more systematic work is often done by adopting a restrospective approach, i.e. by tracing a representative sample of all those who had undergone the relevant experience at some earlier stage and then assessing their psychological condition in order to make statements about outcome. Inevitably, however, there will be variations in that outcome: some children will be more affected than others, some perhaps not at all. If one then wants to explain these variations in terms of the impact of the experience at the time (its length, its severity, the child's immediate reaction to it, and so forth), one requires more reliable data than can be obtained from personal recollection or old records. Hence, longitudinal studies of a *prospective* nature, that observe children undergoing the experience and then follow them up thereafter, are very much superior to retrospective, let alone clinical, studies in their ability to trace the path from onset to outcome. Unfortunately, such longitudinal research, because of its time-consuming nature, is relatively rare; the value of this approach as a source of credible information is, however, considerable.

Dissemination and implementation

To have research findings available is one thing; to see them have an impact on practice is another. This is a general problem: much thought has, for instance, been given to ways in which industry can effectively be served by research in scientific and technological fields and to the mechanisms that need to be developed for the prompt delivery of potentially useful laboratory findings to practical industrial settings. In the social science area the gap between research and practice is probably much wider than anywhere else, so that only too often decisions about particular individuals or client groups – the handicapped, the aged, offenders, children, and so on – are taken in disregard (or, more likely, ignorance) of much useful information that is available. Why the gap exists and how to span it are matters of considerable concern.

One problem concerns dissemination – how best to communicate the results of research to the relevant groups of consumers. The difficulty here is a well known one: research is generally done by academics who are accustomed to (and rewarded for) communicating their work to fellow academics rather than to practitioners. This may be appropriate for research of a pure or theoretical nature where the target audience is solely composed of members of the same discipline. Unfortunately, research that has applicability to practice is often also handled in just the same way, the assumption being that if it is in print it is available to all, and if practitioners do not know about it, it is their fault for not reading widely enough. How to establish lines of communication between research workers and practitioners whereby findings can be conveyed promptly and meaningfully is a complex issue for which there is no one simple answer and which needs to be kept under constant review.

It would, however, be a mistake to think that dissemination is the only or even the major difficulty. The gap between research workers and practitioners is to a large extent due to a variety of factors that together spell out differences in the way in which these two groups function in their working lives – in their mode of operation, in the requirements that they must meet and in the pressures to which they are subjected. If the gap is to be bridged and mutual understanding achieved we need to be aware of these factors. Let us consider the more important ones.

In the first place, the two groups have different aims: research workers are generally concerned with the advancement of knowledge as such; practitioners set out to provide help and to solve problems of everyday life. The former deal with generalities and abstractions, the latter with particular instances and individual cases. What is more, the two mostly work in different settings: in universities and other academic institutions on the one hand and in various field settings on the other. It is not surprising, therefore, that mutual misunderstanding and ignorance can occur under these circumstances. In the industrial field large firms are able to deal with this difficulty by employing their own research staff – scientists who work on particular applied problems for which their employers need a solution but who at the same time are aware of the general developments that are taking place in their speciality and can make use of these to enrich their own work. This situation rarely exists with respect to social scientists who can therefore so easily get drawn into work that appears arid and meaningless to practitioners. Exchange schemes, whereby academics are seconded to field settings and practitioners to research groups, might be one way of dealing with this problem, as would research strategies that involve practitioners in the formulation and planning of investigations as well as in their subsequent execution and evaluation.

In the second place, those working in academic settings often fail to appreciate that in arriving at a decision, professional workers, even when they do have research derived knowledge available, must generally take many other considerations into account as well. The finding that course A is more effective in promoting some desirable result than course B at an acceptable level of statistical significance may seem such a blinding truth to academics that they will expect everyone immediately to drop B in order to adopt A. In real life this does not happen: financial, political, ideological and organizational factors also play a part in determining the choice of alternative courses. Thus, when resources are scarce, there is a general assumption that 'if it is cheaper it is better', and politicians, administrators and the general public alike will not be easily persuaded that this consideration should not be given overriding priority. The influence of ideologies is even more pervasive, as seen, for example, in contrasting ideas about the nature and role of the family – with implications for decisions about keeping children who are at risk with their parents as opposed to admitting them into public care. Thus, whatever knowledge may be available about the effectiveness of particular courses will only too often be ignored in favour of other considerations – an outcome that may bewilder and disillusion academics with their belief in rationality but which reflects the fact that intellectual knowledge can frequently be only one guide to action among several, and not necessarily the most influential at that. The acceptance of particular research results is therefore very much dependent on the prevailing political and ideological climate: the same findings may fall on deaf ears at one time but be enthusiastically accepted at another.

There is, of course, no reason why research workers, on the basis of their findings, should not help to bring about changes in the climate. When they do so, however, they may well encounter yet another source of frustration – namely, the sheer inertia of the system. There is, in other words, dislike of change just because it is change. One saw this, for instance, in the fierce resistance, put up by many paediatricians and nursing staff in the 1950s and 1960s, to the idea that young children separated from their mothers are (at least in the short term) emotionally harmed thereby and that children's hospitals should therefore amend their practices by permitting unlimited access to parents. To research workers the evidence seemed wholly convincing and the implications for action obvious; for hospital staff, on the other hand, such action involved the adoption of some markedly different working practices and (especially for nurses) some radical changes in their role *vis-à-vis* their patients. Thus, not surprisingly it took a very long time to implement the recommendations of research workers and open up children's hospitals to parents. Any threat to status, role or practice of staff will almost inevitably encounter opposition and the evidence from research will accordingly be denied or explained away.

There is another set of factors placing obstacles to mutual understanding of research workers and practitioners which stem from the nature of research itself. Practitioners generally want straightforward answers: yes or no, good or bad. Research rarely provides such answers. Instead, its conclusions are (or at any rate ought to be) full of constraints, hedged in by conditions and caveats and marked by a reluctance to indulge in unjustified generalizations.

From a research point of view this is right and proper: the findings of any one study are, as we have already emphasized, specific to time and place and a function of the particular methods employed and the particular sample investigated. In addition, research findings almost invariably show that the effects on children of particular experiences (such as removal from home, mother going out to work, parental divorce, and so on) depend on multitude of factors surrounding that experience, making sweeping generalizations impossible. As a result conclusions are generally of the 'it all depends' rather than of the 'good or bad' variety. To the practitioner (and perhaps even more so to the average man or woman) this may sound like an infuriating refusal to commit onself; to the research worker it is an essential caution that does justice to the complexities of life events.

Another matter to consider is the different time scale on which the two sets of individuals operate. Practitioners generally require answers here and now; they are confronted with the need to make decisions about particular cases that cannot wait and understandably become impatient with an enterprise that delivers answers after years, if not decades, of effort. Yet given the complexity of research, the duration of longitudinal investigations and the need for replication, the long-drawn-out time scale is a necessary part of that enterprise. Research on human beings can rarely come to quick conclusions; as experience has shown, simple and speedily delivered answers turn out only too often to be simplistic and misleading.

One further point needs mentioning. Research workers generally talk in terms of group comparisons and probabilities whereas practitioners must make decisions about individuals. Let us consider one typical research study, concerned with the nature of abused children's attachment to the abusing mother, in which marked differences were found between the abused group and a non-abused control group in the type of attachment formed. A majority, about two-thirds, of the maltreated children were observed to be markedly insecure in their relationship to the mother, whereas this occurred in only a minority (i.e. about a quarter) among the control children. This was statistically a highly significant difference, and it is then tempting to discuss the results entirely in terms of this group difference. Yet what about the one-third of the abused children who apparently had normal attachments?; and for that matter, what about the 25 per cent of the control group who did not have normal attachments? In so many investigations these exceptions are disregarded even when they form quite substantial minorities. To practitioners exceptions are important, for they cannot be content with statements about probabilities, for example that abused children are *more likely* to have deficient relationships. Operating as they do at the level of the individual, practitioners want information that can help them to make decisions about *particular* children; statements about group trends are not sufficient to predict the developmental course of individuals. Fortunately, research **workers are now** increasingly aware of the need to do justice to both aspects, **to** group differences and to individual variation. Thus, for instance, having become aware of the fact that not all children fall victim to stresses such as deprivation or maltreatment but that some survive in the face of quite horrendous adversity and turn out surprisingly well, the search is currently on for the sources of such resilience. Once these are known it will be easier to predict the outcome for any given individual, and as a result such research findings will be of correspondingly greater use to the practitioner.

Contributions to practice

We have discussed not only the advantages of research as a guide to action but also its limitations, as well as the different orientations that characterize research workers and practitioners respectively. It is necessary to emphasize the negative as well as the positive side, for it would be only too easy to draw an over-optimistic picture of what research can deliver – to allow the pendulum to swing from a total disregard of research as a guide to action to a naïve faith in its infallibility. Such faith would be unjustified and can only be followed by disillusionment. A proper balance needs to be maintained in order not to raise false hopes. Let us therefore summarize the main types of contribution that one can realistically expect from research.

In the first place, research can provide us with specific factual information – information, that it, regarding particular aspects of human behaviour and development where a factual answer is required to some precise question. An example is found in the first Issue that we shall examine in Part 2, below: when do children first become capable of forming an attachment to another person? The answer required is some particular age; it is then up to research workers to mount the necessary investigations and provide that answer. By now it will come as no surprise to the reader that this is not as straightforward as it sounds, especially as 'attachment' is a complex function and it is therefore necessary first for investigators to agree on a way of defining it that enables one to assess its existence in individual children. Until there is agreement on such an operational definition there may well be divergence in the findings obtained from different studies. In due course, however, agreement is reached and a particular age range supplied in answer to the question posed.

In the second place, research can demonstrate the outcome of some particular course of action and make comparisons with other courses of action. Are children of divorced parents better off if custody is awarded to the mother rather than to the father? Will young children be harmed if looked after in a group-care setting instead of a family setting? Should temporary foster parents be encouraged to form an affectionate relationship with the child in their care, or is it preferable for them to adopt a more impersonal attitude? Choice between alternative courses is a dilemma that frequently confronts professional workers, and having information about the consequences of each course is thus most useful. The problem for the research worker in supplying such comparative information is that the groups being compared should be alike in all respects except that being investigated – no easy task in real-life situations; and reports muct accordingly be carefully checked before their conclusions can be accepted. In any case, the findings will only provide us with behavioural descriptions of the consequences of each course; it is then up to the practitioner to determine which is 'better' in relation to the needs and requirements of the individual case. Of course, if the outcome were assessed in terms of some measure of psychological adjustment and the research workers were able to demonstrate that one course leads to greater adjustment than another, there would be no problem about which is 'better'. So often, however, the choice is not so straightforward: children sent to day care are (according to some research findings) likely to become more independent but also more aggressive than those remaining at home; and which course is the 'better' one is then a matter of personal preference as to what kind of child characteristics one wants to foster. Research can provide the comparative data; it is up to others, however, to use that information in order to decide which is the preferred course.

The third type of contribution made by research is of a more general kind. As a result of accumulating specific information in the context of particular research problems we are enabled to make certain overall statements about the general nature of children's development and the conditions under which that takes place. We shall mention some of these in the final section of this book: the focus on family discord as a major cause of children's psychological ill-health, the centrality accorded to the quality of interpersonal relationships, the reversibility of adverse effects brought about by specific stresses (even those experienced during the early, so-called impressionable years), and so on. Such conclusions do not emerge from any one particular investigation but from a broad range of research; they refer not to specific issues but to a general view of human development.

Thus, research provides more than a database; it also indicates the goals towards which we ought to strive in order to promote individual welfare. Thus, for example, the realization some decades ago, as a result of accumulating evidence from a broad range of studies, that children deprived of parental care of a personal and consistent nature may come to psychological harm set up new goals for all those charged with fostering children's optimal development. No longer could good physical care, proper education and strict moral training be regarded as sufficient guarantee of children's successful adjustment. The emotional needs of children, as focused on particular individuals from whose consistent availability they derived their security, had also been highlighted, and as a result a great range of changes was instituted in both the public and the private care of children. In the short history of child-development research, there are few examples as encompassing in scope as the work on maternal deprivation. In due course, however, there will no doubt be other sets of conclusions that will have a similarly profound impact on aims and practice.

In the meantime there are a number of more specific topics where research has made information available that is likely to be of help to practitioners working with young children and their families. In the next part we shall look at this information and consider its uses.

Part 2

Children and their families: issues for research and practice

We shall now examine a number of issues, posed in question form, which are of concern to professional workers in their dealings with young children and their families. The issues are those that have been the subject of research and about which a body of knowledge is thus available. There are, of course, many other problems which research workers have investigated in their attempts to learn something about the nature of children's development; however, these deal mostly with theoretical questions and are thus of only indirect relevance to practitioners. Naturally, anyone concerned with children will benefit from obtaining a total overview of child development, but there are many other books that provide this and can be consulted for this purpose. Here we shall single out those particular aspects that are of more immediate relevance, and while their sum total may still be frustratingly low compared with all one would like to know, they at least represent a reasonable start, given the short history of scientifically conducted research into child development.

In the course of that history different problems have been investigated at different times. Thus, some specific topic may capture the imagination of research workers at some particular time and a great deal of attention is then devoted to its examination. In due course, however, as answers emerge and conclusions are agreed upon, attention switches to other topics and new lines of enquiry are initiated. The various issues we shall discuss thus have different histories: some (for example, that concerned with the age when children first become capable of forming attachments and that enquiring about the effects of separation from parents) were investigated several decades ago; others (such as the parenting abilities of men, the effects on children of divorce and the consequences of non-traditional rearing) are of more recent origin and currently continue to receive much lively attention from research workers. We shall look at 'old' as well as 'new' topics: the former are more likely to provide firmer data and agreed conclusions; the latter, though perhaps incomplete in their findings and having therefore to be treated with greater caution, reflect issues that are currently of special concern to society and about which practitioners require at least interim information.

For each of the issues discussed below we shall follow the same format. First, something will be said about the background to that particular topic, with special reference to the rationale for wanting to investigate it, the kinds of questions posed by research workers in examining it and the approaches taken by them in attempting to provide answers. We shall then look at some of the relevant findings, and do so by presenting summaries of a number of appropriate studies. In this way the reader can obtain a rather more immediate feeling for the kind of research that has been carried out than would be possible from a more global overview of the present state of knowledge. The summaries therefore also contain information about the methods used by the investigators in obtaining their findings, so that these too can be taken into account in evaluating the usefulness of each study. Inevitably, of course, there are problems in choosing reports for presentation; some of the issues have attracted quite a lot of attention and a complete listing would not be feasible. An effort has therefore been made to select those studies that are methodologically most sound and from which reasonably authoritative conclusions can be drawn. However, in the section that follows the summaries some comments on the research are provided, with a view to locating these particular studies in a more general context and also to highlighting any methodological problems that may have arisen in that area and that may affect the conclusions to be drawn. The last section under each issue considers some of the implications for practice of the research findings, though no doubt readers will also want to draw their own conclusions as to the consequences for their own particular fields of professional activity. Finally, for each issue some references are given for the sake of those who want to pursue that particular topic further.

When do children first form
attachments to other people?

Background

The formation of a child's first emotional relationship (more often
than not with the mother) is widely regarded as one of the most
important achievements of childhood. It is from that relationship
that the young child derives its confidence in the world: the sheer
physical availability of the other person spells security. A major
break in that relationship may be experienced as highly distressing
and may constitute a considerable trauma. It is therefore necessary
to know something of its developmental course, including the age
when one can first expect an attachment to another person to show
itself.

The term 'attachment' has traditionally been used to refer to the
child's part of the relationship – as opposed to the term 'bonding',
which has come to be used for the parent's part. There has been a
great deal of research in the last few decades on the nature of early
attachments, and though most of it has taken a non-developmental
form, being concerned more with its manifestation in children at one
particular age (especially around one year) than with changes over
time, we do have some indication as to when and how children's
attachments to significant others first appear.

That an attachment has to be learned, in the sense that it is based
on experience with the other person, cannot be doubted. The questions of interest are how much experience it takes and at what time
children become capable of benefiting from that experience.

Initially, a child's caretakers are interchangeable. At birth the
child does not yet 'know' its mother; a familiarization process has to
take place. There is in fact considerable evidence that such familiarization occurs very quickly and that by 2 or 3 months infants are

already capable of distinguishing familiar from unfamiliar people. (There are even some intriguing findings that immediately after birth infants can distinguish the mother's voice from that of any other voice – something that can only be explained by learning in the womb!) However, being able to recognize the mother by, for instance, smiling at her more readily or being more easily comforted by her touch does not in itself signify that an attachment has been formed to her. Such recognition is only a prerequisite to attachment formation; in all other respects infants remain quite indiscriminate. Thus, they will accept care and attention from anyone, however unfamiliar, and show no sign of upset when separated from the parent or any orientation towards her during her absence.

The interchangeability of caretakers is best seen in separation situations. It is well known that young children (say between 1 and 4 years of age) tend to be extremely upset when removed from their parents, particularly when placed in such strange environments as hospitals or children's homes. The often quite intense and prolonged fretting that then occurs is an indication of the child's need for the parent's presence – a presence which normally provides the young child with comfort and security and a secure base from which it can explore the environment. Without it, security is shattered; the ministrations of strangers, however kindly offered, are rejected and indeed seem to add to the stress experienced. The separation situation thus highlights the fact that a meaningful, emotionally highly charged, lasting relationship has been formed and that a break in that relationship will produce, in the short term at any rate, some highly distressing, undesirable consequences.

The question can therefore be asked: how early in infancy does separation from a mother (or other permanent caretaker) have an impact on children and cause them to be upset? Is it possible to indicate some age when people cease to be interchangeable, when the child's positive feelings have become focused on just one or two specific individuals while others are responded to more negatively? To establish such an age is clearly desirable: it means that we can determine when children become vulnerable to the loss of their mother-figure and what the limits of the earlier period are when changes in caretaker may take place relatively safely. This was indeed one of the first issues to which research workers addressed themselves when scientific investigation of children's attachments began in the late 1950s.

Research findings

(1) SUMMARIES

Schaffer, H. R. and Callender, W. M. 1959: Psychologic effects of hospitalisation in infancy. Pediatrics, 24, 528–39.

In this early study use was made of the separation situation to highlight the extent to which infants of different ages within the first year of life require their mother's presence and refuse to accept attention from other people. In particular the intention was to establish the age at which the mother's absence becomes a cause for distress and strange caretakers are no longer acceptable.

The most frequent separation situation is, of course, hospitalization. Accordingly 76 infants, aged between 3 and 51 weeks, were observed when admitted to a children's hospital. The length of their stay there varied from 4 to 49 days, though most remained for less than 2 weeks. Observation sessions took place on each of the first 3 days following admission and again on the last 3 days preceding discharge. Each session lasted 2 hours and included a feed and the visiting period. The observer kept a running record of the infants' behaviour, with particular reference to their responsiveness to other people, play with toys, feeding and amount of crying. In addition, all infants were subsequently visited at home, first within a week of discharge and thereafter periodically until all overt effects of the separation experience had apparently subsided.

It emerged from the findings that the infants' reactions to hospitalization fell into two quite distinct syndromes, each associated with a particular age range and divided from each other at approximately 7 months. Those above that age showed the classical separation upset: acute fretting following admission, negative behaviour to all strangers, often quite desperate clinging to the mother during her visits, disturbed feeding and sleeping patterns and, after returning home, a period of insecurity shown especially by fear of being left alone by the mother. Infants below 7 months, on the other hand, showed minimal upset. In most cases admission to hospital evoked no observable disturbance; instead, an immediate adjustment to the new environment and the people in it was the typical reaction. On returning home these younger infants showed some isolated symptoms but none of the clinging to the mother that was seen in older babies. In general, it appeared that the separation experience had very different meanings for those in the first and those in the second half-year of life: only at the older age were responses such as to suggest that infants had formed a definite tie to the mother and that a break in that tie was experienced as upsetting.

Schaffer, H. R. and Emerson, P. E. 1964: The development of social attachments in infancy. Monographs of the Society for Research in Child Development, *29, no. 3 (serial no. 94)*

The study described above was a cross-sectional one: infants, that is, were seen only at one particular age when they happened to be admitted to hospital. To trace the way in which a particular function like attachment to the mother emerges in the course of development one really needs a longitudinal study, i.e. seeing the *same* infants at different ages. The present investigation accordingly took such a form.

A group of 60 infants was followed up at 4-weekly intervals throughout the first year of life and then seen once again at 18 months. In the course of home visits reports were obtained from the mothers about the infants' behaviour in a number of everyday separation situations such as being left alone in a room, left with a baby-sitter or put to bed at night; observational checks on the accuracy of the mothers' reports were built into the procedure. For each of the seven separation situations investigated information was obtained on every visit as to whether the infant protested or not, the intensity and regularity of the protest and whose departure elicited it. In addition, the infant's reaction to the research worker was assessed by means of a standardized approach procedure held at the beginning of each visit in order to see how readily the child accepted the attention of a relatively unfamiliar person.

As in the previous study, the age when separation protest was first recorded was of particular interest. For the majority of infants this was at the beginning of the second half-year, i.e. in the same age range as had been pin-pointed by the earlier research. Before that age, protest in separation situations did sometimes occur, but it was indiscriminate in nature in that the infant cried for attention from anyone, whether familiar or not. After that age it was focused on certain specific individuals: it was they and not others who were capable for stopping the child from crying. There were considerable differences in the precise age when infants first began to show such differential behaviour to other people, ranging from 22 weeks of age to the beginning of the second year. In the majority of cases, however, it was somewhere around the age of 7 or 8 months that it first became evident that these infants had now formed a very definite, lasting relationship with certain quite specific individuals.

Tennes, K. H. and Lampl, E. E. 1966: Some aspects of mother–child relationship pertaining to infantile separation anxiety. Journal of Nervous and Mental Diseases, *143, 426–37.*

Replication of any research findings is essential, and this study provides a welcome confirmation that the third quarter of the first year is indeed the period when focused attachments first appear – again on the basis of using children's responses to separation as an indicator and again by means of a longitudinal study.

Twenty-seven infants were followed up between 3 and 23 months at monthly or bimonthly intervals. On each occasion the infants were observed under naturalistic conditions at home and in semi-structured situations in a university observation room. Detailed descriptions of mother–child interactions were recorded by several observers simultaneously. Methods for assessing separation and stranger anxiety were built into the procedure, i.e. by asking the mother to leave the room and by the examiner approaching the infant on first arrival. The behavioural responses of the infants in these two situations were rated on six-point scales.

The majority of infants first developed separation anxiety during the third quarter of the first year. The average time of onset was around 8 months. Here too considerable individual differences were noted, however, ranging from 4 to 18 months. According to an earlier report on this same study, negative responsiveness to strangers appeared somewhat earlier, usually preceding separation anxiety by a few weeks. The indices taken together show how indiscriminate sociability with others, as seen in the early months, gives way to highly discriminating behaviour and appears to do so relatively suddenly once an infant reaches the relevant age range.

Yarrow, L. J. 1967: The development of focused relationships. In J. Hellmuth (ed.), Exceptional Infant: the normal infant, vol. 1. *Seattle, Washington: Special Child Publications.*

A rather different approach was taken in this study, in that it investigated infants' reactions to adoptive placements. In so far as a new mother-figure was immediately provided following the break with the previous mother, it was possible to study the effects of separation *per se*, uncontaminated by the effects of such other conditions as institutional deprivation.

The total sample involved 100 infants, though at any one age the number available was generally somewhat smaller. Observation sessions took place prior to and following that separation; they were conducted in the home setting and were of 1½ hours duration. A series of simple situations was incorporated into each session, involving the presentation of various inanimate and social stimuli, including the mother's and the observer's face and voice. The latency, duration and intensity of a variety of behavioural responses were recorded. Information from the mother was also obtained regarding the infant's behaviour in various everyday social situations.

By the age of 8 months all of the infants showed strong overt disturbances to permanent separation from the mother. At 3 months no infant showed such disturbance, at 5 months 20 per cent did so and at 6 months, 59 per cent. According to comments in a subsequent paper the author believes that the upset found at some of the younger ages, i.e. in the first half-year, may have been elicited by changes in routine and in type of stimulation provided rather than by a change in the mother-figure as such.

Kagan, J., Kearsley, R. B. and Zelazo, P. R. 1978: Infancy: its place in human development. *Cambridge, Mass.: Harvard University Press, 1978.*

The primary focus of this study is on the effects of day care (a subject to which we shall return later), with reference, among other things, to the way in which children's relationships with their mothers is affected thereby. As one of the assessments a separation situation was arranged in order to see whether this highlighted any differences in the child–mother relationship of children with and children without day-care experience.

For this assessment 87 infants were available, including a day-care and a matched home-care control group. Included in the sample were children of both Caucasian and Chinese ethnic origin. Children aged between 4 and 29 months were observed in a specially arranged separation situation, which involved the mother leaving the child alone in a relatively unfamiliar setting while playing happily. The occurrence and duration of crying were recorded by observers from behind a one-way screen. The sample included 59 children who participated on all six occasions that the procedure was administered between the ages of 5 and 20 months.

The incidence of crying in response to separation was found to be low up to 7 months of age, after which it rose sharply, peaking at 13 months and then declining. Every one of the 59 children seen longitudinally cried at least once, and most cried on several occasions. After 7 months children reacted to the mother's departure with crying much more quickly, and especially so in the age range 13 to 20 months. There were no differences between the two ethnic groups, and there were also no differences between the day-care and the home-care children, suggesting that the onset and early course of separation upset is a general phenomenon that appears to be unaffected by the amount of daily contact with the mother.

(2) COMMENTS ON RESEARCH

There is a most welcome degree of agreement among the various research studies as to when children first become vulnerable to separation from a mother-figure: the third quarter of the first year seems to be the crucial time when this is likely to occur. It is then that separation becomes a psychologically meaningful and emotionally disturbing event, as a result of which changes in mother-figure are now no longer tolerated. Investigators concur that before this age any disturbances in behaviour appear to be related to changes in routine or in the general environment rather than to loss of the mother. The disturbances are moreover brief and do not involve the distress which is subsequently such a central feature of the child's reaction. There is some disagreement as to the age at which that distress reaches its peak: according to some reports the intensity of upset is every bit as great at 7 or 8 months as it is in 2- or 3-year-old children, while others locate the peak at the end of the first or the beginning of the second year. The diversity may be due to the different kinds of measures and procedures used (amount of crying or intensity of crying, natural or arranged separations, and so forth), but suffice it to say that the longitudinal studies agree that the onset is relatively sudden – a stepwise development and not a slow and gradual one. Thus, sometime after the beginning of the second half-year, infants reach an important milestone in their social development. From then on their positive responsiveness tends to become restricted to certain familiar individuals while other, unfamiliar individuals elicit mostly negative responsiveness and wariness. The combined effect is to ensure that caretakers are no longer interchangeable; the child has become capable of forming 'proper' social attachments.

Relatively sudden, stepwise changes are by no means uncommon in behavioural development, so the rapid onset of the capacity for separation upset is hardly surprising. A lot of research has found the third quarter of the first year to be a time of considerable change, heralding as it does the onset of a large number of new achievements, including the development of recall memory. This is particularly relevant here: in earlier months infants may have been able to *recognize* persons or objects, i.e. show signs of remembering them when they were present, but in their absence they behaved on the basis of 'out of sight out of mind'. *Recall* involves memory of an absent person or thing, and it is this which is indicated by separation upset. Previously, however excited infants might be by the mother's presence they showed no orientation to her in her absence; but once this particular milestone has been reached, they are capable of missing her.

Stepwise changes do not, of course, mean that the development comes totally out of the blue. It may be the culmination of various prior events without which this particular development could not have taken place. The ability to differentiate familiar from unfamiliar people is clearly one prerequisite; mother must first be known in order to be missed. Yet research has found few experiential variables that seem to have any bearings on when this development takes place. Thus, it has not been found possible to relate variations in the age at onset of separation upset to variations in mothers' child-rearing practices; there are no differences according to whether a mother works or not; infants born blind and thus without visual experience of the mother also develop separation upset at the usual age; and finally, the age at onset is very similar in a wide range of different cultures, despite the considerable diversity of child-rearing practices. It seems that the timing of this particular milestone is primarily determined by the child's inherent developmental programme: given previous reasonably normal experience, the child is bound to reach this point.

Implications for practice

Any break in a child's existing relationships is likely to cause distress. The nature and severity of that distress varies with age: it will be greatest in the early years when children still require frequent access to the physical presence of those individuals who are the objects of their attachment. Such individuals spell security; but with that gone, upset is likely to be intense and prolonged. That alone justifies preventive action, quite apart from any possible long-term consequences, and amongst such actions is the search for a 'safe period' at the beginning of life when social ties have not yet been established and when, from the child's point of view, there is nothing as yet to sever.

Such a period, according to the research findings summarized above, extends over the first half year of life or so. From then on children become vulnerable to separation. It follows that wherever there is a choice, any measure involving the child's removal from home should be taken during the safe period. It is, for instance, always maintained that adoption placements ought to take place as early as possible. The findings we have quoted provide a rationale for such a belief and define more precisely what is meant by 'as early as possible'. Similarly, hospitalizations – or at least those that involve elective procedures where there is a choice as to when the child is to be admitted – should also be timed according to our knowledge of children's emotional vulnerability. While there may, of course, be good medical reasons for wanting to delay admission till the child is somewhat older, these should be weighed against the psychological considerations spelled out above.

Two qualifications should, however, be added. First, as most of the research reports stress, there is a considerable range in the age at onset of separation upset. It is true that the majority of infants reach this point during the third quarter of the first year, but some show signs of distress several months before then, while others appear not to do so until much later. This is, of course, not surprising; the same variation applies to any developmental milestone. It does mean, however, that one cannot precisely predict when any given child will become vulnerable to separations. There is some evidence that children who are developmentally ahead in other respects such as motor functioning are also likely to be ahead in this respect, but the association is not close enough to allow for accurate prediction. All one can do under the circumstances is to indicate the age range (i.e. the third quarter of the first year) when it is most probable that such a development will take place; for the majority of children this will be a justified assumption.

The other point refers to the fact that even in the first 6 months of life there may be some undesirable effects of separation. Feeding and sleeping disturbances have been reported, as well as bewilderment by a changed physical environment. These symptoms are generally brief in duration, but they do indicate the need to prepare the infant's new caretakers for such reactions and, wherever possible, to attempt to preserve routines. If, of course, the child's new environment is unsatisfactory by lacking in stimulation or by providing inconsistent care, deleterious effects will ensue however young the child may be. The 'safe period' refers only to the child's vulnerability to separation from the mother-figure; it does not imply that children at that age are immune from everything. Care must clearly be taken with respect to the environment in which even the youngest infant is placed.

Further reading

Ainsworth, M. D. S. 1973: The development of infant–mother attachment. In B. M. C. Caldwell and H. N. Ricciuti (eds), *Review of Child Development Research, Vol. 3*. Chicago: University of Chicago Press.

Bowlby, J. 1969: *Attachment and Loss: Vol. 1, Attachment*. London: Hogarth Press.

Schaffer, R. 1977: *Mothering*. London: Fontana; Cambridge, Mass.: Harvard University Press.

Issue: How long can the formation of the first attachment be delayed?

Background

As we have just seen, children normally form their first emotionally meaningful relationship around the third quarter of the first year. To do so they obviously require the availability of a parent-figure – a familiar, consistently available person who can convey to the child her or his own deep commitment and love. As a result of experiencing such treatment children will in due course become capable of reciprocating the affection given them throughout the early months.

But what if the child does not experience such treatment during this early period? What of infants who are kept, so to speak, 'on ice' emotionally by being reared in an impersonal environment where there is no caring mother-figure, where they thus have no opportunity for establishing an attachment with anyone and where they then pass the age when one might normally have expected that development to have taken place? How much longer, if at all, can one delay before it is too late and the child's capacity to form relationships atrophies? This applies in particular to children brought up throughout infancy in an institutional environment, where they are looked after indiscriminately by a series of nurses or houseparents whose contacts with them are both impersonal and temporary. Can such a child subsequently be placed in an ordinary family setting and still be capable of developing normal social relationships? Is there an upper age limit beyond which procedures such as adoption are no longer effective?

The emphasis on early adoption is largely derived from a belief in the existence of 'critical periods' in human development. This notion originally arose from observations of certain animal species such as chicks and ducklings, which were found to become 'imprinted' on the first object that they encountered after hatching – normally the mother. This will then form the basis of a permanent attachment. Imprinting, it was thought at one time, has to take place within a sharply delimited period (a matter of a few hours in the case of these birds). If the animal is kept isolated during this time it is subsequently totally incapable of forming any attachments, irrespective of the opportunities it is given later on to encounter other members of the species. The development of human attachments was once considered to follow the same lines: the formation of such attachments was also thought to be confined to a narrow age range. In particular the influential child psychiatrist John Bowlby held to such a critical period view. Citing as evidence a series of studies of children who had spent their first 2 or 3 years in institutions before then being fostered and who apparently subsequently showed grave disabilities in their social relationships, he declared that 'even good mothering is almost useless if delayed until after the age of 2½ years.' (Bowlby, 1951) It would follow that the formation of the first attachment can be delayed somewhat beyond the usual age in the first year of life, but that nevertheless a sharply delimited period does exist beyond which no amount of the 'right' kind of experience is effective if the child has been deprived before then. Late placements are thus inadvisable; the child is condemned to develop a syndrome which Bowlby referred to as the 'affectionless character', distinguished by the permanent disability of the individual to establish deep, lasting, emotionally meaningful relationships with any other person, whether it be as son or daughter, friend, spouse, parent or any other role in childhood or adult life.

This problem is part of a wider concern, namely the extent to which unfortunate experiences early in life leave irreversible effects on an individual's psychological make-up. Largely because of Freud's strong support for such a doctrine it was for long considered an established truth that children are highly vulnerable in the early years, that they are permanently affected by whatever experiences they encounter at that time, and that by the end of the first few years the die is cast as far as their future personality development is concerned. There are now grave doubts as to the validity of this notion. To assess it one must investigate the fate of children who have been subjected to adverse experiences of some kind early on but subsequently were provided with the opportunity to make good by a major change in their upbringing. Thus, as far as the present issue is concerned, one needs to examine children who were prevented from forming emotional attachments during the so-called critical period but were then placed with parental figures to whom they could form meaningful relationships – if, that is, the capacity to do so was still there.

Unfortunately, there is very little research bearing on this issue. In fact only two studies could be found that are directly relevant and of sufficient quality to justify being quoted. However, this is such an important question that, exceptionally, we shall discuss it despite the meagre evidence – bearing in mind, of course, the caution necessary in drawing conclusions.

Research findings

(1) SUMMARIES

Tizard, B. 1977: Adoption: a second chance. *London: Open Books.*
This study set out to test the belief that children reared in institutions in the early years and adopted beyond infancy are so damaged by their experience that they are incapable of subsequently establishing attachments to anyone. All the children included in the sample had been admitted to an institution in the early weeks of life and had remained there for periods ranging from 2 to 7 years. Their care during this time was in the hands of a wide range of people: by age 2 they had been looked after by an average of 24 different people, and for those still in the institution at age 4½ that figure had gone up to 50. Under such conditions of impermanence there were virtually no opportunities to establish an attachment to anyone.

The children were assessed in the institution at 2 years of age, and were then seen again at ages 4½ and 8. Between the ages 2 and 7 some of the children were restored to their own mothers while others were adopted. For the 8-year assessment 25 adopted children were available, 20 of whom had been adopted between 2 and 4 years while the other five were adopted between 4 and 7 (referred to in the report as the 'early' and the 'late' group respectively). At all three assessment points data were obtained about both intellectual and social functioning; some of the information was collected from the children themselves (for example, by means of psychological tests), while other material was obtained from their caretakers. Most of the data about the children's social relationships at the later two assessment points were provided by their adoptive parents and their teachers.

At the age of 4½ most of the children adopted by then had settled well into their new homes. They were said to be easy to manage and intellectually they were also functioning well. The majority of the parents considered that the child had formed a deep attachment to them. Many of the children were, however, said to be rather attention-seeking, both with the parents and with strangers, and in some cases this was allied with a tendency to be overfriendly and even affectionate towards strangers. Nonetheless, the children were by no means indiscriminate and showed a marked preference for their parents.

By 8 years the earlier adopted children were still unusually affectionate but again not indiscriminately so with all comers. Sixteen of the mothers considered the child to be closely attached to them. Of the five later adopted children four were said to have formed deep attachments to their parents; the exception had been adopted by a couple merely as an act of charity. Otherwise, the adoptive parents emerged as a highly motivated group, eager to devote a great deal of time and effort to the child. There were a number of negative findings for the sample as a whole: in comparison with a control (non-adopted) group their concentration at school was reported by teachers to be poor, and they were also said to be restless, inclined to have temper tantrums and various nervous habits, and sometimes to be unpopular with other children. Only a small minority of adoptive parents described their children to be difficult, this referring mostly to disobedience, temper tantrums and over-activity.

There were few differences in behaviour between the early and the late adopted children. The two oldest children at placement, aged 7 and 7½ respectively, had made as successful an adjustment as children adopted at much earlier ages. None resembled the stereotype of the ex-institutional child: overfriendly yet unattached. Four of the mothers seen when the child was aged 8 viewed the adoption negatively – a 16 per cent failure rate on this criterion which, though disappointingly high, should be compared with that among the group of children restored to their biological mothers following institutionalization, where nearly half reported the child to have failed to develop any attachment towards them. It seemed that the success of the adoption depended not so much on the age of placement nor on the child's previous history but largely on the emotional investment that the adoptive parents put into the child.

Hodges, J. and Tizard, B. 1989: Social and family relationships of ex-institutional adolescents. Journal of Child Psychology and Psychiatry, *30, 77–98.*

Adolescence is often said to be a particularly difficult time for adoptive families. The question therefore arises whether problems stemming from earlier experiences might become more prominent then or whether, on the contrary, processes of normalization continue through this period. Hodges and Tizard have attempted to answer this question by following up the children in Tizard's sample 8 years later, assessing them at the age of 16.

Twenty-three of the adoptees were available at that age, two placements having broken down in the mean time. The young people and their parents were interviewed, tested and asked to fill in questionnaires. Information was also obtained from their teachers. Similar data were gathered from a comparison group of individuals who had been with their families throughout childhood and also from a number of adolescents who had been restored to their own mothers following an earlier institutional period.

As at age 8, the great majority of the adopted mothers felt that their child was deeply attached to them. There were four exceptions, and of these one mother had taken the same negative view 8 years earlier while the other three had previously seen their children as closely attached but now doubted the strength of the child's feeling (though in one case the child was described as definitely attached to the father). In general, however, the outcome in this group was considerably better than amongst the children restored to their own mothers, where only five out of the nine 16-year olds were said to be deeply attached to their mothers. Attachment to the father similarly differentiated these two groups: only one adopted adolescent was reported as not attached, whereas this was said of about half of the restored youngsters. The proportion of adolescents able to show overt affection to their parents was rather lower in the adopted group than among their never separated comparison group but considerably higher than was the case among the restored 16-year olds. Thus, in general the family relationships of most of the adopted adolescents seemed satisfactory both for them and for their parents and differed only a little from those of adolescents who had never been in care.

On the other hand both ex-institutional groups showed difficulties in relationships to peers and to adults outside the family. The adopted as much as the restored adolescents appeared to be considerably less popular with others of their own age than youngsters who had never been away from home: they were more quarrelsome and tended to bully others, and were also less likely to have special friends. While the indiscriminate overfriendliness to adults shown by some of them at age 8 was no longer a problem, they still tended to be more oriented towards adult approval and attention than was the case in the comparison group.

It therefore appears that lack of close attachment in the early years had not necessarily led to a later inability to form such attachments with adoptive parents. When the parents wanted the child and were able to put a lot into the parental role the relationship between them prospered. Nevertheless, as much as 12 years after the child had joined the family certain difficulties in social relationships, particularly with peers, could be found. One must conclude from this report that some psychological functions are more vulnerable to long-term effects than others – a conclusion borne out by a companion paper (Hodges and Tizard, 1989) on the emotional and behavioural difficulties of the same individuals, according to which such problems were found to be more prevalent among the 16-year-old adopted group than in young people without an institutional history. IQ, on the other hand, showed no evidence of long-term effects of early institutionlization.

Triseliotis, J. and Russell, J. 1984: Hard to Place: the outcome of adoption and residential care. *London: Heinemann.*

The only other report with relevant data takes the follow-up period of late-adopted children still further, i.e. into adulthood. This is, of course, most valuable, though the price paid in this study was to rely largely on retrospective information from the adoptees themselves.

A sample of 44 individuals, all of whom had been adopted between the ages of 2 and 8, were traced when in their mid-twenties. They were compared with a group of 40 who had been institutionally reared for a major part of their childhood. As ascertained from records of public agencies, most of the adoptees had been removed from their family of origin in the first year and admitted into public care. They came mostly from a highly deprived background, and the delay in placing them for adoption was mainly due to doubts as to whether these 'high-risk' children should be adopted at all. During their period in care all experienced a number of moves between institutions and foster homes, and according to the agency records nearly half were said to have had moderate to severe emotional problems at that time.

When interviewed as adults, the adoptees took a largely positive view of their childhood. Well over 80 per cent expressed fair or considerable satisfaction with the adoption experience (as compared with 55 per cent of the residential group's view of their childhood). Asked for their feelings about the quality of their relationship with the adoptive parents, 45 per cent rated it as very good, 41 per cent as good, 9 per cent as mixed and 5 per cent as poor. In the great majority of cases they considered themselves to have been emotionally close or very close to the parents, to have had warm relationships also with siblings and members of the extended family, and to have regarded the adoptive family as 'theirs'. In 80 per cent of cases this feeling of closeness still prevailed in adulthood. Neither the quality of the relationship with the adoptive parents nor the degree of satisfaction with the whole adoption experience appeared to depend on the age at placement with the family or the number of moves experienced before then.

All in all, the authors of this report feel able to conclude that 'the good adjustment achieved by the vast majority of adoptees, indicates that, given a new and caring environment, children can form fresh attachments and overcome deprivations and deficits.'

(2) COMMENTS ON RESEARCH

It is a pity that so little work can be cited that is relevant to the issue under discussion. There have been other reports of children 'kept on ice' for prolonged periods, either as a result of isolation or because of institutional upbringing, but none of these has specifically addressed the question of late attachment formation. A few provide anecdotal or indirect evidence, and while this tends to bear out the above findings it is not sound enough to justify quoting here. For that matter, the quality of evidence regarding attachment formation in the studies summarized here is not as unshakeable as one might like: reports from parents and from the adoptees themselves (especially about events in the past) may be open to various distortions. Unfortunately, 'hard' tests for attachment formation, at least in children beyond infancy, do not yet exist and one must therefore base one's conclusions on the material that is available.

These conclusions are that even older children appear to be

capable of forming an attachment for the first time when placed with adoptive parents after a period of several years of institutional, impersonal rearing. The critical-period notion, that there is a sharply delimited range (ending, say, at 2½ years) beyond which children are not able to develop emotional attachments, is not supported by these findings. Children placed as late as 8 years, having never before experienced stable and committed care, develop close and discriminative ties to their new parents and show no sign of the 'affectionless character'. It is also significant that no differences in this respect have been found between 'early' and 'late' adopted children within the 2–7-year age range. Judging by these data, the die is by no means cast at the age of 2½. Not that the children emerge entirely unscathed from their early experience: various behaviour problems and difficulties with peers were found in Tizard's sample to be unusually frequent. Precisely what led to these symptoms and what they signify is not known, nor can we tell what their implications are for psychological functioning in adulthood. In the light of the enormous adjustment these children had to make in the transition from institutional to family life, they are probably a small price to pay for otherwise accomplishing this task reasonably successfully.

However limited the evidence, the conclusions do fit in with current thinking about the effects of early experience generally. Such views are derived from research which examines children who had experienced traumata of one kind or another in their early years – deprivation, neglect, isolation, abuse and the like, from which they were rescued in due course and then put into much more favourable environments. These studies are in the main concerned with outcome measures different from those of interest to us here, i.e. mostly with intellectual functioning, language development, acquisition of skills, and so forth rather than with relationship formation. They are pertinent, however, for almost without fail they point to the reversibility of early trauma. The idea that every experience (especially of a traumatic kind) encountered during the formative years leaves an indelible mark on the child that no subsequent change in circumstances can eradicate is not borne out by this work. Children's ability to recuperate has clearly been grossly underestimated, just as the role of the early, so-called formative, years has been considerably overestimated. Thus, the idea that children deprived of normal love relationships in early life quickly become incapacitated in ever forming meaningful emotional ties to others was accepted as long as the former view of human development prevailed, according to which experiences at the earliest stages of a child's life are all-important in their effects on personality growth. Now, with relevant evidence to hand, this view can no longer be sustained. Early experience is reversible under certain conditions by means of subsequent experience, and it can be accepted that this applies to the effects on social behaviour as much as it does to intellectual functioning.

On the other hand, what we do not know is how long adverse experience can continue before it does become irreversible. There are various indications that speak against infinite plasticity: in due course children's personalities do become resistant to change. Thus, the oldest child in Tizard's sample to be placed for adoption was aged 7, but what of children aged 10 or even 15 who have their first chance of family life delayed until then? We do not know the answer. It is certainly difficult to believe that someone brought up for the whole of his or her childhood in a totally impersonal manner would emerge unscathed in the ability subsequently to establish love relationships: such an individual may indeed manifest the characteristics of the affectionless character. However, further research on the question of age limits is clearly required.

Implications for practice

The scarcity of evidence on this issue suggests the need for considerable caution. Nevertheless, it does appear justified to conclude that the reluctance (at one time amounting to complete refusal) to place children older than 2 years or so for adoption is unnecessary. It seems that children up to the age of 7 at least can be successfully integrated into a family, despite a complete lack of previous personal relationships. Without doubt a policy of 'the earlier the better' should be maintained for the sake of *both* adoptive parents and children: the more they share a common history, the easier their mutual adjustment will be. In addition, children's infinite capacity for change should not be assumed: interventions early in life on the whole do meet with greater success, and placement at the earliest possible time ought to remain an overriding aim. However, if for one reason or another a child could not be placed in infancy, it is unnecessary, and even dangerous, to conclude that such a move is now too late – dangerous because the alternative will in all probability be either to keep the child in some institutional environment or to make temporary and therefore fragile arrangements such as fostering. Where the choice is between keeping the child in care or having it adopted, the latter course is surely preferable in the vast majority of cases.

What has also emerged is the vital role that the adoptive parents' commitment plays in ensuring the child's adjustment. Selecting prospective parents is generally undertaken with great care – especially when such parents greatly outnumber the children available. When older children are involved such care becomes even more essential. It is significant that in Tizard's study it was the parents' devotion in terms of time and mental energy that was more closely related to successful outcome than the child's age at placement. As Tizard's observations on children restored to their own mothers showed (and we shall refer to these in detail under another Issue when we discuss the role of the 'blood bond'), merely putting a child together with an adult does not guarantee the development of an affectionate tie; that can only occur on a reciprocal basis whereby the parent clearly displays his or her strong positive feelings to the child who in time will then be likely to return them. Finding individuals with the considerable warmth of character necessary to take on this part is thus an essential prerequisite for the successful outcome of late adoption.

This is especially so because many of the late-adopted children are likely to have behaviour problems which may well represent the scars of their earlier experience. A syndrome of restlessness, lack of concentration, tantrums and nervous habits has been mentioned in this respect, as has an overfriendliness to strangers that is fairly typical of institutionalized children and which adopted children may still show in the early stages of their new life. Tolerance and understanding of such symptoms on the part of the parents is clearly necessary, and this must therefore be another factor to take into account in selection procedures. Preparing adoptive parents for the likelihood of such behaviour occurring, as well as the provision of help and counselling, is a further step that is highly desirable, if not essential.

Further reading

Bowlby, J. 1965: *Child Care and the Growth of Love*. Harmondsworth, Middlesex: Penguin.

Clarke, A. M. and Clarke, A. D. B. 1976: *Early Experience: myth and evidence.* London: Open Books.

Clarke, A. M. and Clarke, A. D. B. 1979: Early experience: its limited effect on later development. In D. Shaffer and J. Dunn (eds), *The First Year of Life.* Chichester: Wiley.

Rutter, M. 1989: Pathways from childhood to adult life. *Journal of Child Psychology and Psychiatry,* 30, 23–51.

Issue: When does maternal bonding occur?

Background

The term 'bonding' has been widely used to designate the process whereby mothers form emotional relationships with their children. More specifically, it has come to refer to certain rapid, irreversible changes said to take place in the mother within a period immediately following birth which lasts no more than a few hours or days at the most, during which prolonged contact between mother and baby (preferably of a skin-to-skin nature) must occur if maternal feelings are to be properly mobilized. Failure of contact through separation at this crucial period allegedly interferes with the formation of the bond, leading to deficient mothering months or even years later.

Bonding therefore describes the mother-to-child part of the relationship (as opposed to attachment, which refers to the child-to-mother part). More importantly, however, the 'bonding doctrine' (as it has come to be known) also describes a particular way in which the mother's relationship is said to develop. This was originally derived from a number of animal studies (concerning mainly goats and sheep) which reported the effects on mother–offspring relationships of contact and of separation during the immediate post-birth period. According to these observations, removal of the young for just a few hours after their birth resulted in the mother subsequently rejecting her offspring. The initial contact, it was concluded, was essential for maternal bonding to be mobilized: any interference with it through separation at that crucial time resulted in atrophy of all maternal feelings towards the young animal which no amount of subsequent contact could reverse.

These findings inspired two American paediatricians, Klaus and Kennell (for references see below under Further Reading) to investigate the role of early contact and separation in human mothers and babies. Their research involved two groups of mothers: one who experienced the rather limited amount of physical contact with their new-born babies that is customary in most Western maternity hospitals, while the other mothers were given 16 hours of additional contact during the first 3 days after birth. Observations and interviews carried out over the next 5 years with these two groups indicated that the extra contact had apparently produced warmer, more caring and more sensitive maternal behaviour and that this in turn resulted in a number of benefits for the children which were not to be found in the limited contact group.

These findings led Klaus and Kennell to claim that extra mother–child contact in the very first days of the baby's life can influence the maternal relationship for years thereafter, and that a critical period therefore exists at that time during which it is necessary for the mother to have close contact with her new-born baby if later development is to be optimal. In the absence of such an experience the bonding process is interfered with: events in the immediate postnatal period exercise such a powerful influence that the mother's fitness to provide effective parenting may be affected for a very long time indeed.

This proposal is, of course, extremely important, for it might account for a wide range of failure in parenting (child abuse in particular has been mentioned in this respect). If borne out, such a view implies that a number of essential, though simple, practical measures ought to be taken in order to improve the quality of parenting. First of all, however, it is necessary to ensure that the bonding hypothesis is indeed valid – at least in the form in which it has been propounded. The studies quoted below address themselves to this question, in that they ask whether the timing of maternal bonding is confined to one particular limited period as suggested by Klaus and Kennell or whether there are no such specific constraints.

Research findings

(1) SUMMARIES

Svejda, M. J., Campos, J. J. and Emde, R. N. 1980: Mother–infant 'bonding': failure to generalise. Child Development, 51, 775–9.

Methodologically, this is one of the soundest investigations in this area. It includes a number of procedural safeguards that the work of Klaus and Kennell lacked, such as random assignment of mothers to the different contact conditions, use of double-blind controls and the precise definition of response measures related to the manifestation of bonding.

Thirty lower-middle-class mothers and their babies were randomly assigned to either routine care or to a programme of extra contact during the first 36 hours of the child's life. Routine care involved a maximum of 5 minutes contact after delivery and thereafter contact only during feeds lasting approximately 30 minutes. Mothers in the extra-contact group held their babies skin-to-skin for 15 minutes immediately after birth and a little later for a further 45 minutes, and during the following days each mother had her baby with her for 1½ hours around feeding times. Double-blind procedures were used in that the mothers did not know that they were taking part in a research project and that they had been assigned to any particular condition, and the research assistants carrying out the observations were kept unaware as to the group membership of any particular mother. Only one study mother at a time was present in the maternity unit, so that mothers experiencing different contact conditions could not compare notes.

Thirty-six hours after birth an interaction session and a breast feed were videotaped. Each session was scored for 28 different response measures that indicated the mothers' affectionate, proximity-maintaining and caretaking behaviour-patterns.

The results of this study are quite unequivocal. They show that *none* of the response measures differed between the two groups. This applied irrespective of such variables as sex of child or age of mother. When the 28 measures were combined into four pooled categories, comparison of the two groups of mothers on each category again failed to reveal any differences. As the authors conclude, there appears to be little support in these findings for the effect of additional early contact on maternal behaviour.

Carlsson, S. G., Fagerberg, H., Horneman, G., Hwang, C. P., Larsson, K., Rodholm, M. and Schaller, J. 1978: Effects of amount of contact between mother and child on the mother's nursing behavior. Developmental Psychobiology, 11, 143–50.

Carlsson S. G., Fagerberg, H., Horneman, G., Hwang, C. P., Larsson, K., Rodholm, M. and Schaller, J. 1979: Effects of various amounts of contact between mother and child on the mother's nursing behaviour: a follow-up study. Infant Behavior and Development, 2, 209–14.

These two papers both refer to the same study, in which three groups of Swedish middle-class mothers were investigated. Two groups (of 20 and 22 mothers) were given extended contact with the baby, which involved the mother being able to keep her naked infant in her bed for 1 hour immediately after delivery. Subsequently, there were a number of differences between the two groups in the nature of the ward routine they experienced, i.e. whether there was extra contact between feeds, whether the nurses advised and supported the mother or not, and whether the mothers were encouraged to breast-feed. The third group (containing 20 mothers) had limited early contact: the baby was held by the mother for only 5 minutes after birth and subsequently was kept in a separate crib by the mother's bed.

Observations were carried out at two points. The first involved breast-feeding sessions during the first 4 days in hospital, and the second, also a feeding session, was held at home when the child was 6 weeks old. Identical observation procedures and scoring categories were used on both occasions. During the first 4 days the behaviour of the mothers differed according to the amount of contact after birth: extended contact mothers engaged in a greater amount of petting, rubbing, rocking, touching and holding the infant than limited contact mothers. No differences according to ward routine were found. When seen again 6 weeks later the amount of contact after birth no longer affected the mothers: none of the response measures differentiated the groups. Thus, a short-term, temporary effect was the only result these investigators were able to detect; a few weeks later this had already disappeared.

Rode, S. S., Chang, P. N., Fisch, R. O. and Sroufe, L. A. 1981: Attachment patterns of infants separated at birth. Developmental Psychology, 17, 188–91.

One of the most common reasons for a child's separation from the mother at birth is prematurity and the need to keep the infant in an intensive-care unit. If the 'bonding failure' hypothesis is correct, such infants should be at high risk of developing unsatisfactory relationships with their mothers. This is investigated in this study.

Twenty-four infants, separated at birth from their mothers and admitted to a neonatal intensive-care unit for an average period of 27 days, were observed when they were 12 months old and again at 19 months in order to assess the quality of the attachments they had formed to their mothers. The assumption was that the early separation of these infants could have disrupted the mothers' bonding behaviour and that this in turn led to the children being unable to form satisfactory attachments to the mother.

The children were seen in the 'Ainsworth Strange Situation', a standard procedure for assessing the quality of infant attachment, based on a series of stressful episodes such as the approach by a stranger, the mother's departure from the room, and so forth. During these episodes the child's behaviour *vis-á-vis* the mother is recorded and subsequently classified. The observations on the present sample showed that the children were comparable in their attachment patterns to children previously studied who had not experienced separation at birth, and that this applied as much to those whose parents visited them minimally during the stay in the intensive-care unit as to those with more extensive contact at that time.

There was thus no reason to believe that the early separation in any way affected the infants' ability to form normal attachments to their mothers: it seemed much more probable to the authors of this paper that 'the quality of the infant–caregiver attachment relationship is a product of the entire history of interaction.'

Leiderman, P. 1981: Human mother–infant social bonding: is there a sensitive phase? In K. Immelmann, G. W. Barlow, L. Petrinovich and M. Main (eds), Behavioural Development. *Cambridge: Cambridge University Press.*

The reference given here is a summary of a number of previously published reports by Leiderman and his colleagues, describing the results obtained over an 8-year follow-up period. The study examined two groups of prematurely born infants: one group of 22 who experienced routine separation in an intensive-care nursery, where the mother's contact with the baby was confined to visual inspection and no handling was permitted; and the other an extra contact group of 20 infants, whose mothers could touch and handle the baby and participate in all care-taking activities. Mother–infant pairs were allocated at random to these two conditions, which continued for the 3–12 week period that the babies remained in hospital. A comparison group fo 24 full-term infants was also included.

A large amount of information was obtained in the course of the follow-up about the mothers' behaviour and attitudes, derived from interviews, questionnaires and observations. All scoring was done blind, without knowledge of the group to which any particular mother–infant pair belonged. The mothers were seen every few months for the first 2 years and those that could be traced were contacted once again 5 to 8 years later.

When seen one week after discharge from hospital a number of differences between the separated and the contact groups were evident. Observations during 1 to 2 hour sessions indicated that mothers from the separated group made rather less physical contact with their babies, but many other behavioural measures of maternal bonding did not differentiate the two groups. The mothers of the contact group showed greater commitment and self-confidence in their maternal role as elicited by questionnaires; but 1 month later this difference had disappeared. One year after discharge from hospital none of the measures differentiated the two groups; 21 months after discharge the only difference found was that the mothers from the separated group were *more* attentive to their children than the other mothers. It was also established at this point that the two sets of children were alike in the scores they obtained on a developmental test. Finally, at the follow-up interview held 5 to 8 years later there was once again no difference on any of the measures taken: whatever differences there were among individual subjects was accounted for by such traditional family variables as social class and parity and not by the post-partum experience of mother and child. For that matter, the social bonds that the mothers of either group of premature babies established in due course were indistinguishable from those of mothers of full-term babies.

Siegel, E., Bauman, K. E., Schaefer, E. S., Saunders, M. M. and Ingram, D. 1980: Hospital and home support during infancy: impact on maternal attachment, child abuse and neglect, and health care utilization. Paediatrics, 66, 183–90.

There are some who have speculated that 'bonding failure', as caused by early separation, may be an important factor in explaining child abuse. This and the following report examine this possibility.

The 321 women included in this study came from low-income backgrounds and were for the most part young, black and unmarried. At the time of delivery they were randomly assigned to a contact group or to a comparison group. Mothers in the former group were given their babies for an extra 45 minutes in the first 3 hours after birth; subsequently and throughout their hospital stay they kept the child with them for an additional 5 hours per day. Mothers in the comparison group had only brief contact with the baby immediately after delivery; thereafter, contact in the hospital was confined to feeds and other routines. Data were collected by interview during the last trimester of pregnancy and by interviews and observations in the home when the infant was 4 months and 12 months of age. The observers, who were blind as to the mothers' group membership, worked in pairs and recorded approximately 30 items of mother–infant attachment behaviour, derived from interaction situations such as bathing, dressing, feeding and play. They also completed a 92-item inventory after each visit that was designed to measure maternal acceptance–rejection and involvement–detachment. In addition, reports of child abuse and neglect were obtained from the records of official agencies throughout the children's first year.

A statistical analysis of the difference between the measures produced by the two groups was undertaken. It was found that differences on such indices as the mother's acceptance of the infant, the amount of her positive interaction and stimulation and her ability to console a crying infant were closely related to such social background variables as education, age, race and marital status. The amount of contact with the baby in hospital, on the other hand, was of relatively little significance (and surprisingly, the same applied to a home-visiting programme designed to provide support to the mothers: this too had little effect on the development of social bonds). A separate analysis of the 88 mothers whose babies had to be placed in an observation nursery for 24 hours immediately after birth because of medical complications showed up no difference in their behaviour when compared with that of other mothers. Finally, the occurrence of abuse and neglect was also not related to the amount of contact during the neonatal period. As the authors put it, 'it appears that programs other than early and extended contact ... must be developed to produce substantial influences on attachment [and on] abuse and neglect.'

Egeland, B. and Vaughn, B. 1981: Failure of 'bond formation' as a cause of abuse, neglect and maltreatment. American Journal of Orthopsychiatry, 51, 78–84.

From a total sample of 267 women two groups were selected: one of 33 mothers providing their infants with high-quality care, the other of 32 mothers who abused or neglected their infants. Judgements about quality of care were arrived at on the basis of home observations carried out 3, 6 and 9 months after birth. Following each visit the observer checked ratings for a variety of items including physical violence towards the child, poor standards of care, bad living conditions, neglect and failure to thrive. The women were all from lower socio-economic backgrounds, mostly young and unmarried, with no older children.

Details regarding birth, delivery and the neonatal period were obtained from medical records. These included prematurity, difficulties at birth resulting in the new-born being separated from the mother and length of stay in the hospital after the mother's discharge – i.e. all possible criteria for potential bonding failure. Comparison of the two groups indicated no difference on any of these criteria, nor on any other item of information obtained such as unplanned pregnancy, length of labour or presence of physical anomalies in the new-born. It must thus be concluded that 'these data ... provide no evidence to support the notion that premature status, perinatal problems or other indices of limited contact immediately after birth are implicated in the etiology of abuse, neglect or other forms of maltreatment by mothers.'

(2) COMMENTS ON RESEARCH

The history of research in this area shows only too well the need for caution in accepting the findings of any one study without subsequent replication. The original reports by Klaus and Kennell were only too appealing because of the simplicity of their message: effective mothering is dependent on events in the period immediately following birth; if mother and baby are separated at that time or even if there is just limited contact between them, that efficiency is seriously interfered with for a long time, and perhaps even irreversibly so. This message has not been borne out by subsequent research. The various studies that have attempted to check on the bonding hypothesis have been near-unanimous in rejecting the notion of a critical period confined to a very limited time after birth when the mother–child relationship becomes 'fixed' for good or ill. Lack of early, extended contact at that time may (at least according to some studies) produce a few immediate, short-term effects, but the idea of long-term effects can now be unequivocally rejected. Even the findings on animals that originally gave rise to these ideas had to be modified in the light of further studies.

There are a number of fairly serious methodological inadequacies in the Klaus and Kennell work which are probably responsible for the results they obtained. It is a feature of much of the later research, such as that summarized above, that these weaknesses have been removed through the adoption of precautions like double-blind procedures, random allocation of subjects to different conditions and the use of robust measurement techniques. This is one reason why one can have confidence in the conclusions reached. Another is that studies using a great diversity of subject populations (middle- and lower-class families; American, British, Swedish and German mothers; full-term and premature babies, and so on) have all come up with comparable findings. Finally, the unanimity exists despite a considerable diversity in the design of the studies and in the research methods employed by them. Thus, there have been variations in the nature and timing of the extra contact provided, in the aspects of maternal and child functioning that have been chosen as outcome measures, and in the way in which the data so obtained have been analysed. It is also noteworthy that the mechanism sometimes advanced to explain the supposed enhancement of maternal feelings after birth, namely an altered hormonal condition which is then maintained by the presence of the baby, has not been substantiated by research. No wonder that Klaus and Kennell, writing 8 years after their original report, found it necessary to modify their previous standpoint. As they put it second time round: 'The many complex factors involved in the bonding process cannot be considered in isolation. It seems unlikely that such a life-sustaining relationship could be dependent on a single process. There are many fail-safe routes to attachment.'

Implications for practice

It is unfortunate that in many quarters the notion of bonding has retained the status of a sacred doctrine – a 'must' to which all mothers are supposed to conform in a particular way and at a particular time and which professional people are expected actively to encourage and, if events have not taken place in the prescribed manner, to condemn as inevitably leading to trouble. The doctrine sees the bonding process as an all-or-nothing one-off event: it should happen immediately after birth, take place quickly and suddenly and involve a total and unreserved commitment on the part of the mother. This super-glue view may well be a travesty even of the ideas originally put forward by people such as Klaus and Kennell, but it is a view that is nevertheless widely prevalent in professional circles. Thus, nurses in maternity hospitals are asked to make sure that 'bonding' takes place in the cases they supervise by enforcing contact between mother and baby; forms used by social workers and health visitors may contain the question 'Has bonding occurred?', followed by a simple 'Yes/No' alternative for checking; and pathology occurring later on in the mother–child relationship such as child abuse is only too often automatically ascribed to 'bonding failure' without any further enquiry into the circumstances surrounding the particular case. In addition, those mothers who do not experience a great upsurge of love for the baby immediately after birth are made to feel guilty and inadequate.

The bonding doctrine, as expressed in its super-glue version, is a gross over-simplification. The establishment of the mother's bond with her child is a highly complex, gradual and ever-changing process; to treat it otherwise merely prevents the painstakingly detailed analysis that is required in understanding any interpersonal relationship. The doctrine provides a glib explanation for cases such as abuse and neglect: a diagnosis of 'bonding failure' may be both meaningless and inaccurate under such circumstances. To believe that bonding can only occur within one highly restricted period may well engender an attitude of pessimism when that requirement has not been met. That is not warranted; if it were one would need to condemn as doomed to failure all cases of adoption, of mothers too ill or depressed after giving birth to care for the baby, of Caesarean sections where the mother is initially unconscious as a result of a general anaesthetic, and of babies whose prematurity or precarious medical condition forces them to be placed in isolation in a special-care unit. In fact, there is plenty of evidence to indicate that bonds can develop in all such cases and that their strength and quality need be no different from what is found generally among mothers and babies.

None of this is to deny the importance of taking measures designed to humanize the birth and post-partum experience of mothers. It is ironically one of the beneficial offshoots of the bonding doctrine that, following the publication of Klaus and Kennell's studies, a great many maternity hospitals in the Western world revised their routines in order to provide more natural methods of care for mother and baby. This may have been done under the misapprehension that the mother–child relationship was thereby put on its right course for good; as we now know, early contact is not such an easy cure-all. Nevertheless, any measure intended to instil confidence in mothers from the very beginning is well worth while. As we have seen, some studies suggest that extra contact may produce short-term effects of a beneficial nature that foster the relationship *at the time*. It is the long-term effects of these early measures that one must question.

Ideally, of course, the mother's care should be adapted to the needs of the individual case, rather than being governed by an automatic routine – whether that involves enforced contact or enforced separation. Individual variability in mothers' *spontaneous* interest in and wish for contact with their new-born babies is considerable. As several studies have shown, a large proportion of mothers report initial feelings of indifference and some may even refuse contact altogether with the baby immediately after birth. In the vast majority of cases these feelings are soon replaced by a much more positive attitude; a desire for immediate contact or its absence thus have no long-term diagnostic significance. The bonding doctrine, in its extreme form, is mistaken in assuming that mothers are bound to fall head over heels in love with their babies immediately after birth; frequently, the process is a much more gradual one. There is no evidence to suggest that the speed of the mother falling in love with her baby predicts the quality of the relationship thereafter, and it follows that there is no point whatsoever in attempting to hurry on bond formation by forcing extended contact on those mothers who are not yet ready for it.

As far as later pathology such as abuse or neglect is concerned, explanations that put responsibility entirely on events immediately following birth are clearly to be avoided. Single-factor explanations, particularly when the supposedly crucial event occurred at some distance of time, are rarely appropriate in any attempt at understanding psychological development. It is quite true that in cases of abuse and neglect a disproportionate incidence of conditions such as low birth weight and neonatal complications tends to occur and that early separation from the mother is therefore more likely. This does not mean, however, that a cause-and-effect relationship has been found, for the same families are also more likely to be distinguished by a great many other aberrant circumstances such as poor housing, inadequate diet, strained family relationships, and so forth. Retrospectively, it is virtually impossible to ascertain the influence of any one of these factors: it takes prospective studies such as that by

Egeland and Vaughn (quoted above) to provide a more definitive answer. Only then can one appreciate how many children with neonatal complications necessitating early separation have *not* been abused and have developed perfectly satisfactory relationships with the mother. Whatever the explanation of child abuse and neglect may be, searching for the cause merely in the hours immediately following birth is not a fruitful undertaking; and by the same token, prevention is likely to be a rather more complex affair than single-factor explanations would have us believe.

Further reading

Kennell, J. H. and Klaus, M. H. 1984: Mother–infant bonding: weighing the evidence. *Developmental Review*, 4, 275–82.

Klaus, M. H. and Kennell, J. H. 1976: *Parent–Infant Bonding*. St Louis: Mosby.

Schaffer, H. R. 1984: *The Child's Entry into a Social World*. London: Academic Press.

Sluckin, W., Herbert, M. and Sluckin, A. 1983: *Maternal Bonding*. Oxford: Blackwell.

Issue: Is there a 'blood bond'?

Background

Children are usually brought up by the parents who bring them into the world in the first place. However, not all parents are able or willing to assume the responsibilities associated with child rearing: children are abandoned, given away or compulsorily removed, and substitute arrangements for their care must then be made. Such arrangements take various forms; and in so far as they ought to reflect the needs of children for permanent, personal relationships, placement in a new family by means of fostering or adoption is the course most widely recommended. But are children brought up by people who are not their 'real' parents thereby handicapped in some way? Do individuals who are not biologically related to a child make 'inferior' parents? In cases of conflict between biological and substitute parents, should the 'blood bond' be taken into account, perhaps to override all other considerations and thereby permit the biological parents to retain or reclaim that child at will?

The widespread belief in the blood bond is based on the notion that there is a natural affinity between child and biological parents which makes the latter more fit to be responsible for the child's care and upbringing than any outsider. Such fitness is assumed to be due to the common heredity found in parent–child pairs: whatever experiences a child may share with some other adult, and whatever affectionate ties then develop between them, are considered to be of secondary importance to the blood bond which is said to exist from the moment of conception. As a result, courts of law have removed children from the foster parents with whom they have spent virtually all their lives and to whom they have formed deep attachments, in order to place them with the natural mother, despite the fact that the child may have spent no more than the first few hours or days following birth with her. In addition, the reluctance to remove children from parents patently unsuitable to care for them and place them in another family may sometimes be based entirely on belief in the validity of the blood bond. But does such a bond have psychological reality?

The question for research to answer is therefore as follows: Will parenting by non-biologically related individuals always and inevitably be second best? There are two ways of answering this question: by examining the parents and by examining the children. The former is more direct; it seeks to establish how adoptive parents compare with biological parents in their child-rearing practices, in particular to determine whether the absence of a genetic relationship is in any way a handicap in bringing up a child. Unfortunately, there is very little evidence available on this point; only the last of the summaries to be presented below provides some relevant data. The other line of enquiry, that involving the examination of children, is far more common. It seeks to determine the effects on children of being brought up by non-biologically related individuals (usually adoptive parents) in order to establish whether their psychological functioning is in any way inferior or developmentally retarded compared with what one might otherwise have expected. The effects on intelligence in particular have received quite a lot of attention, but as the summaries below demonstrate, research workers have also concerned themselves with the effects on social adjustment, behaviour problems and academic achievement. If adopted children do badly in these respects then (so the argument runs) it is the adoptive parents who are most likely responsible.

Research findings

(1) SUMMARIES

Seglow, J., Pringle, M. K. and Wedge, P. 1972: Growing up Adopted. *Slough: National Foundation for Educational Research.*

This study deals with the behaviour and adjustment of adopted children at home and at school. Its value lies in the fact that the sample was drawn from a highly representative group included in a national survey, namely all those children born in 1 week in March 1958 in England, Scotland and Wales. Data were obtained periodically about all these children from birth to adulthood, the information coming from a wide variety of sources including medical records, test scores, school assessment, parental questionnaires, and so on. A further advantage of the study is that the adopted children may be compared with various control groups of non-adopted children for whom comparable information is available.

The 145 adopted children included in the study were assessed at the age of 7. Their records showed that 42 per cent of them had been of 'vulnerable' status at birth, i.e. there were various pre-natal and/or perinatal problems such as prematurity, toxaemia, and so on – a very much higher proportion than found in the rest of the birth cohort. By 3 months of age 74 per cent of these children had been placed with the adoptive parents; only 9 per cent were placed after 1 year.

The adjustment of the children at age 7 was measured by asking teachers to complete the Bristol Social Adjustment Guides (in which a large number of concrete descriptions of behaviour are presented to the teacher, who is asked to underline that description which fits the child in question; a deviance score can then be calculated from the answers). No difference in adjustment was found between the adopted children and the rest of the birth cohort. On the other hand, children who had been born illegitimate but had stayed with their mothers (perhaps the most relevant comparison group) were found to show a markedly higher degree of maladjustment. The adopted boys, however, were rather more likely to show deviant behaviour than the adopted girls. The early history of the children did not appear to affect their adjustment. Thus, the number of moves prior to placement seemed to be of no relevance, nor whether or not they went straight to the adoptive home from their own mothers. The one aspect that did seem to play a part was age at placement: those adopted after 6 months of age showed somewhat higher maladjustment scores than those adopted before that age. When the total adjustment scores were broken down into 'syndrome' scores denoting more specific types of behaviour, no difference between adopted and non-adopted children was found for ten of the 12 syndromes; the remaining two ('hostility to other children' and 'anxiety for acceptance by children') indicated the adoptees to have somewhat more problems in these areas.

The teachers were also asked to supply information about the children's educational ability and attainment. Ratings of the level of general knowledge showed the adopted children to do better than others in the cohort and the same also applies to the children's power of self-expression. On tests of reading attainment and of arithmetic attainment, as well as on ratings of creative ability, there were no differences between the adopted and the non-adopted groups. On the other hand, on each one of these comparisons the illegitimate children who had not been adopted came out significantly more poorly.

Thus, despite the fact that so many of the adopted children had been 'vulnerable' at birth, the initial handicap had been almost entirely overcome by age 7. In this connection it may well be relevant that home visitors had judged 90 per cent of the adoptive homes to be happy and normal and that teachers rated a considerably larger proportion of adoptive mothers as 'very interested' in their child's education as compared with other mothers (60 per cent versus 39 per cent).

Brodzinsky, D. M., Schechter, D. E., Braff, A. M. and Singer, L. M. 1984: Psychological and academic adjustment in adopted children. Journal of Consulting and Clinical Psychology, 52, 582–90.

This study also investigated the social and educational adjustment of adopted children. It was undertaken in the belief that much of the earlier work suffered from various methodological deficiencies which accounted for sometimes contradictory findings and that a better designed study was therefore required.

A total of 260 children, 130 adopted and 130 non-adopted, was included in this investigation. They were carefully matched for age, sex, race, social class, family structure and number of siblings. Half of the children in each group were boys and half girls. Most of the adopted children had been placed very early on and all had been informed of their status by their parents. Two assessment measures were used: one consisted of social competence and behaviour problem itmes which mothers were asked to rate, while the other scale was based on observable classroom behaviour and academic achievement and had to be completed by teachers. At the time of assessment the children were between 6 and 11 years old.

The results show the adopted children to have been rated lower by their mothers in social competence and as having more behaviour problems than the non-adopted children. A similar picture emerges from the assessments by the teachers: on each of the 12 subscales (dealing with such aspects as inattention, originality, anxiety about failure, and so on) which they completed, adopted children did rather worse. This picture was relatively consistent across the age range studied and holds equally for boys and for girls. Thus, the adopted group was in general more prone to emotional, behavioural and educational problems; but the authors stress that these children, 'although rated as more poorly adjusted in comparison to non-adopted children, are still well within the normal range of behaviour. In other words, adopted children are typically not manifesting severe pathology, but are only displaying slightly more extreme forms of behaviour than are found among non-adopted children.'

Singer, L. M., Brodzinsky, D. M., Ramsay, D., Steir, M. and Waters, E. 1985: Mother–infant attachment in adoptive families. Child Development, 56, 1543–52.

This paper comes from the same team as the previous report and is an attempt to check on the suggestion that the higher incidence of psychological problems found by them among adopted children of school age may be due to insecurity in the relationship with the adoptive parents formed during infancy. The quality of early attachments was therefore assessed in a group of adoptive mother–infant pairs and compared with that found in a comparable but non-adoptive group.

The adoptive group comprised 46 pairs, including 19 children of Oriental or Hispanic origin who had been adopted into Caucasian families (the 'transracial' group). All children had been placed for adoption between 3 days and 10 months following birth and had lived with their adoptive parents for a minimum time of 4 months (average 12 months). Non-adoptive children were matched to the adoptive group in terms of age, parental education, father's age and family's social class.

At an age between 13 and 18 months all children were assessed in the 'Strange Situation' – the method widely used to highlight the quality of a child's attachment to its parent by observing its reaction to a series of mildly stressful situations involving the departure and subsequent reappearance of the parent. An elaborate scoring system is employed to assign children to a threefold classification: secure, avoidant and ambivalent. This scoring system, using videotaped recordings, was applied without knowledge of the children's adoption status.

No differences were found in attachment classification when non-adopted controls were compared with adopted children who had been placed in families belonging to the same ethnic grouping. Such differences were only evident when the transracially adopted children were compared with the non-adopted group, in so far as 58 per cent of the former were classified as insecurely attached as opposed to 26 per cent among the latter. Thus, in those families that adopted children of the same ethnic background as themselves the quality of the mother–infant relationship was similar to that found in non-adoptive families. Transracial adoption, on the other hand, may sometimes impose a strain that can affect the nature of the developing relationship between mother and child. These results do not therefore give support to the idea that any behaviour problems that may subsequently be evident are derived from a basically unsatisfactory relationship with the mother in any but a minority of exceptional cases.

Schiff, M., Duyme, M., Dumaret, A. and Tomkiewicz, S. 1982: How much could we boost scholastic achievement and IQ scores? A direct answer from a French adoption study. Cognition, 12, 165–96.

There have been many attempts to examine the effects of adoption on intelligence, mainly in order to sort out the respective influences of heredity and environment by seeing whether children's IQs resemble more closely those of their biological parents or those of their adoptive parents. This French team of research workers addressed the same problem but used a somewhat different approach.

The aim was to establish whether rearing in a socially more advantaged home than that into which the children had been born can affect intellectual development, and the method used was to compare a group of adopted children with their biological siblings who had remained in their families of origin. The 32 adopted children had all been abandoned at birth by their natural mothers and placed with the adoptive family before the age of 6 months. The families of origin all belonged to the lower end of the social-class spectrum, both parents being unskilled workers. The adoptive parents, on the other hand, were from the upper-middle-class range, the fathers spanning the top 13 per cent of the socio-economic scale.

The children were tested at ages 6 to 13 years. The mean IQ for the adopted group was 110.6, whereas for their siblings it was 94.2. School failure (defined as being one or more grades behind) showed a rate of 13 per cent in the adopted group but 55 per cent among their siblings. Additional comparisons with national norms for the general population show the adopted children to be well ahead in this respect too, with mean IQ scores being 14 points higher and the rate of school failure four times less when compared with the figures available for children for unskilled workers. These substantial differences, the authors believe, can only be explained by the drastic change in social environment experienced by the adopted children. They thus reflect the superior intellectual opportunities provided by the child-rearing practices of the adoptive parents.

Bohman, M. and Sigvardsson, S. 1980: A prospective, longitudinal study of children registered for adoption. Acta Psychiatrica Scandinavia, 61, 339–55.

This is a very ambitious study from Sweden, consisting of a long-term follow-up investigation of adopted children whose social and intellectual development was monitored right through childhood and compared with a number of control groups.

All children who had been registered for adoption in the City of Stockholm during a 2-year period were included in the sample. Only about a quarter of these children were in fact placed for adoption, while just over a third returned to their mothers and the remainder went to foster homes. At the ages of 11 and 15 years, to which this paper refers, there were 160 adopted, 214 returned and 205 fostered children available for investigation. The biological parents of all children came from poor economic and social backgrounds, most being unskilled without regular employment. The socio-economic status of the adoptive parents was very much superior in comparison, with those of the foster parents somewhat below that standard.

For each of these children two class-mates of the same sex were chosen at random. Information about the trios was collected mainly from teachers, who were asked to rate the children's adjustment and behaviour on nine scales referring to such aspects as aggressiveness, social maturity, intelligence and concentration. The teachers knew nothing about to which group each child belonged. School grades were also obtained for all children.

At age 11 all three groups were found to perform poorly with respect to both educational progress and social adjustment in comparison with their class-mate controls. It appeared that these children were more at risk at this age of developing behaviour disturbances and symptoms of maladjustment, regardless of whether they were growing up in an adoptive home, a foster home or with their own biological mother. At age 15, however, the difference had disappeared as far as the adopted children were concerned but not with respect to the returned and fostered children. Thus, for example, adjustment problems categorized as 'severe' were now no more prevalent among adopted children than among their class-mates: among children returned to their biological mothers and among those reared by foster parents such problems were two to three times as frequent as among their controls. Similarly with respect to school grades: the adopted children performed at about the same level as the control group at age 15; the other two groups, however, showed highly significant differences in this respect.

Thus, whatever psychological difficulties adopted children showed at the earlier age, the outcome in adolescence turned out to be good. Their superior status in comparison with children initially placed for adoption but then returned to their own parents is presumably a reflection of more optimal rearing conditions and thus a measure of the positive effects of adoption. For the returned children, on the other hand, there is a considerable risk of maladjustment and school failure. What is rather puzzling is the unexpectedly poor showing of the foster children. One possible explanation is that this is due to the uncertainty of their status and the consequent insecurity felt by both children and foster parents.

Tizard B. 1977: Adoption: a second chance. *London: Open Books.*

We have already referred to this study, but it is relevant to the present issue, and especially so as it is one of the very few reports to give some detailed information about the child-rearing practices and attitudes of adoptive parents. In addition (like the above paper by the Swedish investigators), it provides a comparison with a returned group, i.e. children who left their biological mothers very early on but were subsequently restored to them. In all cases the children were put into care because the mothers were unable to provide a home for them, generally for reasons connected with the illegitimacy of the child and the financial and emotional resources of the mother. Thus, both the adopted and the restored group of children spent their first few years in institutions under highly impersonal conditions. During this time, some of the biological mothers of the children who eventually returned home kept in regular and frequent touch with them, while in many, visiting was only sporadic and infrequent.

The children left the institution at varying ages between 2 and 7 years and were assessed at home at 4½ (where appropriate) and at 8 years. In comparing the restored with the adopted children, the former were found to be inferior in their intellectual performance, emotional adjustment and social relationships. When tested in the institution at the age of 24 months, for instance, the two groups were intellectually similar, having an average mental age of 22 months. At age 4½ those children who had been restored to their own mothers by then were found to have a mean IQ of 100; the adopted children, on the other hand, had made considerable gains, scoring well above the average with a mean IQ of 115. Behaviourally, the restored children were also inferior, in that considerably more had problems such as bed wetting, tantrums, fears and anxieties. They were also found to be more clinging, more demanding and to have poorer concentration than the adopted children. At the 8–year assessment most of these differences were still evident: intellectually the adopted children had above-average IQs and reading attainment scores, whereas the restored children's IQs were average and their reading attainment below average. The restored children also continued to show a greater incidence of behavioural problems.

These findings bear out those reported by others, namely that adoption often results in a considerable improvement of psychological functioning. It goes further, however, in linking this to a description of the adoptive parents' behaviour, which was then compared with that of the biological parents who had their children restored to them. A far greated investment of time, energy and emotion on the part of the adoptive parents is the most striking feature of such a comparison. These parents had considerably more resources – not only financial but also in the way of more support from friends and kin. They had greater reserves of energy and were thus able to provide their children with a wider range of experiences such as taking them out on outings and on holidays. In general, the adoptive parents spent more of their leisure time with their children than the biological parents: they talked more together, there was more reading and play, they involved them more in joint household activities and also more often helped them with school work. Even in comparison with a sample of middle-class 'natural' families the adoptive parents were found to spend more time with the child on various types of joint activities. It seemed to the investigators that this high frequency of joint parent–child activity stemmed from the fact that the adoptive parents were motivated to enjoy parenthood to an unusual degree and that they thus took considerable pleasure in their children's company. This in turn, of course, had all sorts of beneficial effects as far as the children's psychological development was concerned.

(2)   COMMENTS ON RESEARCH

As we have already indicated, the research literature does not provide a great deal of direct evidence that would enable us to answer unequivocally the question about the relative aptitudes of biological and non-biological parents. Most of the research refers to the effects on children brought up by these two sets of individuals rather than to the parents themselves. Nevertheless, the work on children does give us some indication of the effectiveness of rearing by those not connected to the child by a 'blood bond' such as adoptive parents.

Going to an adoptive home almost invariably means going to an environment socially and economically superior to that of the family of origin. The research literature is virtually unanimous in finding that such a step can bring considerable benefit to children. The effects are most clearly reflected in intellectual development; thus, the study by Schiff et al. quoted above is typical of a number of similar investigations, all of which have found that when children move from a disadvantaged background to a home of higher social status, their IQ is likely to rise by around 15 to 20 points. The level of intellectual functioning thus comes to approach that of the adoptive parents more closely than that of the biological parents, and Schiff's findings are particularly telling in this respect in that they are based on a comparison of adopted children's intelligence scores with those obtained by their siblings remaining in the family of origin. The outcome for the adopted children is clearly better in this respect than for those left behind in the disavantaged environment.

A similar conclusion applies to educational progress. Measures of attainment, motivation and school failure rates all indicate that the superior intelligence of adopted children is translated into classroom performance and that their progress in the educational system is considerably better than what one might have predicted had they continued to live in the family of origin. The evidence is not so clear when it comes to emotional adjustment. In this respect there is some disagreement in the literature (stemming partly from differences in methodology), in that some studies find no difference in the incidence of behaviour problems between adopted and non-adopted children while others show adopted children to be more vulnerable to emotional difficulties. However, even if one accepts the latter conclusion there are two considerations to bear in mind. One is the finding by Bohman (quoted above) and confirmed by one or two other studies that such difficulties are of a temporary nature and tend to disappear in later childhood. The other is that there is no indication that the symptoms are necessarily derived from the relationship with the adoptive parents and that they must be interpreted as reflecting the parents' ineptness. Emotional vulnerability in adopted children, if it does exist, may have other causes, and among these the child's confusion regarding its sense of identity is probably a particularly common and potent one.

It should not be concluded, of course, that the process of adoption wipes the hereditary slate clean and that the new home environment is able completely to override genetic influences in all respects. It has been shown, for instance (in a publication by Rutter and Madge, 1976), that such influences are of minor importance in juvenile delinquency but play a much more significant part in the causation of severe and persistent adult criminality. Thus, adoption into a socially conforming home makes it very much less likely that the children of antisocial biological parents will themselves come to indulge in delinquent activities; on the other hand, the adopted children of serious criminals have been found to show a greater incidence of criminality than one would have predicted from their adoptive family. In psychiatric disorder too there is a strong hereditary influence which manifests itself in severe mental illness but far less so in mild behaviour disorders. Adoption is therefore likely to influence the latter more than the former.

The research findings thus suggest that, judging by the effects on children, adoptive placement produces psychological improvement in many though perhaps not in all respects. There is therefore no indication that rearing by non-biologically related individuals is in any way a handicap. Direct examination of adoptive parents and their child-rearing practices may have been undertaken by far fewer investigators, but the study by Tizard summarized here is unequivocal in its conclusions: adoptive parents are in many respects 'super-parents', in that most show a devotion that is frequently well above what one finds in ordinary families. Tizard's sample was small and one must therefore be cautious about generalization; but her comparison of adopted children with restored children is a particularly telling one, for it indicates that parents who are forced to send their children into care may (perhaps by force of external circumstances such as financial or health problems) in some instances not be able to provide the same devotion and level of care that one finds in many adoptive parents. The blood bond by itself is not guarantee of sound parenting practice.

Implications for practice

Naturally one should start with the general principle that it is best for children to be brought up by their own parents. The rights of parents must be respected; for outsiders arbitrarily to interfere in the family unit is in many respects repugnant. Simply moving children around because it may be possible to improve their prospects to some degree smacks of social engineering at its worst and will be anathema to the vast majority of people.

There is, however, another principle which occasionally clashes with the first one, and that is that children need security in their personal relationships and a sufficiently adequate standard of care to ensure their satisfactory development. Where these requirements are not met in the family it may be necessary under certain circumstances to consider alternative arrangements for care. In practice it is often quite extraordinarily difficult to decide when the point has been reached that justifies such a drastic course. Adequacy of care, after all, is not a matter of either–or but refers to a continuum defined by a great many criteria, and where one draws the line along that continuum depends to a considerable extent on value judgements that will always be subject to debate. The point to be made here is that in such a debate the notion of the blood bond can have no place: a child's parents are not inevitably and under all circumstances the people most fit to bring it up merely by virtue of their biological relatedness.

To refuse to remove a child from its biological parents under *any* circumstances must clearly be rejected. In cases of cruelty and abuse amounting not only to threat to life but to severe physical and psychological harm, removal may well have to be resorted to and is generally accepted as justified by present-day society. It is perhaps natural that professional workers often feel guilty in terminating parents' contact with their own child, yet the biological relationship cannot be said to confer on the parents an inalienable right to do as they wish. Respect for the family unit, however essential a requirement, ought not to be such that it is used as the *only* argument for keeping the child within it. Considerations concerning safety, security and adequacy of care take precedence. This applies equally to removing a child from home and to restoring it there. Thus, a child who has spent a considerable period of time with foster parents, formed deep emotional attachments to them and has had little or no contact with its biological parents during that time cannot be automatically regarded as 'belonging' to the biological parents. What needs to be taken into account is the existence of mutual feelings of attachment which have formed between child and caretakers through the simple process of living together. It is a history of social interaction, not kinship, that breeds attachment, and to break these bonds cannot be done light-heartedly – certainly not on the basis of a myth, namely a psychological blood bond.

Further reading

Adcock, M. and White, R. (eds) 1980: *Terminating Parental Contact*. London: British Agencies for Adoption and Fostering.

Feigelman, W. and Silverman, A. R. 1983: *Chosen Children: new patterns of adoptive relationships*. New York: Praeger.

Goldstein, J., Freud, A. and Solnit, A. J. 1980: *Beyond the Best Interests of the Child*. London: Burnett Books.

Mech, E. V. 1973: Adoption: a policy perspective. In B. M. Caldwell and H. N. Riciutti (eds), *Review of Child Development Research, Vol. 3*. Chicago: University of Chicago Press.

Issue: Should mothering be confined to one person?

Background

The belief that the mother–child unit is basic and unique is long-established and deeply ingrained in both popular and professional thinking. Any arrangement of child rearing which does not foster this unit is thus frowned upon, and in particular one that dilutes maternal care by spreading it over several people rather than concentrating it all in the hands of the one individual. Shared care is regarded as harmful, and studies demonstrating the adverse effects of institutional upbringing, where children are cared for by a range of people, are often cited to bolster this argument.

In fact such studies are irrelevant to this issue, for institutional care means far more than the absence of a single mother-figure. For one thing, the number of individuals responsible for the care of any one child over a period of time is often very large; for another, the relationships are mostly impermanent and sometimes extremely brief; and finally, the emotional commitment to individual children displayed by their caretakers tends (not surprisingly under the circumstances) to be minimal. Generalizing to family-reared children with opportunities to form several attachments is hardly justified.

The belief in the uniqueness of the mother–child relationship is based on two assumptions, both fostered by Freudian theory. One is that children by nature are initially incapable of forming more than one emotionally meaningful attachment; all other relationships will appear only subsequently and will always be subsidiary to that with the mother which, by virtue of being first, serves as a prototype for these later bonds. The other is that any attempt to impose more than one caretaker on a child at the beginning of life will inevitably lead to confusion in children too young as yet to sort out the roles played by different adults, thus weakening the relationship with the mother and leading to insecurity. It is indeed sometimes further argued that the conventional Western family, with its division of roles among the parents according to sex, has specifically evolved in order to cater for children's particular emotional needs by making the task of child care the monopoly of one person, the mother. It follows that any arrangement of sharing that task is to be discouraged: mothers ought to assume sole responsibility and devote themselves wholly to their mothering duties. Shared care, according to this argument, is diluted care: it will lead to a weakening of the tie with the mother and must thus be regarded as emotionally damaging.

There are several questions arising from these assumptions which research needs to examine. Some relate to the effects on children of shared care arrangements; they involve the consequences of mothers going out to work and the implications for children's development of being looked after by other people during part of each day, whether in group-care settings or on an individual basis. We shall return to the issues of maternal employment and of group care later on; here, our concern is with another question, i.e. whether the suggestion that children are at first incapable of forming more than one emotionally meaningful relationship is indeed a valid one. Thus, we need to ascertain whether it is part of children's inborn make-up that they must initially derive their security entirely from one single source (normally the mother), or whether even an infant can already sustain a number of relationships and become attached to several individuals without sign of confusion or emotional damage.

The studies summarized below address themselves to this question. As we have seen, it has been established that children first become capable of forming attachments around the beginning of the second half-year. We can now proceed to ask about the nature of such relationships, with particular reference to the person or persons with whom they are formed.

Research findings

(1) SUMMARIES

Schaffer, H. R. and Emerson, P. E. 1964: The development of social attachments in infancy. Monographs of the Society for Research in Child Development, *29, no. 3 (serial no. 94).*

We have already referred to this report in discussing the age children form their first attachments. It is relevant here too in provides data with respect to the number and identity of the individuals to whom such attachments are formed.

Of the 60 infants followed up at 4-weekly intervals during the first year and again at 18 months, just under one-third directed their initial attachments at more than one person, some even selecting as many as five individuals for this purpose. Three months after the first focused relationships emerged, i.e. when children were approaching the end of the first year, over half the sample were showing attachments towards more than one person; by 18 months only 13 per cent were attached to just a single individual while nearly a third of all children now had five or more attachment figures.

As to the identify of the individuals so selected, the mother was (not surprisingly) by far the most frequently chosen. However, the importance which fathers came to assume in these infants' lives was also very evident. Initially as many as 27 per cent of the sample chose father as an attachment object jointly with the mother, and by 18 months this proportion had gone up to 75 per cent. In addition, such other regular companions as grandparents and older siblings were also chosen by quite a few of the children. Although the most intense attachment was generally formed to the mother, this was by no means inevitable: fathers in particular were also occasionally found to be the child's principal attachment figure. This happened despite their limited availability during the day, for amount of time spent with the child seemed to play only a minor role in determining choice of attachment object, and participation in routine activities such as feeding played none at all.

The findings thus show that children are not initially confined to forming only a single relationship. They indicate that even very early on multiple attachments are by no means uncommon, apparently occurring to the extent to which children have the opportunity to experience pleasurable interactions with other people. One other point which also emerged from this study was that an especially close relationship with one person (say the mother) by no means prevents other relationships being formed – quite to the contrary, it appears to foster them, for in large part the children with the closest relationship with the mother were also the ones who had the largest number of other attachments.

Cohen, L. J. and Campos, J. J. 1974: Father, mother and stranger as elicitors of attachment behaviors in infancy. Developmental Psychology, *10, 146–54.*

This study is specifically concerned with fathers as attachment objects. It set out to compare the behaviour of infants to the mother at various ages with behaviour to the father, using for this purpose a mildly stressful situation that induced the infants to seek comfort and reassurance. The question asked was the extent to which fathers were seen as individuals able to provide the required security.

Twenty infants at each of three age levels, i.e. 10, 13 and 16 months, were investigated. Each infant was observed under three conditions, which varied according to the persons present in the room, these being mother, father and two strangers. The presence of the strangers and the unfamiliar environment were considered to constitute sources of stress, to which the infant could react by seeking the proximity of a parent. Various measures of differential proximity seeking were used as attachment indices.

From the results it is quite clear that even at the youngest age, 10 months, father is already an object of attachment for most infants. In the presence of a stranger, and without the mother present, he functioned as a source of security, and responsiveness to him was overwhelmingly greater than that shown towards the stranger. On the other hand when both parents were present, mother was generally the preferred person: it was to her that the infants mostly went for reassurance. Even then, however, a small number of infants relied more heavily on the father than on the mother. The incidence of attachment to the father was high right through the age range covered while the incidence of *exclusive* mother attachment, on the other hand, was consistently low (occurring in about 10 per cent of infants).

There is thus no support in these findings for the notion that the first relationship formed is an exclusive one. As in the previous study summarized, we find that multiple attachments are already the rule in infancy, though it is also notable that most infants do not just treat these individuals as completely interchangeable, in that they have definite preferences for one over another.

Lamb, M. E. 1977: Father–infant and mother–infant interaction in the first year of life. Child Development, *48, 167–81.*

This report is also concerned with fathers as possible objects of attachment, but it is based on extended observations in the natural setting of the home and provides a more detailed analysis of the interactions of infants with fathers and mothers respectively. It refers to 20 infants who were seen on two occasions between 7 and 8 months of age and again twice around 12 and 13 months. Each time, the infant was observed at home with both mother and father present, the parents having been asked to continue with their usual routines around the house. During this time the observer dictated into a tape-recorder a detailed narrative account of the infant's behaviour as well as of the parents' reactions. These accounts were subsequently analysed to provide estimates of the incidence of various kinds of infant responses to each parent. Another research worker, acting as a 'strange visitor', was also present on each occasion.

Already at 7 months, i.e. the age when focused attachments first emerge, the infants showed such attachment responses as proximity seeking, touching, wanting to be held and reaching to *both* parents. In this respect they clearly differentiated between the parents on the one hand and the strange visitor on the other. At neither of the two age points was there a preference for one parent over the other: in this study both served equally as attachment figures. On the other hand such responses as smiling, laughing, looking at and vocalizing (referred to collectively as 'affiliative behaviour') were more likely to be directed to the father. This appeared to be accounted for by the different kinds of experiences fathers tended to provide in comparison with mothers: as analysis of the observed interactions showed, while mothers most often held the babies to perform some caretaking act, fathers held them in order to play with them.

Here too, then, we have evidence showing that the mother–child relationship is by no means an exclusive one and that, under 'normal' conditions of family life, fathers also quickly assume significance to their infants. However, the fathers observed here were not merely mother substitutes, for they interacted with the infants in a qualitatively distinct manner, thereby extending the infants' opportunities to learn about the nature of their social world.

Fox, N. 1977: Attachment of kibbutz infants to mother and metapelet. Child Development, 48, 1228–39.

The Israeli kibbutz system offers a most useful opportunity to observe the effects of shared care, for here children are brought up communally by a professional caretaker (the *metapelet*) but remain in constant touch with their parents, with whom they may spend several hours every day. The metapelet is thus primarily responsible for the child's physical care and training, while the parents' role is more concerned with affection and companionship. This situation lends itself well to investigating the possibility of multiple attachments being formed and the extent to which even quite young children can sort out the role of different people.

In this study 122 children between 8 and 24 months of age were observed in a number of social situations specially set up to record their reactions to separation from and reunion with the mother and the metapelet. Measures included such indices as amount of crying, duration of play, proximity to mother or metapelet and reaction to a stranger, these serving as indications of the nature and strength of the relationship to the children's caretakers.

The findings show that for most children, including the youngest, mother and metapelet were interchangeable attachment figures, in that each provided a 'secure base' from which to explore and to which to return for reassurance. The children were equally upset by the departure of either person from the room but in general did not protest when left by one with the other. Only their behaviour at reunion following a brief separation showed some difference, in that most children appeared to be more attached to their mother than to the metapelet under such circumstances.

What is striking is the fact that the quality of the relationship to the mother was in no way affected by the fact that she was not the only, and in certain respects not the principal, caretaker. To a considerable extent the two adults were interchangeable, and at the same time there were also indications that the infants were well able to differentiate between them and were largely more attached to the mother.

Smith, P. K. and Noble, R. 1987: Factors affecting the development of caregiver–infant relationships. In L. W. C. Tavecchio and M. H. van IJzendoorn (eds), Attachment in Social Networks. Amsterdam: Elsevier.

The studies quoted above were all concerned with attachments to individuals who had been with the infant from birth. The present report concerns an attempt to investigate what happens when a new person is introduced as a potential attachment object after an infant has already formed its initial focused relationships to parents. Thus, rather than dealing with the finished product an attempt was made by these investigators to observe the possible buildup of an additional relationship.

This was done by recruiting six caregivers to act as temporary childminders for 72 infants aged about 15 months. Each infant was visited at home on 15 occasions by a particular caregiver, the visits lasting 3 hours and taking place either once or three times a week. During that time the mother was present for only the first half-hour. Following her departure the caregivers followed a particular sequence of routines and carried out systematic observations for which they had previously received training.

The results show that most of the infants settled reasonably well with the new caregiver. While about half of the infants typically cried at the mother's departure, their upset was mostly brief. The prevailing mood when left with the child-minder was neutral or mildly positive. As sessions continued the infants became increasingly relaxed, gradually settling into the new relationship. The mother was clearly preferred in terms of all attachment criteria investigated, but in her absence the caregiver fairly quickly came to be used as a source of security by the majority of infants.

Some infants, however, did not adjust so well. About 10 per cent cried regularly at the child-minder's arrival and about 20 per cent were upset for some prolonged period when the mother departed. A number of factors appeared to be related to this failure to settle into the new relationship, including the infants' temperament, the kind of relationship they had with the mother and the amount of their previous experience of non-parental care. In general, however, there was no indication that the relationship to the mother was such an all-consuming one that it left no room for the buildup of any new relationship, despite the fact that the contact with the caregiver in the course of any week was neither very frequent nor prolonged.

Hill, M. 1987: Sharing Child Care in Early Parenthood. *London: Routledge and Kegan Paul.*

The research outlined so far was mainly concerned with the question: Are children capable of forming multiple attachments? In the final report in this section we turn from children to parents in order to ask how parents view the situation – do they insist on confining child care to the mother? How prevalent is shared care? Quite a lot is known about the incidence of group care but far less about the informal arrangements that parents may make with relatives, friends, neighbours and child-minders. The study summarized here provides some relevant data about that aspect.

The investigation concerns the care arrangements made by a group of 63 families for their children during the first 3 years of life. The families came from two districts of Edinburgh, one working class and the other middle class. Information was obtained through detailed interviews and from diary records that the mothers were asked to keep for a typical 2-week period.

The extent to which shared care was resorted to by the families varied considerably within the sample, but the majority of the children had experienced care from people other than their parents for a major part of their second and third years at frequencies that ranged from several times a week to once a month. The carers were often relatives, especially on the mother's side such as the maternal grandmother, who were called upon even though they lived at considerable distance. Non-relatives acting as carers were mainly mothers with young children who lived nearby, as well as immediate neighbours whom the child knew well and frequently visited quite spontaneously. The carer was, however, not always the same person: according to the diary information over a third of children had been looked after by more than one person on separate occasions in the past 2 weeks.

By the age of 2 over half the children had experienced some sort of care provided by a person other than their parents; one in six was being looked after for 5 days a week for part of the day while both parents were at work. In the first 3 years not only did shared care become more frequent but the number of different people looking after the child became larger too. In addition, over three-quarters of children at the age of 3 were attending some form of group care (mostly nursery school, for which there was an unusually high level of provision in the locality). Shared care tended to occur more frequently among the middle-class families but was made use of rather later in the child's life than was the case with working-class families.

None of the parents considered that shared care in any way harmed their children; on the contrary, they believed it produced benefits as far as social experience and play opportunities were concerned. It was striking that children described as shy, clinging and anxious were mostly those who had been almost exclusively with their mothers. However, most parents felt more comfortable about sharing care with second or later children.

These findings give some indication of the extent to which parents are prepared to have their children looked after by other people. The precise figures for shared care are likely to vary from one population to another; what may well be general is the high level of care from people outside the immediate family which even quite young children experience as a matter of routine.

(2) COMMENTS ON RESEARCH

Studies such as those quoted above have produced in recent years a marked shift of opinion in the psychological literature – away from a belief in the exclusiveness of the mother–child relationship and towards a realization that children can and do form multiple attachments even in infancy. The former view, it is now realized, was based on dogma rather than on empirical evidence; it may have applied to one particular family structure, i.e. the kind of middle-class family that prevailed many decades ago where child care was regarded as exclusively the mother's business and where fathers played a distinct and distant part vis-à-vis their children. However, even then this was found only in certain social class and cultural settings; and in this connection it is worth quoting the findings of two anthropologists, Weisner and Gallimore (1977), who pointed out that amongst all human societies on whom we have relevant data, mothers function as exclusive caretakers of their children in only 3 per cent and as predominant caretakers in only 60 per cent of societies. Such cross-cultural data help to put the mother's role in its proper perspective.

In any case the situation within our own Western society has greatly changed in recent times, with mothers working, the increased use of day-care facilities and child-minders and, above all, the far greater involvement of fathers in the rearing of their children. It has taken research some time to catch up with these social changes, but now that the issue has been examined empirically there is substantial agreement: the notion of exclusiveness cannot be maintained, there is no biological necessity to confine attachment to one person only, and indeed under the usual conditions of family life by the end of their first year the majority of children already sustain several emotionally meaningful relationships and moreover are encouraged by their parents to do so. One individual (usually but not invariably the mother) may generally be the principal source of the child's security, but some degree of interchangeability among attachment figures is common.

It is perhaps not surprising that most attention has been given to the father as a possible object of attachment, and quite an industry in father research has sprung up in recent years. We shall return to some of this work later, for it is relevant to other issues to be discussed. Even more recently the special psychological significance that siblings can have for young children has come to be appreciated and documented; however, it is also clear that anyone in regular and affectionate contact with a child is in a position to become the focus of its attachment. Yet the question as to why the child chooses some individuals rather than others, or why some are preferred as the main source of security, is by no means settled. It appears not to be based on providing for the child's physical needs such as for food, nor is it necessarily a matter of time spent with the child. Obviously the other person must be available for a certain minimal amount of time in order to become familiar, but otherwise, attachment choice appears to depend primarily on various subtle aspects of the relationship developing between adult and child: the warmth and sensitivity of the adult, the temperament and expectations of the child, and so forth. It is the merit of studies such as that by Smith and Noble that in experimentally introducing a new person to the child one can investigate the way in which the relationship builds up and so determine the factors that influence this process. This is also the merit of 'unusual' arrangements of child care such as the Israeli kibbutz system, where the care functions are divided up among several individuals and where one can therefore see what role such factors as time spent together and lack of participation in physical care appear to play in the development of attachments. Above all, such 'experiments of nature' have demonstrated that the necessity of exclusive mothering is a myth.

Implications for practice

The results of the psychological research on this topic may be pretty well unanimous, but they have by no means yet reached all potential consumers. Many mothers go on feeling guilty about any move they make towards sharing the child's care: they refrain from taking on activities outside the home during the early years of the child's life, frequently to the detriment not only of themselves but of the child as well. The myth of exclusive mothering remains prevalent, yet objectively speaking there is no obvious reason why maternal care *must* be confined to one person. If young children commonly and spontaneously form attachments to several people, then one is not going against nature by exposing them to more than one caretaker. On the contrary, there may well be advantages to such an arrangement: it acts as a kind of insurance policy in case something goes wrong with one relationship, as the child will then have alternative sources of security; it provides opportunities for the child to be exposed to different people's practices and expectations and so helps to develop a greater range of social skills in dealing with these; and by lessening the strain which child rearing can sometimes impose on a mother it facilitates a smoother relationship between her and the child. Certainly, the fear that that relationship is in some way going to be 'diluted' by the simultaneous existence of other relationships is quite unjustified: a child's attachment is not some limited quantity that has to be divided up amongst people. Thus, mothers who share their care-giving role need not fear that they put their children at risk thereby. Some may prefer exclusive mothering because that suits their personality and their life-style, but there is no reason why each family should not adopt that course with which it is most comfortable, and certainly no reason why active steps should be taken to prevent a child from forming relationships with people other than the mother. As has been repeatedly established, what matters is the *quality* of interaction with the child, not its *quantity*.

What is much more difficult to stipulate are the limits beyond which sharing does produce detrimental effects and at what point the number of 'mother–figures' becomes so great that the child becomes bewildered and insecure. Sharing with one other person, such as a relative or a child-minder, is clearly no problem with respect to even the youngest child, and this tends to be the most common practice. The extent to which one can go on increasing the number of substitute caretakers remains unknown. Most likely there is no one specific upper limit, for much depends on such factors as a child's age and temperament and the precise nature of the care arrangements made. All one can assert is that when stability and quality of relationships are satisfactory, children's well-being is not put at hazard by multiple-care arrangements. Moreover, it has also become apparent that children are able to sort out the differing roles of people at much earlier ages than they had been given credit for. Thus, their differential reaction to various individuals (mother as opposed to father, parent as compared to child-minder, and so on) shows that, however interchangeable these people may be for certain purposes, they are clearly discriminated between. It seems that even infants already feel themselves to be part of quite a complex social world; there is thus no need to fear that exposure to a range of individuals will produce confusion as to the nature of that world.

Further reading

Scarr, S. and Dunn, J. 1987: *Mother Care/Other Care*. Harmondsworth: Penguin.
Schaffer, R. 1977: *Mothering*. London: Fontana; Cambridge, Mass.: Harvard University Press.

Issue: Do women make better parents than men?

Background

Traditionally, the rearing of children has been regarded as women's business. It is a biological necessity that women give birth; it used to be a biological necessity that they were responsible for feeding the baby; and the role segregation of the two sexes so begun was then continued into the later years of children's lives. Women were thus considered as 'natural' parents: fathers (as the anthropologist Margaret Mead once put it) may be required for conception but thereafter they are just a nuisance. According to the traditional view, men's business is to provide economic and emotional support for the family, but otherwise their involvement in child care is peripheral and indirect, at most confined to a few specific tasks such as discipline and the teaching of some 'masculine' skills.

It is in fact doubtful whether a division of labour as rigid as this ever really prevailed in more than a minority of families, even in middle-class Victorian circles. Nevertheless, the stereotype has persisted, and many attempts have been made to find scientific support for it. Thus it has been argued that this kind of sex-role segregation is universal among human beings – an assertion which, on closer examination, turns out to be untrue: in some non-Western societies, for example, men traditionally participate fully in the care of their children. It has also been argued that amongst animals it is inevitably the female who is solely responsible for the rearing of offspring – another assertion which cannot be sustained, for there are several species where the paternal animal takes an equal or (in a few cases) even a major part of the responsibility. And finally, a lot of attention has been paid to the notion that at birth certain hormonal changes take place in the mother, as a result of which she is 'primed' to engage in caretaking and will do so more effectively than someone who has not gone through the birth process. A 'maternal instinct' would thus be called into being, i.e. a biologically based competence for child care specific to females and in no way shared by males. Once again, however, the evidence for such a view is thin. Most of the work on hormonal changes accompanying birth has been done with animals and has doubtful relevance to human beings; and in addition, as we have already seen in our discussion of the 'blood bond', the idea that non-biologically related individuals are bound to be less competent as parents cannot be maintained.

It is unlikely that sex-role segregation is fully accounted for by biological factors; it is more likely that whatever sex differences do exist nowadays can be largely explained by social convention. The great changes that have taken place in recent times in the nature of the family would certainly suggest that. Fathers these days are in- volved in child care to a far greater extent than they used to be: the distant disciplinarian is a rarity and full participation in all aspects of children's upbringing is becoming more and more common. Mothers, including those of quite young children, are increasingly seeking employment outside the home, and as a result the pressure on fathers to take a part in child rearing is also increasing. Indeed, in a few families a complete role reversal has occurred, in that mother goes out ot work (possibly because she is the only one who can find employment) while father stays at home doing the housework and caring for the children. Economic pressures may be one factor underlying such social changes, the ideals of feminism another, and technological advances accounting for the widespread availability of labour-saving domestic devices that free mothers from the drudgery of housework and enable them to undertake outside commitments constitute a third factor. Whatever the reasons, however, the changes indicate that the traditional role differences between the sexes are not immutably fixed but can be adapted to differing social circumstances.

One further change is also relevant, i.e. the steeply rising divorce rate and the increasing number of disputed custody cases. It is the latter which perhaps gives most point to the issue which we are examining here. Despite fathers' greater participation in child care, there remains the deep-seated conviction that a mother is invariably the 'natural' parent and should therefore be given priority in custody decisions. That conviction is well illustrated by one of the studies summarized below (that by Fry and Addington), in that it highlights the mother-centred orientation found among professional people and the prejudice against fathers. Until fairly recently, fathers were completely neglected as a research topic, and it is only in the last decade or two that attempts have been made to examine the competence of men as parents and to compare them in this respect with women. The following summaries give some indication of the way in which this question has been tackled and of the sort of answers yielded by research.

Research findings

(1) SUMMARIES

Frodi, A. M., Lamb, M. E., Leavitt, L. A., Donovan, W. L., Neff, C. and Sherry, D. 1978: Fathers' and mothers' responses to the faces and cries of normal and premature infants. Developmental Psychology, 14, 490–8.

One of the problems in assessing something as complex as parental competence is to find adequate measures. There are many constituents to this concept, amongst the most basic of these being the sensitivity which an adult displays towards a child. Does the sheer sight of a baby affect him/her? Is he/she aroused by a baby's crying? This study examines such responsiveness in order to determine whether sex differences can be found in this respect. As another aim was to investigate the effects of premature infants on adults, both prematurely born and normal infants were included.

Sixty-four parents were shown a videotape of either a full-term or a premature infant crying. While the parent was viewing the tape various physiological measures were taken, i.e. heart rate, skin conductance and blood pressure, these being indices of the arousal that an individual experiences when confronted by some environmental stimulus. The parents subsequently filled in a mood-adjective checklist to report on their feelings while watching the tape.

The physiological measures showed that parents generally responded to the infant's cries with increased arousal, and that this applied in particular to the distinctive crying of the premature infant. This was borne out by the self-reported feelings on the checklist, which showed the parents to experience distress and concern then. None of the physiological measures yielded any differences between fathers and mothers: the former were as responsive in this respect as the latter. On the self-reports, both sets of parents reported the same kinds of feelings, except that mothers were said to be more attentive when the baby began to cry.

To summarize these results in the authors' own words: 'Though there are obvious dangers in reaching conclusions based on the absence of differences, we believe that there is reason to doubt the notion that adult females but not adult males are 'biologically predisposed' to respond nurturantly to infant signals.'

Feldman, S. S. and Nash, S. C. 1978: Interest in babies during young adulthood. Child Development, *49, 617–22.*

In this study too responsiveness to young infants is assessed, but here an actually present baby was used in order to observe the behavioural reactions of males and females. Moreover, the adults were drawn from different stages in the formation of a family, in the belief that sex differences in responsiveness may vary according to the demands of parenthood.

Four groups of 30 young adults, representing different stages, were investigated: cohabiting singles, childless married, married and expecting the first child, and parents of a child. The groups contained an equal number of males and females. Each individual was observed in a specially set-up waiting-room situation in which he or she was placed on some excuse and in which a baby and its mother were also present. Interest in and responsiveness to the baby were recorded by observers from behind a one-way mirror by noting down each instance of such responses as looking, smiling, touching and talking to the baby, as well as offering or showing objects and moving near. Each adult was subsequently given a batch of slides showing various objects and people, including babies, and allowed to view each slide as long as he or she wished. The percentage time spent looking at slides depicting babies was recorded. Prints of these pictures were then given to the adults and they were asked to select their favourites.

In the three childless groups no differences were found between men and women on any of the various measures. Only among those who were parents did women surpass men in responsiveness to the baby (though even here the difference was not great). Thus, whatever sex difference does exist is specific to a given period of life and not present at all times, resulting probably from the particular demands made on women as mothers and from the increased exposure to babies that these women had had. Responsiveness, these authors believe, is therefore experience-based rather than hormone-based.

Field, T. 1978: Interaction behaviors of primary versus secondary caretaker fathers. Developmental Psychology, *14, 183–4.*

There is a considerable amount of literature which suggests that fathers and mothers have different styles of interacting with young children. The question arises whether this is due to being a father as opposed to being a mother, or whether it reflects the fact that it is usually the mother who is the primary caretaker and the father the secondary caretaker. This study sets out to provide an answer by investigating fathers with primary responsibility for their child.

Three groups of parents were assessed during face-to-face interactions with their 4-month-old infants. One group consisted of mothers who were their baby's primary caretaker, another of fathers who were primary caretakers and a third of fathers who were secondary caretakers. There were 12 parents in each group, all middle class and college educated. The sessions were videotaped and subsequently analysed for differences between the three groups.

The results show some differences between both sets of fathers on the one hand and the mothers on the other (for example, the fathers tended to hold the infants less but to engage them more in play). However, in most respects the differences found were those between the primary caretakers (mother *or* father) and the secondary caretakers. Thus, the former adopted a style of interaction that involved a lot of infantile behaviour on the parent's part (high-pitched vocalization, grimacing, lots of smiling, and so on), whereas the latter behaved in a less informal manner. As the author puts it: 'These similarities between mothers and fathers when they are both primary caretakers suggest that father–mother differences are not necessarily intrinsic to being a father or mother. Instead they might derive from the differential amount of experience they have with their infants as primary or secondary caretaker.' Thus, this report arrives at the same conclusions about the role of experience as the last one, despite their different methodological approaches.

Santrock, J. W. and Warshak, R. A. 1979: Father custody and social development in boys and girls. Journal of Social Issues, *35, 112–25.*

It is in custody issues that the question of sex-related parental fitness becomes especially important. This paper supplies some relevant data by comparing three groups: families in which the father had been awarded custody after divorce, families where the mother had custody and intact families. The sample of 60 (equally divided between the three groups) was predominantly middle class. Parents were all in their 30s and those in the two divorced groups had been apart approximately 3 years. No cases of remarriage were included. The children were aged between 6 and 11 at the time of the investigation. A considerable number of methods were used to obtain data about the children's adjustment and the nature of parent–child interaction, but the present report is based primarily on observations of parent and child in a session during which they were asked, first, to plan an activity together and, second, to discuss the main problems of the family. Sessions were videotaped and systematically analysed according to a variety of behaviour scales.

The most striking findings are that children living with the same-sex parent (boys in father-custody homes and girls in mother–custody homes) are better adjusted than children living with the opposite sex parent. When father-custody boys were compared with boys from intact families, the former were found to be *more* socially competent, mature and independent than the latter. Girls under the father-custody arrangement, however, fared less well than their counterparts in intact families. When children from mother-custody families were compared with children from intact families, few differences emerged. When the father-custody children were compared with the mother-custody children, boys living with their fathers were uniformly found to show more competent social development than girls in father-custody homes; by contrast, girls living under a mother-custody arrangement were more competent than boys in that type of family.

Thus, the adjustment of children from divorced families depended very much on whether they were living with the same-sex parent or not: for boys, according to this study, fathers appeared to be a more suitable choice.

Fry, P. S. and Addington, J. 1984: Professionals' negative expectations of boys from father-headed single-parent families: implications for the training of child-care professionals. British Journal of Developmental Psychology, 2, 337–46.

Unlike the other reports quoted here this paper is not concerned with a direct comparison of mothers and fathers. Instead, it deals with another but highly relevant question, namely the expectations that people generally have as to the competence of mothers and fathers in the task of bringing up children.

The study involved 300 professional workers (half teachers and half social workers) and 300 lay persons. Each individual was shown videotapes of four 10-year-old boys, filmed while playing and interacting with other children both at home and at school. After viewing the tapes the adults were asked to make a number of judgements about each of the boys, rating them along various perso- nality dimensions and predicting how they would behave in several everyday situations. However, the adults had been divided into three groups according to the kind of background information they had been given about the boys before seeing the tapes: one group was told that the boys' parents were divorced and that they were being looked after by the father, a second group that the boys were looked after by their divorced mother and a third group that the boys came from an intact home.

The results concern the different kinds of judgements made by these three groups when viewing the same boys. The respondents judged boys from intact families as *most* well-adjusted, happy and able to assume responsibility and leadership, while boys from father- headed families came out *least* well in these respects. Thus, boys thought to be in the sole care of their father were rated lowest on happiness, getting along with others, achievement needs and emo- tional adjustment but highest on delinquency. These boys were also judged as being poorest in situations demanding obedience, the ability to cope with stress and to co-operate with adults and other children.

Thus, judgements about the *same* boys varied according to the kind of information provided to the judges, demonstrating how potent the influence of preconceptions may be. These preconceptions favoured boys thought to come from intact families; they worked against children from single-parent homes but most of all against those being reared by a father. It is worth emphasizing that these preconceptions were as evident among the professional people, so- cial workers and teachers, as among the lay persons.

(2) COMMENTS ON RESEARCH

How does one assess something as complex as parental competence? The difficulty in doing so is the main obstacle to providing an unequivocal answer to the question of whether women make better parents than men. Much of the work has been concerned with

responsiveness to children, i.e. whether there are sex differences in
the extent to which adults are interested in, excited by and attentive
to babies and young children. This does at least tell us something
about the initial orientation of men and women towards children,
and here the evidence from a variety of studies (not only those
quoted above) is reasonably clear: the popular notion that only
women are primed to be interested in children cannot be upheld;
men too show such special responsiveness, and any differences between the sexes that do appear are more likely in response to social
convention than an expression of some inborn propensity.

The findings reported in the study by Frodi et al., namely that men
respond physiologically as much as, and in a similar fashion to,
women to infants' distress (a result replicated by several investigators) are particularly pertinent in this respect. If at this very basic
level of arousal no sex differences can be found, then it becomes all
the more likely that differences emerging in other respects are cultur-
ally determined. This is also substantiated by the finding that responsiveness to young children varies according to family life cycle:
the study by Feldman and Nash (described above) receives support
from investigations of other age-groups which show, for example,
that there are no differences between boys and girls in their responsiveness to babies till the age of 5 or so and that among adolescents
too there are age changes which suggest social pressures to be at
work. It is, of course, not easy to demonstrate the truth or falsehood
of the notion of a biologically based sex difference, but on the whole
the evidence does make this an unlikely explanation.

Unfortunately, there is far less material available that tells us
about the *adequacy* of men as opposed to women in bringing up
children. A number of studies indicate that single fathers are on the
whole successful and competent with respect to their domestic responsibilities and child care tasks (though a period of adjustment
may well be required when they first assume such responsibility).
However, these investigations are mainly based on self-reports by
these fathers and their validity must thus be questioned. The study
by Santrock and Warshak, summarized above, is one of the few
exceptions, in that it is based on observation and thus not likely to
be influenced by the parents' own bias. The conclusion of this study,
that children of divorced parents fare best when in the care of the
same-sex parent, is an interesting and potentially a very important
one. It must be pointed out, however, that these results are in need
of replication before they can be accepted without hesitation. For

one thing, the sample used was a relatively small one and exclusively middle class and for another the assessment was derived from a rather limited observation period at just one point of time. There is indeed a general problem in our ability to generalize from the research available so far: fathers who act as primary caretakers of young babies (as in the study by Field) or to whom custody of their children is awarded may well be rather unusual individuals and not representative of fathers in general. For these sort of reasons one must be cautious in arriving at hard-and-fast conclusions about the parental competence of men in general. What the evidence does suggest is that statements about women inevitably being 'better' parents by mere virtue of their femininity appear to be no more than facile generalizations.

Implications for practice

It is clear from what has been said above that considerable caution has to be exercised at present in basing practice on the research results obtained so far. The total amount of research in this area is by no means great and what research does exist has dealt with only limited aspects of a highly complex problem. Nevertheless, there is sufficient consensus in the available evidence for us at least to conclude that masculinity is by no means to be regarded as some kind of disqualification as far as parental fitness is concerned – just as femininity is no automatic guarantee of satisfaction in that role. To many this may seem obvious, and yet practical issues about parenthood are only too often determined by a kind of black-and-white thinking that takes for granted the existence of gross sex differences. There is no indication that these are inevitable; instead, each case should be treated on its own merits, without making sweeping generalizations based on nothing but the sex of the individuals concerned. It is the unique and total circumstances of each family that must be considered in reaching decisions.

This applies especially to those cases where a comparative judgement about a mother and a father is required, such as in custody disputes. The assumption that mother is almost invariably the fitter person to assume sole parental responsibility has dominated judgements in the past; fathers were considered unfit unless proved otherwise. The changes in family life-styles that have occurred in recent times have shown that this is not necessarily so; fathers can be adequate care-givers too. It follows that a father with the appropriate inclination and personality ought to be considered for sole parenthood as seriously as his ex-wife. It may well be that the majority of children will continue to go to their mothers following a divorce, for in most families the mother was always the main person responsible for the child and there is much to be said for maintaining continuity in such an arrangement. But when both parents apply for custody it is not the parents' sex but their individual circumstances that are of prime concern. Amongst these the nature of the child's existing attachments and preferences are particularly important, though in establishing these, great care needs to be taken not to confront the child directly with the choice between the parents. The vast majority of children deplore the need for their parents' divorce and want to retain both mother and father: asking children to choose between their parents is likely to give rise to considerable feelings of guilt *vis-à-vis* the non-preferred parent that will haunt the child for years to come.

The idea that children are better off with the same-sex parent, as suggested by some of the research, must as yet be treated with caution. As we have stressed, this finding is still in need of replication and cannot be used as a firm basis for action until the research has been repeated with other samples and other data-gathering techniques. At present, other things being equal, it could be given consideration – but when are other things ever equal?

The other situation giving rise to the question of male competence in the parental role concerns the admittedly rare instances of single men wanting to foster or adopt children. The same general principle applies here as in custody cases; the individual's sex ought not to debar him from consideration. Motivation and personality are of greater importance, and an application from a single man ought to be treated in the same way as one from a single woman. It may not be easy to shed cultural prejudice against men as primary, let alone sole, caretakers of children, and the suspicion that there is something 'peculiar' about a man wanting to assume such a responsibility may therefore linger on. This is a pity: if there is no evidence that men are inevitably less fit to assume the parental role, if it is likely that social convention rather than biological constraint determines the division of labour as far as child care is concerned, then such a prejudice ought not to find a place in decisions about children's future.

We have seen from the last of the studies summarized above how pervasive such prejudices can be. In the long run the chance of their diminishing depends on changes in society: only when the roles played by men and women, within family life and outside it, come to assume greater similarity than is the case now will such thinking spontaneously disappear. In the short run, one needs at least to draw the attention of professional workers to the existence of these preconceptions; the fact that they are often quite unconscious makes them all the more powerful, and training courses in particular ought to incorporate techniques for bringing them out into the light of day.

Further reading

Berman, P. W. 1980: Are women more responsive than men to the young? A review of developmental and situational variables. *Psychological Bulletin*, 88, 668–95.

Bronstein, P. and Cowan, C. P. 1988: *Fatherhood Today: men's changing role in the family*. Chichester: Wiley.

Lamb, M. E. and Sagi, A. (eds) 1983: *Fatherhood and Family Policy*. Hillsdale, New Jersey: Erlbaum.

Parke, R. D. 1981: *Fathering*. London: Fontana; Cambridge, Mass.: Harvard University Press.

Issue: Do children need a parent of each sex?

Background

A 'normal' family contains both a mother and a father. Much of psychological theory, attempting to account for the course of children's development and socialization, has assumed that this is not merely normal but essential: each parent has a distinctive role to play; the roles are not exchangeable; and so it follows that for proper development to occur children require both these individuals, one of each sex.

This applies particularly to the acquisition of sex roles by children. Boys, it has long been held, should grow up to be masculine (assertive, competitive, action-oriented), girls to be feminine (co-operative, compliant, feeling-oriented). For any individual not to fall into the appropriate category must then be regarded as socially deviant and a sign that the course of development has somehow become misdirected. Under normal circumstances, however, this does not happen because children are typically motivated to identify with the parent of the same sex – or so Freud believed, and it is his theorizing in this as in so many other respects that has dominated thinking for most of this century. At first (according to Freud) both boys and girls need to form an attachment to the mother. Girls continue thus, but boys switch their identification over to the father during the course of the early years because they fear him as a competitor for the mother's love and deal with this conflict by appeasing him through wanting to become like him. Thus, both boys and girls require a model with which to identify and to imitate, in order to acquire the kind of personality characteristics that society regards as appropriate to their sex. The adoption of such sex-appropriate behaviour will, moreover, be reinforced by parents and other adults through praise, just as inappropriate behaviour will be stamped out by disapproval and punishment.

If this account is correct, the absence of a parent on whom the child can model itself is likely to have undesirable effects: difficulties in psychosexual development, as shown in atypical sex-role behaviour, can be expected to manifest themselves sooner or later under such circumstances. It follows that being brought up in a single-parent family could thus be a psychologically hazardous business – an important consideration in view of the large and increasing number of individuals who spend at least part of their childhood in such families. Are these children indeed adversely affected? It is well known that in many single-parent families difficulties arise from the social and economic problems that their status so often entails. They are more likely to be in poor housing, have financial worries, be forced to make unsatisfactory arrangements with child-minders, and so forth – all of which may well have implications for the child's mental health. In addition, when there is only one provider the child is more likely to be vulnerable in case something happens to that individual; having two parents is an insurance against such a mishap. But what about the effects on the child's personality, with particular reference to the development of sexual identity, if there is no person of the same sex in the family to act as a model? In so far as most single-parent families are headed by a mother it would seem that boys are likely to be particularly affected, becoming feminized because of the absence of a father-figure. In the case of girls too, however, there are suggestions that father can play a vital role in encouraging feminine behaviour in his daughter. His absence might therefore affect her development of femininity and, *inter alia*, result in the girl's failure to acquire proper interactional skills with males.

There is one other 'atypical' family that is relevant to this issue, namely one where the child is brought up by two parent-figures of the same sex. There are very few of these (though their number might well rise with increasingly permissive attitudes towards homosexuality), and those that do exist are generally females couples. However, the same issue arises: are the children adversely affected by not having a parent of each sex?

The effects on children of both these situations, i.e. of being raised in a single-parent family or in a lesbian household, have been examined in various research studies. A range of possible consequences have been considered, with particular attention given to delinquent tendencies and school achievement in fatherless children. Of most relevance, however, is the development of sex-role behaviour, and it is this which is singled out by the studies described below.

Research findings

(1)   SUMMARIES

Santrock, J. W. 1977: Effects of father absence on sex-typed behaviors in male children: reason for the absence and age of onset of the absence. Journal of Genetic Psychology, *130, 3–10.*

Earlier studies of the effects of single-parenthood took a somewhat crude approach, in that they would (for example) lump together all fatherless children and compare them with a group of children with fathers, paying no attention to the different circumstances under which children lose a father – circumstances which might well be crucial to the outcome of such an experience. In this study two aspects were taken into account that might influence outcome: the reason for the father's absence (death or divorce) and the child's age when this occurred.

The subjects were 30 boys aged 10 and 11 years, mainly from working-class families. Half had lost their father through death and half through divorce, this having occurred at various ages up to 9 years. A control group of 15 boys from intact families, matched in terms of IQ, age and school, was also included in the study. Measurement procedures focused on three characteristics of the boys: masculinity–femininity, aggressiveness and dependence. Each of these was assessed both by teacher ratings and by a structured doll-play interview (the latter involved the setting up of situations with dolls designed to elicit the relevant three characteristics).

The results give no support to the contention that a father's presence in the home is necessary for the son to develop masculine sex-typed behaviour. On the contrary, the boys in this sample without fathers were assessed as *more* masculine, aggressive and independent, though this finding was reflected primarily in the teachers' ratings rather than in the play measures. The authors concede that the greater aggressiveness of the fatherless boys might encompass antisocial behaviour – a possibility not investigated here. What is clear is that there is no sign of more feminine characteristics developing in the absence of a father in the home. On the other hand the effects of age at and reason for father separation were not clear-cut. As to age, it was found that the earlier that father absence occurred the more disobedient the child was, but the later it happened the more aggressive he was. With respect to reason, boys from divorced homes were found to be more aggressive than boys from widowed homes, but no other difference occurred between these two groups.

Hetherington, E. M. 1972: Effects of father absence on personality development in adolescent daughters. Developmental Psychology, 7, 313–26.

As in the previous study, father absence due to death or divorce was investigated, though this time in girls. The girls ranged in age from 13 to 17 years and came from three groups with 24 subjects in each: an intact family group, a divorced family group and a widowed group. A considerable number of measures were obtained, including observation of each girl in a recreation centre, ratings based on interviews both with the daughter and with her mother, indices of non-verbal behaviour during the interview with the girl, and scores on a number of inventories (including a Femininity Scale).

There is no indication in the findings that the girls without fathers were in any way affected in either their sex-typed behaviour or their preference for the feminine role. Sex-appropriate behaviour and interaction with other females were no different in these girls when compared with the girls from the intact family group. A difference was, however, found in relationships with males, though the nature of the difference depended on other factors. Thus, girls with divorced parents showed early heterosexual behaviour and attention seeking from males, while girls whose fathers had died were inhibited and avoidant with males. In addition, the girls' age at separation from the father had some effect, in that earlier age was on the whole associated with more marked consequences.

The author points out that other studies with younger girls had found no effect of father separation. It appears, therefore, judging by the results obtained here, that whatever consequences this experience does bring about, these do not emerge until adolescence. Even then, however, they are confined to the girls' skills in relating to males and do not manifest themselves in other deviations from appropriate sex typing or in interactions with females.

Kurder, L. A. and Siesky, A. E. 1980: Sex role self-concepts of single divorced parents and their children. Journal of Divorce, 3, 249–61.

Any effects that single parenthood does produce in children may be brought about by factors other than the loss of the parent as such. In particular, one needs to consider the impact on the other parent, for his or her reactions may well determine how the child is affected.

The present study takes account of this possibility by investigating not only the sex roles of children but also those of their divorced parents. A total of 74 custodial parents (60 mothers and 14 fathers) were selected, together with their 92 children (43 boys and 49 girls). The ages of the latter ranged from 10 to 19 years. All were given the Bem Sex Role Inventory – a much-used questionnaire which contains a list of 60 adjectives, each describing a stereotypical masculine or feminine or neutral characteristic. Parents and children were asked to rate each adjective on a seven-point scale to indicate how true a description they considered it to be of themselves. A control group of children from non-divorced families, matched on age and sex, was aldo included in the study.

As far as the parents are concerned, the divorced mothers as well as the divorced fathers scored highly (in relation to published norms) on *both* masculinity and femininity. Thus, the parents emerged as primarily androgynous, i.e. as possessing a blend of masculine and feminine characteristics rather than being at one end or the other of the male–female distribution. The same applied to the children: both boys and girls were significantly more androgynous than children whose parents were not divorced. Of special interests are the boys from divorced families, nearly all of which were headed by mothers. They were found to be less masculine in their self-concepts than their controls, but this 'non-masculinity' was found to be equated *not* with a trend towards femininity but with a trend towards androgyny.

The either–or view of male–female sex typing thus does not do justice to these children or to their parents: both kinds of characteristics can be found in one and the same individual. This is particularly likely in single parents who have to assume a dual parental role: it seems that their behaviour may then bring about similar psychological traits in their children.

Brenes, M. E., Eisenberg, N. and Helmstadter, G. C. 1985: Sex role development of preschoolers from two-parent and one-parent families. Merrill-Palmer Quarterly, *31*, 33–46.

The concept of sex role has frequently been treated as though it were a unitary entity, giving rise to sweeping generalizations about individuals' masculinity–femininity. It has, however, become increasingly clear that this is an over-simplification and that the concept has a number of distinct constituents, some of which may be affected by membership of a single-parent family while others may not.

This was investigated in the present study, which concerns 41 children aged 4 years. Seventeen of these came from a mother-headed single-parent family and 24 from a two-parent family. Each group contained both boys and girls. Three separate aspects were examined: (1) the children's understanding of their own sexual identity (assessed by a standardized interview constructed for this purpose); (2) their knowledge of sexual stereotypes, i.e. what behaviour and functions characterize each sex (also assessed by a series of questions); and (3) the children's adoption of sex roles (measured by observing their choice of toys, masculine or female, during play).

Compared with the children from two-parent families, the children from the single-parent families were no different in the understanding of their own sexual identity. The pattern of dvelopment was thus similar in this respect for both groups, indicating no confusion in either the boys or the girls of single parents. With regard to sexual stereotypes, the single-parent children showed *greater* knowledge – an unexpected finding, which the authors attribute to the greater salience that notions of sex roles may have in homes where one parent is absent. Finally, as far as the actual adoption of sex roles by these children is concerned, those from single-parent families tended to be less sex typed in their choice of toys, i.e. they played more with neutral toys or with toys appropriate to the opposite sex than two-parent children. It is important to note, however, that boys from mother-headed families were not 'feminized' in their play, for they were still more likely to choose masculine toys than were girls and their play with feminine toys was comparatively infrequent.

In general, the study demonstrates the complexity of the sex-role concept and supports the notion that some aspects may be affected more easily than others. There is no indication, however, of any obvious confusion in this respect on the part of children brought up by one parent only.

Golombok, S., Spencer, A. and Rutter, M. 1983: Children in lesbian and single-parent households: psychosexual and psychiatric appraisal. Journal of Child Psychology and Psychiatry, 24, 551–72.

In lesbian households children are also without a father and instead may be brought up by two females. Among a number of reports on the psychological consequences of such upbringing the present one is perhaps the most informative.

Twenty-seven lesbian households were compared with 27 single-parent households headed by a heterosexual mother. The former contained 37 children aged between 5 and 17 years, and there were 38 children in the single-parent group. The two sets of mothers were similar on all measures reflecting current psychiatric status, and both were judged to show similarly warm feelings towards the children. No attempts were made by the lesbian mothers to hide their sexual orientation from their children, and in those cases where the mother lived with another woman (12 out of the 27) all but two showed open affection to one another. In most of these households, parenting and housekeeping roles were shared between the two women.

Three aspects of the children's psychosexual development were investigated: (1) sexual identity (i.e. the individual's concept of him/herself as male or female); (2) sex-typed behaviour (the adoption of activities that tend to differentiate the sexes); and (3) sexual-object choice (i.e. the individual's homosexual or heterosexual orientation). In no instance was any difference found between the two groups of households and in none of the three areas of enquiry was there any indication that the children of the lesbian mothers developed in any way inconsistent with their biological gender. All reported that they were glad to be of the sex they were and none would have preferred to be of the opposite sex. Sex-typed behaviour was assessed on two scales based on an interview with the mother and a separate interview with the child. Clear differences emerged between boys and girls in the kinds of activities in which they customarily engaged, and these were moreover of a type generally regarded as masculine and feminine respectively. As to sexual-object choice, those beyond puberty showed no indication of homosexual interests. In addition, various measures of the children's emotional adjustment and social relationship suggested that those from lesbian households had *fewer* psychological problems than those from single-parent households; otherwise, no difference emerged between the two groups.

It can be concluded that rearing in lesbian households *per se* did not lead to atypical psychosexual development in this sample nor did it constitute a psychiatric risk factor.

(2)   COMMENTS ON RESEARCH

By far the greater part of the research in the area of single-parenthood has dealt with the effects of father-absence; mother-absence is a much rarer occurrence and thus less often investigated. Our conclusions must therefore be restricted primarily to the former. In addition, while a variety of possible consequences has been examined (social adjustment, educational progress, and so forth), most attention has been given to children's sex-role development, as it was considered that this aspect of personality functioning would be particularly vulnerable to a parent's absence.

As we have seen from the studies quoted, the research on the whole does not bear out this expectation. In particular, the notion that boys without a father are likely to become feminized is not supported. Generalizations about the psychosexual development of children from single-parent homes are only too often simplistic and unjustified.

There are, however, a number of additional considerations to take into account. For one thing, simply to compare single-parent children with two-parent children is crude; it neglects the fact that the former may have plenty of contacts with other male figures (a grandfather, an uncle, a neighbour, even an older brother), while some of the latter may hardly ever see their father. The assessment of actual contact with father-figures would form a much sounder basis for research.

Second, it has become clear that the effects of father-absence depend on a number of conditions other than the absence of the father itself. These include the reason for that absence (for example, death or divorce), the mother's own reaction, the child's age and sex, the financial and other practical consequences for the family, and so on. The impact of these other conditions may well outweigh the influence of father-absence on its own. In short, it is the context in which this experience occurs that is all-important, and this has not always been taken into account by research studies.

One other point which has to be considered concerns the difficulty of measuring a child's sexual identity. On the one hand, there are several different aspects to this: the child's behaviour, the child's knowledge, the child's self-concept, and so on, each of which may be affected in different ways – hence the importance of measuring all of them, though unfortunately this has not always been done. And on the other, any one aspect may be measured in different ways: by observation, interview, inventory, test, and so on. Some of the measuring devices are sounder than others, but the very fact that such variety is available makes for inconsistency among the reports emanating from different investigations – an unfortunately all-too-familiar story at the present stage of scientific research on human behaviour!

Despite these difficulties in evaluating the literature, the thrust of findings is such as to cast doubt on the belief that deviations in psychological development inevitably occur when a child is not brought up in the traditional family set-up which includes a parent of each sex. This applies, it appears, even to children brought up by lesbian couples, for the report by Golombok et al., summarized above, is borne out by a number of other (though less well executed) studies. Again it is worth pointing out that the children in the Golombok et al., study were by no means reared in total isolation from masculine influence: nearly half of them saw their fathers at least once a week. Even so, it seems unlikely that imitation of and identification with a same-sex parent play the all-important part once ascribed to them. A boy brought up by a single mother, for instance, may well develop masculinity simply because she treats him as a male; the quality is fostered because someone of influence over the child considers it important. Thus, according to more recent thinking there may well be several different pathways to the development of sexual identity; and if that is so, the rationale for expecting absence of a parent to lead to deviant psychosexual development is no longer valid.

Implications for practice

Perhaps the most important implication of recent research on children brought up in fatherless homes is that we must rid ourselves of the expectation that such children will turn out to be psychologically 'inferior' – just because of the absence of a father-figure. There is a widely prevalent belief that the continuing presence of a father is a 'must' for mental health, particularly as far as boys are concerned and particularly with respect to the development of their sexual identity. The failure of research to bear this out is echoed by research on other aspects of behaviour. Thus, for instance, the prevalence of delinquency has also been investigated among fatherless children – though the very fact that a link has been hypothesized for fatherlessness and delinquency could be regarded as yet more evidence of the prevalent prejudice. Yet again, once adequate methodological safeguards are taken in carrying out the research (such as matching control groups for things like social class), no causal effects can be attributed to single parenthood. Thus, if adverse effects are found in the children, it is essential to ascertain whether they occur as the result of the parent's absence or whether they are linked to the many economic and other practical disadvantages so often experienced by single-parent families. Action directed at these would appear to be the more crucial course to take if one is to promote optimal psychological development in this group of children.

If being the child of a single parent is not *per se* an at-risk factor, then there is no reason to attach undue weight to it in decision-making, given other satisfactory circumstances. It is, for example, wrong that the children of single mothers are more likely to be taken into care than those of two parents – at least when the only thing that distinguishes them is the number of their parents. It is also wrong to allocate a child in a contested custody case to a remarried parent rather than to a single parent, this difference between the parents being of little importance compared to the many other considerations that are likely to distinguish their circumstances. One other point is also relevant. Research findings have shown consistently that children in single-parent families function more adequately than children in two-parent but conflict-ridden families. Again, the sheer number of parents present in the home does not tell us everything about the conditions that promote a child's well-being. It is clearly necessary to take note of the great changes that have taken place in recent decades in traditional family structure and not base action on what is now in some respects an outdated model. This will be a recurrent theme for us, but it is particularly well illustrated by what is one of the more extreme deviations from the norm, namely children reared by lesbian couples. As we saw, there is no evidence that the sex-role development of such children (or, for that matter, other aspects of psychological functioning) is thereby adversely affected. It is true that as long as this type of household is a relatively rare social phenomenon its unconventional status may have indirect consequences for the child by, for instance, being teased or even ostracized by other children. However, this again shows that it is people's attitudes to particular forms of families rather than those forms themselves that are the operative factor. In any case, there is no justification for measures such as outright refusal to award custody to a lesbian mother on the grounds that she would endanger her child's psychological health.

In some respects there have been definite changes in society's ideas as to what is acceptable behaviour among males and females respectively. Sex roles are no longer divided as sharply as they were at one time: instead of seeing masculinity and femininity as opposite poles, a far greater degree of flexibility and overlap is now generally tolerated. The qualities that we foster in our children through our rearing practices reflect these changing social values. Accordingly we are

now moving towards a somewhat more mixed, androgynous personality make-up and regard this as more in keeping with optimal
adjustment in today's society. In so far as there is evidence that the
children of one-parent families are more likely to develop androgynous characteristics, we have yet another indication that such families are by no means to be regarded in a purely negative light. There
are positive aspects too, and it would be unfortunate if our preconceptions would cause us to overlook these.

Further reading

Ferri, E. 1976: *Growing up in a One-Parent Family: a long-term study of child development*. London: National Foundation of Educational Research.

Herzog, E. and Sudia, C. E. 1973: Children in fatherless families. In B. M. Caldwell and H. N. Ricciuti (eds), *Review of Child Development Research, Vol. 3*. Chicago: University of Chicago Press.

Huston, A. C. 1983: Sex-typing. In E. M. Hetherington (ed.), *Socialization, Personality and Social Development*, Vol. IV of *Handbook of Child Psychology*. New York: Wiley.

Ruble, D. 1984: Sex-role development. In M. H. Bornstein and M. E. Lamb (eds), *Developmental Psychology: an advanced textbook*. Hillsdale, New Jersey: Erlbaum.

Issue: Does separation from parents cause psychological trauma?

Background

The relationships which young children establish with their parents are generally considered as so vital to their well-being that any severance of these bonds, however temporary, is regarded by many as highly undesirable, and indeed as potentially dangerous. Separation from parents may take place under various circumstances: the child's hospitalization, the mother's hospitalization, admission to public care on account of some family inadequacy or break-up, parental divorce, death of a parent, and so on. In all cases, however, two questions arise: first, are the effects on the child's psychological state serious, and second, are they inevitable under all conditions of bond disruption? There are various ways of answering these questions on the basis of what we have learned from research: here we shall deal with the problem of children's immediate reactions; the next Issue will deal with long-term consequences.

Once again it was Freud who provided the rationale for this line of enquiry. Freud drew attention to the extraordinarily strong emotional feelings surrounding the child's relationship with the mother – feelings of such intensity that they are difficult for an adult to appreciate but which ensure that any threatened break in the relationship will be resisted by the child to the utmost. Both Freud and, subsequently, John Bowlby (the latter drawing together the research evidence linking maternal deprivation and subsequent psychopathology) emphasized the importance for healthy personality development of a close and satisfying relationship with the mother during the formative years of childhood, with the corollary that loss of maternal care would have disastrous consequences for the child. No longer having access to an attachment figure was seen as a trauma which a child was just not mentally equipped to deal with. Such an experience would therefore give rise to an intense degree of separation anxiety that, even after only a temporary break, would remain with the individual in some form and (according to Freud) lead to a range of neurotic problems surfacing many years after the event. Separation from the mother was therefore to be avoided at all costs.

Research in this area originally started with a number of clinical reports, whch seemed to show that the experience of separation from an attachment figure plays a crucial part in the development of various psychopathological problems. In so far as these reports were derived from an examination of adults or older children while the separation experience took place early on in life, the connection had to be inferred and the information about separation obtained retrospective – an obviously uncertain undertaking! In addition, such an approach tells us nothing about those individuals who remained unscathed and therefore never came to the notice of clinicians. It was not till the 1940s and 1950s that the first systematic research projects involving direct observation of children during separation were mounted, and it was only then that reports became available which documented in detail how children respond to such an event. It was also only on the basis of following up such children in the context of longitudinal studies that one could consider the extent to which the experience continued to reverberate mentally.

Much of that work involved children admitted to hospital or to short-term public care – the two most common settings for separation at the time, both giving rise to considerable unease among some people as to their impact on children. That unease, as we shall see below, was justified by the results of the research produced; however, the often quite harrowing descriptions of children's reactions to separation tended to suggest that trauma and distress of an intense degree were an inevitable outcome and that no mitigating circumstances could possibly prevail. Thus, the loss of a mother–figure *per se* was regarded as of such overwhelming proportions that it would invariably disrupt the child's emotional life, whatever the conditions surrounding the separation. This clearly has practical implications: it suggests that there is little one can do to alleviate distress, that there are no useful measures to be taken to help children in such a situation. Only subsequently, in another wave of research, was attention eventually paid to the possibility that mitigating circumstances do exist. The notion of uniformity of children's responses was no longer taken for granted and questions were asked about the possibility of setting up 'benign' separations.

Below we shall first present a number of studies undertaken in order to document in detail 'typical' reactions of children and then an influential investigation which demonstrates the role played by the specific conditions surrounding a separation experience. Our attention will be on young children's reactions to hospitalization and to being taken into residential care; separation from a parent through divorce raises different questions and will be discussed in a later Issue.

Research findings

(1) SUMMARIES

Robertson, J. and Bowlby, J. 1952: Responses of young children to separation from their mothers. Courrier Centre International l' Enfance, 2, 131–42.

This is one of the first reports that set out to provide precise descriptive data about the way in which young children behave on being separated from their mothers (note that fathers were not even considered at that time). The study is based on 49 children aged between 1 and 4 years, 25 of whom were observed in residential nurseries and the remainder in hospital.

Of the 45 children whose initial responses were observed, all but three fretted. This *protest* phase was generally marked by crying of different degrees of violence, continuousness and duration, also by periods of subdued whining and grizzling. Children who could speak called for their mothers with varying degrees of insistence. In some cases this phase lasted for a few hours, in others up to 7 or 8 days. During this period children appeared panic stricken and intensely frightened, expressing needs which apparently only the mother could satisfy. The children subsequently entered a phase of *despair*, characterized by continuing desire for the mother but coupled with increasing hopelessness. They became withdrawn and apathetic, with monotonous and intermittent crying. Eventually a third phase was reached, namely *denial* (renamed *detachment* in subsequent reports), during which the children began to show some interest in their surroundings and cried less. Although generally welcomed as a sign of recovery by staff, the authors of this report consider this reaction to be really a device for coping with distress that has become too intense for the child to continue tolerating. The distress is therefore dealt with by repressing all feelings for the mother and, when eventually confronted by her, behaving indifferently towards her (i.e. in a detached manner). When the children were discharged (mostly after periods of 2 or 3 weeks) their true feelings for the mother only gradually broke through. Initially, love tended to be mixed up with anger and hostility, as well as with great demandingness.

The three phases of protest, denial and detachment thus form a predictable sequence of reactions to the trauma of separation. Each represents a means of adapting to the intense stress experienced by the child. However, even the last phase, with its deceptive calmness, constitutes a highly undesirable pattern which, if continued as a result of prolonged separation, can lead into permanent psychopathology.

Heinicke, C. M. and Westheimer, I. J. 1965: Brief Separations. *London: Longmans.*

This is probably the most detailed (book-sized) account of children's behaviour in separation situations that has been published. The number of children studied is small, but the investigation was conducted with exceptional care and provided a wealth of data.

The sample consisted of ten children in the second and third years of life who were placed in a residential nursery for relatively brief periods during their mother's hospitalization. They were matched with a non-separated group according to age and sex. All were first visited at home in order to obtain interview data from the parents and to carry out baseline observations on the children. After admission the separated children were observed at regular intervals by each of two research workers, who recorded behaviour systematically according to a coding system that yielded the frequency of particular types of reactions and so made possible quantitative comparisons. This record was supplemented by more global descriptive accounts, as well as by data from periodically conducted doll-play sessions designed to tap the children's fantasy level. Information was also obtained from the staff of the nurseries. Following reunion each child was seen at weekly intervals for a minimum period of 20 weeks and similar contacts were maintained with the non-separated group for comparable periods of time.

Of the ten separated children, nine reacted with intense distress, often screaming loudly and particularly so at the actual moment of separation. Longing for the return of the parents, in the form of frequently quite desperate crying for them, dominated the children's behaviour during the first 3 days. Following visits paid by fathers, distress became especially acute. Rather less upset was found in those children who were accompanied by their siblings. After the fifth day the intense crying gradually decreased, to be replaced by fretting without crying. During the initial period most of the separated children refused food, all suffered from sleep disturbances, toileting was resisted and there was considerable thumb- and finger-sucking. Initially also, the children refused to have anything to do with the staff, in particular refusing to be approached, picked up or comforted. Subsequently, resistance to contact was mixed with efforts to seek reassurance, and preference for one nurse gradually developed. However, even after 2 weeks one-third of the nurses' requests were still being resisted.

After return home, most of the children cried when either parent left them alone. At the same time the relationship with the mother was marked by an inability to respond to her affectionately. This gradually decreased over a period of weeks, taking longer in those children who had been separated for the longest periods. Such inability was not present in the relationship with the father. Eating, sleeping and toileting were all disturbed during this period, but these too gradually improved.

In general, the findings support the three-phase sequence of protest, denial and detachment which Robertson and Bowlby have proposed, though they also emphasize the considerable variability among children in the way these patterns are expressed.

Schaffer, H. R. and Callender, W. M. 1959: Psychologic effects of hospitalization in infancy. Pediatrics, 24, 528–39.

We have already referred to this study in relation to the first Issue, which examined the age when children begin to show signs of attachment to specific individuals. The study is also relevant here because it provides further data on the upset caused by separation and does so in respect of children even younger than those studied elsewhere, i.e. infants in the first year of life.

The findings show that separation from parents becomes a psychologically meaningful event from about the age of 7 months onward, and we shall therefore concentrate here on the 37 infants beyond this age. During the first 3 days following admission, only those children were investigated who were admitted for 'benign' reasons (for example, elective surgery) and whose reactions to hospitalization were therefore not contaminated by illness and pain. Systematic observations were carried out during a 2-hour daily period which included both a feeding session and a visiting hour. This was repeated for the last 3 days preceding discharge from hospital. Thereafter, infants were visited periodically at home.

The observations point above all to the acuteness of distress in these babies caused by the separation experience. At all ages beyond 7 months, crying generally began as soon as a nurse took the child from the mother, and it then frequently continued virtually non-stop for a considerable time. Only one infant did not fret overtly, but reacted by becoming subdued, withdrawn and continually sucking his thumb. Most infants became frightened and negative when approached by a nurse and food refusal was therefore common. During visiting hours the children mostly clung desperately to the mother and became extremely upset on her departure. At the end of the infants' stay in hospital (which mostly lasted for 2 or 3 weeks), crying and withdrawal were still evident, though not as marked as at the beginning and least so in those who had been in for the longest periods. After return home all children showed considerable insecurity centred on the presence of the mother: whenever left alone by her they cried, at other times they often physically clung to her and refused to be put down, and they were also unusually fearful of strangers. In some cases this pattern lasted for only a few days, in others several weeks.

It thus appears that as soon as children are old enough to have formed a definite attachment to their parents, separation from them becomes a traumatic event that elicits just as much distress as in 2- or 3-year-old children. The lessening of crying and signs of subsequent apathy once again fit in with the three-phase sequence referred to above.

Robertson, J. and Robertson, J. 1971: Young children in brief separation. Psychoanalytic Study of the Child, *26, 264–315.*

The studies quoted so far have all pointed to acute upset as the 'normal' reaction to separation. The Robertsons set out to determine whether this appears regardless of circumstances or whether, on the contrary, separation situations might not be arranged in such a way as to reduce and minimize the occurrence of distress.

Accordingly, they themselves undertook the foster care of four children, aged between 1½ and 2½ years, whose mothers were going into hospital for periods of between 1 and 4 weeks. They also obtained additional material from a further group of nine children who were looked after in their own homes by a relative. In all cases the intention was to eliminate as far as possible 'contaminating' factors, i.e. those aspects of the total experience which were additional to the separation itself and which were sources of stress in their own right: an unfamiliar environment, new routines, strange caretakers, personal illness, and so on. The Robertsons therefore got acquainted with each of their four foster children a month or so prior to the expected separation date and introduced them to their own home. At the same time they found out from the parents the child's characteristics, toilet habits, food fads, sleeping pattern and comfort habits. On coming into care each child brought his or her own bed and blankets, toys and cuddlies, and a photograph of the mother. During the separation the foster parents sought to keep alive the image of the mother by talking about her and showing the photograph. Fathers were free to visit as much as they wished. A running account was kept by the foster parents of the child's behaviour, daily check-lists were completed and the child was also recorded each day on film.

The report contains detailed case histories of the four children. Of course, each of them responded in his or her own way, but what is very apparent from all the records is that none showed the acute distress and despair generally described in other reports. There was certainly some adverse reaction to the separation: sadness, lowered frustration tolerance, some aggression, overactivity, occasional turbulent behaviour – all these were noted, but they did not add up to the syndrome of great unhappiness, bewilderment and panic that had been described by other writers. The affectionate relationships established with the foster parents were clearly of considerable importance in producing this relatively positive picture. The foster mother in particular was able to provide the children with a source of security which helped them over a difficult time. As a result the reunion with the mother caused few difficulties: the children were for the most part able to resume the relationship with her almost immediately, showing only a few behavioural problems after return home and only a little of the insecurity so commonly experienced by other separated children.

The Robertsons warn that this relatively favourable outcome does not mean that the hazards attached to early separation can be eliminated entirely: even the best of the substitute care is not a certain prescription for neutralizing the risk. What it does mean is that separation situations can be created which greatly minimize the traumatic nature of this experience.

(2)   COMMENTS ON RESEARCH

Much of the research on children's reactions to separation was carried out some decades ago, when conditions in hospitals and residential establishments were rather different from what they are now. The fact that changes have taken place since those days is a tribute to the effectiveness of that research, which showed very clearly that separations in these 'traditional' environments are highly traumatic events for young children and are responded to with great distress. The three-phase sequence proposed by Bowlby and Robertson (protest–despair–detachment) has found general acceptance as an adequate description of the way in which children's behaviour develops under such circumstances, and though the observations on which these authors based their conclusions were globally descriptive rather than systematic and quantitative as in later research, in broad outline they have nevertheless been repeatedly confirmed. There remains some doubt as to whether the sequence is in fact quite so neat and universal. However, the occurrence of great distress, particularly in children between the ages of about 6 months and 4 or 5 years, on being separated from parents and looked after by unfamiliar people in an unfamiliar environment may be regarded as axiomatic, as are their subsequent struggles to come to terms with such distress.

What has become evident as a result of subsequent research is that separation is never a 'pure' experience that has only the one ingredient, i.e. the mother's absence. On the contrary, it is inevitably accompanied by a host of other circumstances, each of which may also play a part in affecting how children interpret and react to the situation. Separation, that is, always occurs in a context, and this must also be taken into account because it may modify the child's behaviour – for better or worse.

Research efforts in this area have therefore had to shift from a disregard of context to an analysis of context. There are factors surrounding the separation experience that may worsen the impact and even, in some instances, account for a major part of subsequent pathology: for instance, preceding family conflict, the permanent loss of a parent (through desertion or death), the disruption of routines, removal to a strange environment, care by unfamiliar people, illness and pain and (in hospitals) the imposition of unpleasant procedures. On the other hand, there are also factors that mitigate the separation experience, in particular those which involve the retention of as many features of the child's original life as possible, with particular reference to the continuing availability of other familiar people. Relevant here is the relatively recent appreciation of the fact that the relationship with the mother is not the only meaningful emotional tie formed by even quite young children, and that as a result the continuing availability of father, siblings, grand-mother or other attachment figures may considerably alleviate upset caused by the mother's absence. Thus, the reasons for the separa-tion, the quality of previous family relationships, the conditions under which the separation takes place, as well as such factors as the child's age and temperament, make each separation experience a unique event. Having first dealt in generalizations by pointing to the harmful effects of separation, research has subsequently found it necessary to do justice to the considerable variability in response and so consider the many associated factors that may also determine outcome.

Implications for practice

Whatever the long-term effects of separation may be (and we shall turn to these below), the immediate effects on children commonly found provide plenty of justification on their own for preventive action aimed at keeping young children with their families. It is difficult to convey by words alone the intensity of panic and the degree of bewilderment which a young child experiences when sud-denly removed from home – indeed, it is no coincidence that the most influential means of changing the old-fashioned practice of handling separation situations was by visual means, i.e. a series of films made by James Robertson that appeared in the 1950s and that portrayed in live detail children's reactions to such situations. Long-term effects or not, anything that can be done to prevent that much distress being imposed on a young child is justified in its own right – hence the value of measures such as the introduction of unlimited visiting in children's hospitals, the establishment of mother–baby units, the treatment of children on an out-patient rather than an in-patient basis wherever possible, and an emphasis on keeping families together rather than too readily taking children into care.

Prevention of the need for separation to occur at all is the overriding criterion. Unfortunately, there are situations when children do have to be removed from home or, for that matter, when parents leave home. Severance of bonds may always be distressing; what is also now apparent is that the way in which this is carried out is all-important in affecting the child's reactions. The Robertsons' report show what can be done in an ideal situation: preparation of the child beforehand; assignment to one specific mother-substitute; preservation of previous routines and habits; retaining of own toys and clothes; frequent visiting by whichever parent is available, and efforts to keep the child oriented to the absent parent by means of talking about her and showing photographs. Thus, distress can be greatly alleviated by paying attention to those circumstances surrounding the separation that produce distress in their own right: a strange environment, a strange routine, strange caretakers, and so forth. Loss of contact with a parent will never be a negligible experience even when these other sources of stress have been eliminated, but their elimination will make the experience a less traumatic one than is the case otherwise. That separation is *potentially* a traumatic event is not to be doubted; that it must *invariably* be so has not been demonstrated.

Distress in a child can be a highly unpleasant experience to witness, and it seems natural to take every possible step to prevent it occurring. This is the justification often advanced for not permitting parental access to separated children: each renewed contact and each break that then follows brings with it yet more distress – hence the argument that it would be better for separations to be total while they last, even at the price of young children no longer being oriented to their parents and behaving as though they had forgotten them. However, what the research has highlighted is that such a practice merely postpones the difficulty and adds to the dangers of the separation situation. When eventually reunited with the parents, the child who has 'forgotten' them will show all the signs of detachment: a lack of trust in the parents, a reluctance to see them as a security figures, a display of aggressiveness rather than affection – in short, a most abnormal and undesirable kind of relationship that need not, of course, be irreversible but that will take longer to put right the greater the duration of the separation. Hence the emphasis on maintaining contact with parents during temporary separations, even at the price of continuing upset. If the choice is between grieving for a lost parent and becoming totally detached from her, the former must be judged the more desirable, however painful for all parties concerned it may be.

Thus, the emphasis needs to be as far as possible on preserving continuity – of relationships, of environments, of routines – in fact, all those factors that make for predictability. Children in the first few years of life have difficulty in adjusting to marked discontinuity – hence, the traumatic nature of the traditional separation experience where just about everything changes for the child to a quite drastic degree. As the Heinicke and Westheimer report shows, children admitted to residential care with their siblings suffer less than those on their own, and as the Robertsons made clear, visits by fathers were clearly of benefit – as well as the retention of the children's own toys, clothes and even beds and blankets. Separations often occur under circumstances where such measures are not possible; nevertheless, the notion of as much continuity as can be achieved in the given conditions remains a useful guiding principle.

Further reading

Bowlby, J. 1979: *The Making and Breaking of Affectional Bonds.* London: Tavistock.

Rutter, M. 1981: *Maternal Deprivation Reassessed,* 2nd edn. Harmondsworth: Penguin.

Yarrow, L. J. 1964: Separation from parents during early childhood. In M. L. Hoffman and L. W. Hoffman (eds), *Review of Child Development Research, Vol. 1.* New York: Russell Sage Foundation.

Issue: Does maternal deprivation bring about long-term damage?

Background

We have seen that, under certain conditions at any rate, separation from parents can be a highly traumatic event. Given the widespread assumption that children in the early years are of an extremely impressionable nature and that as a result the experiences they encounter at that stage of life may leave irreversible effects on the developing personality, it is hardly surprising that separation has been looked on as a pathogenic event that may produce long-term, even permanent consequences.

This belief is particularly firmly entrenched because the establishment of the child's primary social relationships, usually with the parents, are generally considered to constitute the foundation on which all psychosocial development is based. These relationships ought thus to be marked by *basic trust* – the belief by the child that the parents are constantly available for comfort and security, that their presence constitutes a haven of safety always ready to receive the child in the face of threat. According to some writers the soundness of all subsequent relationships, even in adulthood, depends on that trust being established at the beginning of life. Any break in the bond formed with the parents early on will not only profoundly disturb the child's faith at the time but also adversely affect the capacity to form later love relationships. It is as though the individual, having once been let down, can no longer emotionally commit him- or herself fully to the formation of other bonds. As Bowlby (in the paper summarized below) put it: 'A break in the continuity of the mother–child relationship at a critical stage in the development of the child's social responses may result in more or less permanent impairment of the ability to make relationships' – an impairment which, at its most extreme, can take the form of the 'affectionless character', marked by a total inability to form any meaningful, permanent emotional commitments, be they in love, marriage, parenthood or friendship.

That there are individuals whose capacity to form relationships is in some way impaired cannot, of course, be doubted. In so far as such persons may cause social havoc, bringing considerable unhappiness to those coming into contact with them, it clearly becomes important to identify the causes of such behaviour, and the efforts to learn about maternal deprivation were originally fuelled to a large extent by the belief that a cause-and-effect link had been detected between early loss of mother and subsequent personality disorders. Stamp out the pathogenic influence (so it was thought) and one can eliminate such disorders, rather as cholera or typhoid have been got rid off by identifying the bacilli responsible for these diseases.

Research in more recent years has shown that such a comparison is not a meaningful one. The simple, one-factor causes that bring about diseases such as cholera or typhoid are rarely to be found in the psychological field. As we saw when discussing short-term effects of separation, such an experience is composed of a great diversity of factors, each one of which may have a bearing on the outcome. This makes generalizations about long-term effects even more hazardous: the eventual outcome depends in the first place on all the circumstances that led up to the separation; second, on the circumstances of that separation itself; and finally, and most importantly of all, on whatever the separation in turn leads to subsequently. Separation, especially when one asks about long-term effects, cannot be considered as an isolated event, however prolonged or traumatic it may be. It has to be seen as embedded in an array of circumstances that give meaning to it.

Concern about long-term consequences of separation is, of course, understandable. If children can be so upset by such an experience it is certainly legitimate to ask whether their future security may not be put at risk thereby and whether it is this consideration, rather than the wish to prevent distress at the time, that should provide the principal rationale for attempts to prevent breaks in relationships from occurring. The research concerned with this problem has primarily examined two possible kinds of after-effects: those involving emotional adjustment, including behaviour problems and delinquency, and those found in the ability to make meaningful interpersonal relationships. The studies summarized below refer to both kinds.

Research findings

(1) SUMMARIES

Bowlby, J., Ainsworth, M., Boston, M. and Rosenbluth, D. 1956:
The effects of mother–child separation: a follow-up study. British
Journal of Medical Psychology, 29, 211–47.

Bowlby initiated this investigation as a direct test of the link he
had hypothesized between early maternal deprivation and later
psychosocial difficulties, with particular reference to the ability to
form interpersonal relationships.

A group of 60 children, who had experienced prolonged separation from home in the first 4 years, was located when the children
were aged between 7 and 14 years. The separations had occurred
because of the children's tuberculosis, and the period spent by them
in the sanatorium lasted from several months up to over 2 years.
During this time contact with the parents was at most once a week
but in many cases a lot less frequently. Nursing was on an impersonal basis, in that no substitute mothering was provided. For purposes
of comparison a control group was selected from the children's
class-mates, matched for age and sex.

The data for the follow-up were derived mainly from reports by
teachers and educational psychologists. The differences found between the two groups of children were on the whole minimal and
certainly not as great as the authors had anticipated on the basis of
previous theorizing. What differences there were tended to show the
separated group in a less favourable light. Thus, they were regarded
by their teachers as somewhat more withdrawn, to day-dream more
and concentrate less, and according to the psychologists' reports
they responded not as adequately during testing as did the control
children. In large part, however, the statistically significant differences between the two groups were few in number. In particular,
there was no indication that the prolonged break away from home
in early childhood had resulted in any gross pathology such as
delinquency or an inability to make friends. The relationships of the
separated children were on the whole satisfactory. Although some of
these children showed signs of maladjustment these were not severe,
and in any case, others who had undergone the same experience
appeared not to be affected at all and to be functioning normally in

all spheres. In addition, neither the length of separation nor the number of separations experienced by the children was significantly related to any index of maladjustment.

Thus, the authors are forced to conclude that:

> Statements implying that children who are brought up in institutions or who suffer other forms of serious privation and deprivation in early life *commonly* develop psychopathic or affectionless characters are seen to be mistaken .... Outcome is immensely varied, and of those who are damaged only a small minority develop those very serious disabilities of personality which first drew attention to the pathogenic nature of the experience. [original emphasis]

Douglas, J. W. B. 1975: Early hospital admissions and later disturbances of behaviour and learning. Developmental Medicine and Child Neurology, *17, 456–80.*

This study takes the follow-up period into adolescence, in order to determine whether there is any evidence to suggest that separation in the first 5 years produces later psychological disturbance. It is based on a national sample of children, namely all those born in Britain during one particular week in 1946. Amongst these children there were 958 who had been separated from their parents as a result of hospitalization – mostly for short periods (a mean of 21 days), though 20 per cent were readmitted at least once before the age of 5. Assessment of the young people was on the basis of four sources of information: teachers' ratings of behaviour, reading tests, police records of delinquency and employment records.

The results indicate that 'nervousness' (as rated by teachers) shows no association with early separation, but that all other measures taken, namely 'troublesome behaviour' (also rated by teachers), poor reading scores, delinquency and an unstable job history, were more marked among separated than among non-separated individuals. It was also found that these adverse indices become more marked as the number and the length of admissions to hospital increase. Thus, a single hospital admission of 1 week or less was *not* associated with an increased risk of later psychological disorder, whereas prolonged or repeated admissions did show such a relationship. The fact that hospitalized children are more likely to come from certain kinds of families (for example, those with several children, where the father is a manual worker and where parents take little interest in school progress) was not found to influence these findings.

The data thus do indicate long-term effects of early separation – a surprising conclusion in view of the relatively mild and brief nature of these separations. The following study was undertaken in order to see whether the findings could be replicated.

Quinton, D. and Rutter, M. 1976: Early hospital admissions and later disturbances of behaviour: an attempted replication of Douglas' findings. Developmental Medicine and Child Neurology, *18,* 447–59.

The authors of this report wanted to replicate Douglas's study for two reasons: first, because the results obtained by Douglas apply to children who were admitted to hospital a generation previously, and second, because no account had been taken of the possible presence of family discord – the variable known to be most strongly associated with disturbance in adolescence.

Representative samples from two areas were combined for the purposes of the study, i.e. all children aged 10 years in 1969 in an inner-London borough and all 10-year olds from the Isle of Wight. Amongst these, 451 were available for intensive investigation. Measures were obtained from a questionnaire completed by teachers and from a detailed personal interview with the children's mothers. The latter also provided information about family circumstances. Scores for various kinds of psychological adjustment–maladjustment were then calculated from the data supplied by both teachers and mothers.

The results confirm some of Douglas's findings, in particular that single hospital admissions lasting a week or less are not associated with any form of psychological disturbance later on, but that *repeated* admissions do show such an association. The risk is, however, greatest in the case of those children who come from disadvantaged homes. It appears that children who for one reason or another are already insecure or troubled are the ones who are most likely to be damaged by separation experiences, and it also seems that the reason for such insecurity concerned family discord. However, the report stresses a positive side too: three-fifth of children experiencing repeated hospitalization do *not* show emotional disturbance in later childhood. All in all, there is little evidence that repeated early separations are a common causal influence in the development of psychiatric disorder later on in childhood.

Lambert, L., Essen, J. and Head, J. 1977: Variations in behaviour ratings of children who have been in care. Journal of Child Psychology and Psychiatry, *18*, 335–46.

Here too advantage is taken of a national sample, i.e. all children born in Britain during one particular week in 1958. The interest in this study is in children who had been deprived of home life because they had been taken into public care for a period, which they spent either in a children's home or a foster home.

The investigation took a longitudinal form and included data-gathering points at ages 7 and 11. At both ages teachers were asked to complete a standardized questionnaire (the Bristol Social Adjustment Guides), and reports were also obtained from parents, including information about any time spent by the child in the care of a public authority or voluntary society. Amongst approximately 16,000 children taking part in the follow-up, 253 had been in care by age 7 and, altogether, 414 by age 11.

When comparing teachers' reports on children who had been in care with those on children who had never been in care, the former were found to have been assessed more unfavourably. In general they were regarded as less well adjusted, though this applied particularly to their social relationships with both adults and other children and to 'outgoing' (antisocial) behaviour rather than to 'ingoing' (neurotic) behaviour. However, it was also established that children who were not admitted to care till after the age of 7 were already judged by their teachers as being more poorly adjusted at age 7. This suggests that the poorer ratings these children obtained subsequently at age 11 were due not so much to the children's separation experiences but to their background and family circumstances. Reports on home behaviour also showed the in-care children in a more unfavourable light than children who had never been in care. However, when account was taken of such associated variables as social class, illegitimacy, crowding in the home and family size, this difference disappeared.

It seems that the children who were removed from their families and taken into public care were already vulnerable by virtue of their home circumstances and that it is these that accounted primarily for subsequent difficulties. However, it may also be that the children's problems were increased by their in-care experience.

Wolkind, S. and Kruk, S. 1985: From child to parent: early separation and the adaptation to motherhood. In A. R. Nicol (ed.), Longitudinal Studies in Child Psychology and Psychiatry. *Chichester: Wiley.*

One possible consequence of lack of mothering in the early years refers to the ability of individuals with such a history themselves to function adequately as parents. It is this hypothesized link which is examined here in a group of women admitted to public care in childhood.

For the purposes of the research, women were considered to be especially at risk if they had been separated from one or both parents for at least 1 month before the age of 5 or for at least 3 months between the ages of 5 and 16 in a context suggesting continuing family disharmony. Criteria used for this included parental divorce, parental death, the prolonged illness of a parent and the child's admission to boarding-school for social reasons. Three groups were then constructed: a non-separated group (comprising 78 women); a 'disrupted' group (49 women) who had experienced separation but had mostly remained with their family; and an 'in-care' group (33 women) where separation had involved admission to public authority care. All women were seen during their pregnancy, and at 4, 14, 27 and 42 months after the birth of their first child. Assessments included semi-structured interviewing and systematic observations.

A number of background factors were found to differentiate the three groups. In the non-separated group 10 per cent of women were unmarried; in both the other two groups this percentage was 63. Among the non-separated women 22 per cent were in their teens when they became pregnant; this compares with 51 per cent for the disrupted and 70 per cent for the in-care group. Not surprisingly the incidence of unwanted babies was considerably greater in the latter two groups than in the former. Yet it is also significant that by the seventh month of pregnancy, fewer of the disrupted group were feeling negatively towards the idea of having a baby. Their rate of 32 per cent for such negative feelings is very much closer to the 26 per cent of the non-separated group than the 61 per cent found among the in-care women.

In general, the in-care group provided the least favourable picture during the follow-up compared with both the other two. Thus, for example, not holding the baby during feeding, rare in the non-separated group and only slightly more common in the disrupted group, was the method used by a quarter of the in-care women. At 4 months, maternal stimulation of the baby, by means of vocalization or physical contact, was very low in the in-care group and highest in the non-separated group. Observations also showed that the in-care women were the least sensitive to the needs of the baby, with the disrupted group more similar to the non-separated one. At later ages the children of the three sets of women were similarly ordered with respect to such indices as the incidence of behaviour problems and the frequency of admission to hospital. Again, the major difference is to be found between the in-care group and the other two, with the former showing all the disadvantages.

It appears that for the women who had been in care the separation had constituted just one episode in a generally disharmonious childhood. Even as adults they were more likely to have poor marriages and to lack support from others, helping to account for their difficulty in developing competence as mothers. The unfavourable picture of their parenting qualities appeared not to be directly due to the separations they had experienced as these had also taken place in the disrupted group. It seems rather that their admissions to care were an index of a certain extreme type of unsettled childhood, which then led on to further unsettled living in adulthood.

Dowdney, L., Skuse, D., Rutter, M., Quinton, D. and Mrazek, D. 1985: The nature and quality of parenting provided by women raised in institutions. Journal of Child Psychology and Psychiatry, 26, 599–626.

This report is also concerned with the parental competence of women separated from their own parents in childhood, and examines the manifestations of that competence in considerable detail.

The study refers to a group of 81 women who had been in care in 1964 in one or the other of two children's homes and who could be traced in 1978 when aged between 21 and 27. They were contrasted with a group of 41 women who had never been in care. All had children aged between 2 to 3½ years at the time of the study. The women's parenting skills were investigated by means of lengthy standardized interviews and (for a subset of each group) by a number of observational techniques carried out in the home.

Ratings of parenting style, based on interview material, showed that four times as many of the ex-care mothers were regarded as 'poor' compared with the control group. It is also noteworthy that nearly one-third of the ex-care women were assessed as 'good'. A number of measures of rather more specific aspects of parenting showed no differences according to the interview data; these included the warmth expressed to the children, the amount of joint play and the type of discipline. On the other hand there was a considerable difference in the interview ratings of the mothers' sensitivity, especially in their handling of distress and disputes. Of the ex-care women 42 per cent were judged to be low in this respect as opposed to 7 per cent of the controls. This was borne out by the observational data: the ex-care mothers were twice as likely to ignore their children's attempts to gain their attention even when repeated a number of times. The observations also showed the incidence of negative behaviour (disapproval, threat, physical punishment, and so on) to be 70 per cent higher in the ex-care group, and in addition, these women were rather more irritable but less effective in disciplining. Yet in many respects the two groups were comparable, for instance in how much the mothers talked to their children, how much they praised them and the extent to which they provided support for them.

The findings thus provide a mixed picture of women who had undergone periods of institutional care as children. On the one hand the majority were both affectionate with their children and actively involved with them, and the evidence gives no suggestion of any gross defect of parenting in most of them. On the other hand many were not particularly skilful in picking up cues from the children and in responding in ways that circumvented difficulties rather than involved direct confrontation. Especially noteworthy, however, is the heterogeneity of outcome for women with this kind of childhood history. The mere fact of separation is clearly not sufficient on its own to cause parenting difficulties as an adult; other factors are also involved.

(2) COMMENTS ON RESEARCH

Investigating the effects of early childhood experience on later psychological functioning is no easy task. For one thing the lengthy time span presents problems: a longitudinal study in which the research workers are present at the time of the early experience and then follow up the children concerned is obviously preferable because the events can be recorded accurately as they happen; it does, however, consume a great deal of resources to stay with the sample over a period of many years. No wonder that a retrospective approach is often chosen instead, whereby data about the early experience are obtained at the same time as the after-effects are assessed. However, as this is dependent on the accuracy of records or of people's memories it is only too easy for gaps and distortions to be introduced. Where the early events are defined in gross terms (for example, was the child separated or not?), this may not be too great a problem; but where more subtle data are required (for example, the nature of family relationships at the time or children's reactions to the separation experience), caution must be used in accepting the information as reliable.

The other difficulty about research on early experience is that all sorts of different things may happen between that experience and the time when later assessments are made which also have a bearing on the final outcome. Thus, in comparing a separated and a non-separated group it is highly likely that there will be many more differences between them than just the fact of separation. In particular, separation involving admission to care is frequently just one link in a chain of unfortunate events: the admission may lead to all sorts of other undesirable experiences such as an institutional and impersonal upbringing, frequent breaks with various foster parents, and so forth. It then becomes extremely difficult to determine whether any subsequent pathology is due to the separation or to the various events that follow it. For that matter, such children may already be different *before* the separation, in that the families from which they come are in some way distinctive (for example, more vulnerable to stresses or more disturbed in their interpersonal relationships) or the children themselves more prone to illness or other personal difficulties. It is thus by no means easy to ascertain which of these many influences gave rise to whatever end-result emerges. Merely comparing separated with non-separated groups is insufficient; allowance must also be made for the other influences at work.

It is in this respect above all that recent research (such as illustrated by some of the reports summarized above) is rather more sophisticated than previous work. From such research it is now becoming clear that, however traumatic separation from parents may be to young children and however violently they react at the time, the separation *per se* is rarely associated with long-term consequences: the family situation which may have given rise to the need for separation and to which the child may subsequently return is more likely to be the crucial influence in determining subsequent pathology. Separation as an isolated event, even when occurring at a 'vulnerable' age and even when as prolonged as was suffered by, say, some of the hospitalized children in the study by Bowlby et al., does not condemn the individual to distorted personality development. Only when that separation forms part of a long sequence of misfortunes are children much more likely to be adversely affected.

The research on this topic is thus another instance of the useless-ness of the 'critical period' way of thinking about human develop-ment – the notion that anything adverse leaves permanent marks on children if it happens at an early and therefore vulnerable age. The findings indicate that it is the totality of a child's experiences that matters rather than single events, however, upsetting those events may be at the time and however early in life the child encounters them. Factors such as the presence of distorted family relationships are much more likely to be influential because they, after all, can exercise that influence throughout the whole of childhood instead of impinging only at one particular point.

Implications for practice

It follows that we ought again to make the point that any attempt to understand and help must take into account not just specific events but the total context in which these events are embedded. Breaks in relationships are frequently associated with other adverse factors; there is not much point in preventing a break at all costs if these other factors are left unattended. Confronted by a childhood history of separation through removal into care it would be as well to regard the separation events more as symptoms than as causes – symptoms, that is, of a family situation that exercises overarching influence on the course of the child's psychological development through lack of stable, harmonious relationships. It is these that need promoting, for they may adversely affect children even without any actual separation ever taking place. As we shall see in discussing the next Issue, the same applies to divorce: it is the influence of family discord more than the actual break-up that is responsible for suffering and unhappiness in children.

It is clearly essential that ideas about the irreversible, or at least long-lasting, effects of separation be discarded, leading as they do to feelings of helplessness and inactivity on the part of service providers. As will become apparent subsequently, some children at least have considerable recuperative powers in the face of stress, and it is also apparent that later experiences may considerably mitigate the effects of earlier misfortunes. The search for mitigating influences is still in its infancy: in the mean time the notion that it is never too late to provide help to a child following an unfortunate experience like separation is given a further boost. If we accept that separations often form part of a chain of harmful events, then in each individual case ways need to be found to break that chain. To take an example, positive school experience has been found to be one possible means of accomplishing this – presumably because of the effects of achievement on a child's self-esteem. It is therefore all the more regrettable that the education of children in care is still an area where the quality of provision and the degree of interest shown by caretakers are greatly inferior to what is experienced by most other children – as though a child once removed from home is condemned to being beyond help, when in fact such help is all the more urgently required.

One other implication refers to the reluctance of many staff of residential institutions and of foster parents to establish close relationships with the children in their care, in the belief that any child temporarily separated and due eventually to return to its parents would only be further damaged by yet another separation, this time from parent substitutes. That there may be grief, especially when the child has been with the parent substitutes for a lengthy period, can hardly be denied; that long-lasting damage will be brought about is unlikely. It is indeed more probable (though firmer evidence on this point is badly required) that the child will be damaged by being kept 'on ice' emotionally through not having any opportunity to form attachments albeit of a temporary nature. Better the grief of yet another separation than a period of emotional solitude.

Further reading

Bowlby, J. 1951: *Maternal Care and Mental Health*. Geneva: World Health Organization.

Clarke, A. M. and Clarke, A. D. B. 1976: *Early Experience: myth and evidence*. London: Open Books.

Rutter, M. 1981: *Maternal Deprivation Reassessed*. 2nd edn. Harmondsworth: Penguin.

Issue: Should mothers go out to work?

Background

Maternal deprivation takes many forms, and though historically the literature dealt mainly with the more extreme manifestations, by a process of generalization questions also came to be asked about the effects of such minor separation experiences as occur when a mother takes on employment outside the home. Do children in the early years need the reassurance of mother's constant availability? Is it necessary for a mother to be in attendance 24 hours a day? If the answer to these questions is in the affirmative, then mothers must clearly be discouraged from seeking employment, and should regard their parenting task as a full-time job and appreciate that mothering cannot be diluted.

There are indeed many who believe that all sorts of ills of society (juvenile delinquency, addictive habits, truancy and so on) are due to inadequate parental supervision, with the mother's absence at work a major factor. Their opinions are reinforced by theorists who believe that children's emotional stability and security is at first wholly dependent on a continuous bond with the one mother-figure: interrupt that bond, however temporarily, and vulnerability to psychological damage is sure to follow.

Yet one of the features of family life in the last few decades has been the enormous growth of female employment, with the greatest proportionate increase taking place among mothers of pre-school children. Far from being an unusual phenomenon, found only among those with pressing financial needs, it is fast becoming the norm in all sectors of the population in most countries throughout the world. There are no doubt various reasons for this increase: the greater educational opportunities for women, the availability of labour-saving devices in the home, the rise of feminism, and so forth. Whatever the reasons, however, there are practical and policy consequences, and especially so with regard to the provision of child-care facilities outside the home. Public authorities have responded to this challenge in ways that often have very little to do with knowledge as to what is good for children and much more with quite extraneous financial, economic and political considerations. Thus, during the Second World War, at a time when women were badly needed in factories and on the land, the British government encouraged mothers to take paid employment, providing nurseries and crèches and looking on their dual role as perfectly acceptable. Contrast that with the situation in the 1980s, when the high incidence of unemployment made it desirable to keep as many women as possible off the unemployment register: mothers were urged to stay at home, devote themselves to their children and appreciate the virtues of a close family life. At the same time the availability of public nursery places dropped sharply. With an anticipated skills shortage in the 1990s it looks as though the pendulum will swing once again, with the idea of working mothers becoming respectable once more.

It is apparent that there is still considerable confusion on the part of both parents and public authorities as to the effects on young children of a period of daily separation as a result of the mother's absence at work. Fortunately, research is now beginning to yield a body of findings that enable us to replace personal opinion with facts. Almost inevitably the picture turns out to be rather more complex than was first thought, so that straightforward answers in terms of 'good' or 'bad' cannot be given, for much depends on the circumstances surrounding a mother's decision to work outside the home. However, at least there is now considerable agreement among research workers as to the conclusions to be drawn from their studies.

Research findings

(1) SUMMARIES

Hock, E. 1980: Working and nonworking mothers and their infants: A comparative study of maternal caregiving characteristics and infant social behavior. Merrill-Palmer Quarterly, 26, 79–101.

Not surprisingly, the younger the child, the greater is the concern about the possible effects of maternal employment. This report is therefore useful in that it provides data about children of working mothers during the first year of life. The sample consisted of 42 mothers employed outside the home from the time the child was 3 months old, the infants being cared for in a home setting on an individual basis during the mothers' absence. In the comparison group of 55 non-working mothers and their infants the mothers did not work at all outside the home during the child's first year.

Assessments were carried out at 3, 8 and 12 months following birth. A variety of methods were used: semi-structured interviews with the mothers; observations of maternal care-giving behaviour as the mother went about her daily routine; a more detailed observational procedure focusing on the feeding situation; maternal attitude scales; the infants' behaviour in the Strange Situation (designed to assess the quality of the child's attachment to the mother); and the Bayley Scales (a standardized scale to measure infants' psychological and psychomotor development).

The results show that infants of employed mothers do not differ from those of non-employed mothers in the nature of their attachments to them, in that the amount and intensity of the behaviour which the two groups directed at the mother were similar. The only difference in social behaviour found was that infants of employed mothers were more positive in their reactions to strangers: when alone with an unfamiliar person they were more likely to permit her to comfort them when stressed than was the case with infants of non-employed mothers. The two groups of infants were also very similar in their developmental status as assessed by their scores on the mental and motor scales of the Bayley test. As far as the mothers were concerned, there was nothing in any of the observations to suggest that employed mothers differed in any way from non-employed mothers with respect to the nature and quality of their caretaking activities.

Thus, as the author concludes, 'results of this study support the belief that work status per se is not significantly related to maternal attitudes and caregiving behaviors, to infant developmental level, or to the quality of the mother–infant relationship.'

Belsky, J. and Rovine, M. J. 1988: Nonmaternal care in the first year of life and the security of infant–parent attachment. Child Development, 58, 157–67.

The extent to which the mother's daily absence from home may have a disruptive influence on the infant's relationship to her has

been investigated in quite a number of studies. In this one 149
infants from working- and middle-class families were followed up
from birth into the second year. On the basis of the mother's
employment outside the home, four groups were established: a full-
time group (35 or more hours weekly spent on a job), high part-time
work (between 20 and 35 hours per week), low part-time work
(10–20 hours weekly), and mother-care (5 hours or less per week).
The care arrangements for the infants of the employed mothers
varied, though the most common was placing the child with a
baby-sitter either at home or outside the home. Assessment of infants was based on the Strange Situation, when they were subjected
to a series of episodes designed to evaluate the quality of their
attachment to the mother (assessed at 12 months of age) and to the
father (assessed at 13 months). By the use of conventional scoring
criteria the infants' behaviour was then classified as secure or insecure.

In their relationship to the mother, infants from the full-time
employment group were classified as insecure in 47 per cent of cases,
as compared with 35 per cent in the high part-time, 21 per cent in
the low part-time and 25 per cent in the mother-care groups. With
respect to infant–father attachment, different results were found for
the two sexes. The boys with full-time employed mothers were most
likely to be insecure: 50 per cent were so classified, as opposed to 29
per cent in the remainder. Among girls, on the other hand, those
with employed mothers were found to be insecure in their attachment to father in 14 per cent of cases, as opposed to the mother-care
group with an unexpectedly high incidence of 50 per cent.

Thus, the findings, unlike those of the previously summarized
study, seem to indicate that maternal absence for the major part of
the day during the first year of life is associated with patterns of
attachment that show some degree of insecurity in the relationship.
It should be added,however, that more than 50 per cent of infants
with an employed mother nevertheless established a secure relationship with her, that 50 per cent of the boys with employed
mothers showed no ill-effect in the relationship with the father; and
that almost two-thirds of all boys experiencing extensive daily
separations from the mother established a secure relationship with at
least one parent. Those most likely to succumb to the risk of insecurity were boys, had been characterized as being fussy or difficult
in temperament, and had mothers who were less satisfied with their
marriage and were more career-oriented than other mothers. It

should also be pointed out that the increased insecurity was only found in infants left by their mothers for more than 20 hours per week.

Schachter, F. F. 1981: Toddlers with employed mothers. Child Development, 52, 958–64.

This investigation looked at a slightly older group, namely children aged 2½ years. Thirty-two children whose mothers worked full-time were compared with a matched group of 38 children whose mothers had no out-of-home employment. The children came from middle-class families of high educational standard and were contacted through a university-based playgroup.

A battery of measures was obtained from each child. Language development was assessed by means of an analysis of naturally occurring speech samples; no difference between the two groups was found in this respect. This also applies to emotional adjustment, for which measures were obtained from the teachers in charge of the playgroup. Cognitive development was assessed with standardized intelligence tests, and here the children of the non-employed mothers were found to be superior to those of the employed mothers (mean IQs being 115 and 106 respectively). Finally, social development was measured by classroom observations and by teacher ratings. Again, a difference emerged, though this time in favour of the children of employed mothers, who showed a greater degree of self-sufficiency and solicited help and protection from adults less frequently than the children of non-employed mothers. In addition, they were also more oriented towards other children and more ready to initiate approaches to other children.

Gold, D. and Andres, D. 1978: Relations between maternal employment and development of nursery school children. Canadian Journal of Behavioral Science, 10, 116–29.

Particular attention was paid in this study to the effects of maternal employment on children's sex-role development, as according to some theories a mother's constant presence is an important factor in such development. Thus, a scale to assess each child's sex-role orientation was administered, as was a scale to sample the children's ideas of the activities appropriate for males and females. In addition, the children's IQs were tested and teachers were asked to complete a behaviour rating scale that measured the child's adjustment at school. Mothers and fathers also completed questionnaires, which assessed their own parental roles, sex-role concepts and child-care attitudes.

There were 52 children whose mothers were working at a full-time job on an uninterrupted basis, and 58 whose mothers had had no paid employment since the child was born. At the time of the study the children were between 4 and 5 years of age, and all came from middle-class, two-parent families. All attended nursery schools, where they were individually tested.

Comparison of the two groups shows a mixed picture. Boys with employed mothers had less stereotyped ideas about sex roles, expressing a less marked preference for masculine activities than boys of non-employed mothers; this difference did not emerge to a significant degree among girls. Boys with employed mothers scored lower on IQ tests than their controls; again this difference was not found between the two sets of girls. As far as adjustment ratings were concerned, the children with employed mothers were described as better adjusted on nine of the 11 items that distinguished the two groups, and this applied equally to both sexes. An additional finding was that the employed mothers reported themselves significantly more satisfied with their role than the non-employed mothers with theirs, most of the latter expressing a wish to seek employment once their children were older. Furthermore, it is interesting to note that the husbands of employed wives also expressed more satisfaction with their wives' roles. Thus, it appears that parental attitudes, both to job and to the rearing of children, are all-important.

Gottfried, A. E., Gottfried, A. W. and Bathurst, K. 1988: Maternal employment, family environment, and children's development infancy through the school years. In A. E. Gottfried and A. W. Gottfried (eds), Maternal Employment and Children's Development. *New York: Plenum.*

There can be no doubt that longitudinal investigations have many advantages when it comes to throwing light on topics such as the effects of maternal employment, for the nature of these effects might well change according to the child's developmental stage and as wide an age range as possible should thus be covered. This is the value of the present study, in that it is an ambitious attempt to follow up children from 1 to 7 years of age and so describe what impact the mother working outside the home has on the course of children's development.

The study is a large-scale one, in that it is based on a sample of

130 children who were repeatedly assessed (first at 6–monthly and later at yearly intervals) till they reached their seventh birthday. The children were from white, middle-class families, 78 per cent of whom remained intact (no divorce or separation) throughout the research period. Employment of the mothers showed a progressive increase, with just over a third being employed at the outset and just under two-thirds at the end of the follow-up period. A considerable battery of assessment techniques was applied to both children and parents, covering the children's cognitive functioning, temperament, social competence, behavioural adjustment and academic achievement (from age 5), and various aspects of the home environment, parental attitudes and parent–child relationships.

Despite this complexity the findings can be summarized very easily: no significant differences emerged at any stage and in any psychological domain between children of employed and of non-employed mothers. As the authors put it succinctly: 'There is simply *no negative effect* of maternal employment status.' (Original emphasis) What did matter was the quality of the home environment, together with socio-economic status and, to a lesser extent, the number of children in the family. The study did show that employed mothers held higher educational aspirations for their children, giving rise to the speculation that these children may ultimately show enhanced development compared with other children. Otherwise, however, the two groups of children were basically alike, as were their relationships with their parents and the atmosphere of their homes. From their findings the authors therefore conclude: 'We believe that any family can provide a favourable environment for children's development regardless of mothers' employment status.'

Lerner, J. V. and Galambos, N. L. 1986: Child development and family change: the influence of maternal employment on infants and toddlers. In L. P. Lipsitt and C. Rovee-Collier (eds), Advances in Infancy Research, *vol. 4. Norwood, New Jersey: Ablex.*

The data presented in this report also come from a longitudinal investigation (the well-known New York Longitudinal Study), in which a sample of 133 children from middle-class families was followed up from early infancy onwards. A great many measures were obtained at frequent intervals, including interviews with parents and later on with teachers, psychometric measures of cognitive functioning such as IQ tests, achievement test scores and observational data. The present report is based mainly on the 100 families that were available for study at ages 3 and 5 years, when over a third of the mothers were found to have resumed employment, many doing so in the first or second years of the child's life.

Comparing the children of employed mothers with the rest on the very many measures that had been obtained, no differences emerged on any. The children did not differ on IQ scores, educational achievement, adjustment at home and at school or on any aspect of mother–child interaction. The children of employed mothers were said to be temperamentally 'easier', though it is difficult to know how to interpret this. On the whole the data support the notion that the kind of relationship established between mother and child had a stronger influence on child development than maternal employment status *per se*. Thus, a warm and accepting attitude on the part of the mother appeared to exert a definitely positive influence on the child, and it was those mothers who were highly satisfied with their roles, *whether they were employed or not*, who displayed higher levels of warmth and acceptance than did dissatisfied mothers.

(2)   COMMENTS ON RESEARCH

The nature of research on this topic has changed drastically in the last decade or two. Previously, the question that preoccupied investigators was: In what way are children deprived when mother goes to work? As a result only ill-effects were looked for, the assumption being that such an experience was bound to harm young children and that it was therefore the negative consequences that had to be documented. Now a rather less blinkered attitude prevails: credence is given to the possibility that there may be gains and not just losses, and as a result the myth that maternal employment necessarily implies a form of maternal deprivation is at last – albeit slowly – disintegrating.

The considerable body of evidence which has now accumulated shows that children over the age of 1 year will not necessarily be harmed by the mother's daily absence from home, provided certain conditions are met. These conditions refer above all to the nature of substitute care arrangements, the stability and quality of which are essential. It is true that one or two studies suggest some degree of intellectual inferiority on the part of the children of employed mothers, but this has neither been confirmed by other studies nor has it been satisfactorily explained. Social behaviour, and especially the development of independence, has sometimes been found to be more advanced; on the whole, however, the indications are that there are few differences, intellectual or social, between children of employed and non-employed mothers.

It is only with respect to children under the age of one that the possibility of ill-effects has been raised more seriously. Some recent studies have found infants with an employed mother to develop an attachment to her that is marked by insecurity. This would suggest that the mother's regular daily absence at the time that the relationship is being built up may be deleterious to the development of that relationship. However, a number of considerations need to be taken into account. For one thing, as the authors of the relevant reports are careful to point out, by no means all infants are adversely affected; approximately 50 per cent develop secure relationships. For another, the effect is seen mainly in infants whose mothers have full- rather than part-time jobs, and there is also some indication that boys are more likely to be affected than girls (a sex difference in vulnerability we have noted before). In addition, there is by no means unanimity in the findings of different studies: several have reported no differences in the kinds of attachment relationships formed by infants of employed and non-employed mothers. And finally, let us also note that far too many studies rely exclusively on one single form of assessment, namely the Strange Situation – a procedure which is by no means without its critics and which in any case ought always to be used as just one in a battery of tests.

Research in this area has also changed in one other respect. A simple cause-and-effect model, where maternal employment is the cause and the nature of children's development the effect, is now seen as far too simplistic. The fact of a mother's employment is embedded in a great mass of associated factors: the reason for mother going out to work, the extent to which she experiences 'role strain' as a result of taking on the dual responsibility of worker and parent, the father's attitude and his willingness to participate in child care, the child's temperament, the kind of substitute care arrangements made for the child, and so forth. All these factors play a part in bringing about the end result, making it difficult to arrive at simple, sweeping generalizations about maternal employment of the 'good or bad' kind. In particular, it is now realized that it is not sufficient merely to examine what goes on between mother and child but that a family perspective needs to be adopted. A mother's employment has implications for the family as a whole: the father, for example, may have to take on a different role and whatever consequences one sees in the child could well be mediated by this rather than by the fact of mother's daily absence. Research on maternal employment therefore needs to do justice to the total situation in which the employed mother and her child find themselves.

Implications for practice

It is clear that mothering need not be a 24-hours-per-day activity and that children are not inevitably harmed by the mother's daily absence at a job outside the home. It is not so much the quantity as the quality of the interaction with the child that matters, and attention should therefore focus on improving that quality. Thus, it may well be that where a mother feels psychologically hemmed in by being constantly at home, the relationship may actually be enhanced by the mother having other outlets. There is no reason why the mothers of young children must at all costs resist going out to work, or why, if they do go out to work, they should feel guilty about doing so. As long as the child has a continuing relationship with the mother, being cared for also by others does not necessarily produce any adverse effect and may even be an enriching experience.

It is true that there is still uncertainty as to the effects of full-time work on infants in the first year, and this uncertainty needs to be resolved through further research. In the meantime it is perhaps as well, given the choice, to postpone going out to work on a full-time basis until the child has passed the first birthday, but let us also assure mothers that if they cannot do so nobody has yet claimed that any effects found in the first year are necessarily long-lasting. On the contrary, the reversibility of early experience has been demonstrated repeatedly.

However, many mothers do not have a choice in this matter. Single parents in particular may have to resume earning a wage as soon as possible, and they would be ill-served by alarmist statements about the adverse consequences of taking such a step. With such mothers especially, emphasis should be placed on ensuring good, stable substitute care, and these mothers should also be helped to have mutually satisfying experiences during the times when they are together with the child (and in this respect it is interesting to note some evidence that when working mothers are together with their children their interactions tend to be more intense, frequent and positive than those of mothers and children who remain together all day – a sort of compensation phenomenon).

However, need for money is not the only 'genuine' reason that makes mothers go out to work. Obtaining intellectual and social stimulation may be just as important for a woman's well-being. It is now well known that the incidence of depression among mothers of young children, particularly in working-class families, is extremely high and that it is directly related to being housebound and having little access to external stimulation. The debate about mothers going out to work should, after all, not just be about the effects on children; it is also about the effects on mothers. A frustrated and depressed mother may well do her child a greater disservice by remaining at home against her inclination than by absenting herself at an enjoyable and satisfying job. The wisdom of a mother's decision to seek employment depends on many factors, and it is right and proper that knowledge about the likely consequences for the child should assume particular importance. However, the implication for the mother herself ought not to be disregarded: cultural stereotypes which tie women exclusively to home and children are no longer appropriate in a society where mothers in ever-growing numbers have decided to seek employment outside the home, with such resulting benefits as increases in self-esteem and income.

Satisfaction in whatever role a mother assumes is important because it in turn is likely to lead to a more positive relationship with the child. Yet one can hardly deny that having a dual role, as mother and as worker, can also place a strain on women. The availability of support – from husband, relatives, child-minders and nursery facilities – is clearly essential; it is the absence of these that provides the most likely context for the development of undesirable effects of maternal employment on children. The provision of good-quality nursery and day-care facilities in particular ought therefore to be regarded as a priority: for policy makers, in the interest of public economy, to fail to recognize the increasing prevalence of maternal employment and the consequent need for proper care arrangements is dangerously short-sighted. When, as a result of such an attitude, children are exposed to unsatisfactory care and their psychological adjustment then suffers, the eventual cost, financial as well as emotional, will offset by far the savings made.

Further reading

Hoffman, L. W. 1984: Work, family and the socialization of the child. In R. D. Parke (ed.), *The Family: review of child development research*, Vol. 7. Chicago: University of Chicago Press.

Hoffman, L. W. 1989: Effects of maternal employment in the two-parent family. *American Psychologist*, 44, 283–92.

Kamerman, S. and Hayes, C. (eds) 1982: *Families that Work: children in a changing world.* Washington, DC: National Academy Press.

Scarr, S. and Dunn, J. 1987: *Mother Care/Other Care.* Harmondsworth: Penguin.

Issue: Is group day care bad for young children?

Background

The majority of young children, at least those under 3, whose mothers go out to work are looked after by a relative, father, child-minder or some other individual able to provide personal care. The remainder – a substantial number in many countries – are in some form of group care where they are unlikely to experience the same amount of intimate, one-to-one treatment, having instead to share the same adult with a number of other children and probably being looked after by several different caretakers. Most of the worries about out-of-home care have focused on the way in which these relatively impersonal conditions may affect young children, with particular reference to those in the first 3 years of life.

There are various fears that have been expressed: that children's development would be retarded in the absence of one person wholly devoted to their progress; that emotional needs would not be adequately met when care is divided among a number of different adults, none of whom can ever be as sensitive in recognizing these needs as a single caretaker; and that children become insecure, anxious and aggressive during daily periods spent away from their parents under conditions very different from those of ordinary family life. Group care, that is, has been seen by some as a form of institutionalization and the children exposed to it as deprived. Given the twin assumptions, at one time so prevalent, that a child's early experience has profound implications for its subsequent psychological development and that that experience must occur in the context of a small family unit and on the basis of an enduring relationship with a single mother-figure, it is not surprising to find widespread suspicion of any form of experience – such as day care – that deviates from this norm.

Yet notwithstanding these suspicions a great many mothers have either freely chosen or been compelled by personal circumstances to put their children into day care. There was thus an urgent need to ascertain whether these children were indeed psychologically at risk, and as a result a considerable amount of research has come to be devoted to this question. The findings have now been reviewed by a number of writers, and though there are still various gaps and deficiencies in our knowledge there is also considerable agreement as to the kinds of conclusions to be drawn from the findings. In general this amounts to allaying most of the fears about the effects of day care; indeed, under certain circumstances at least, such an experience may well be beneficial. There are various reservations to such a statement; nevertheless, the research on this topic substantiates the conclusions drawn from work on some of the other Issues mentioned here, namely that care at home from one mother-figure does not have to be the only experience provided to children in their first few years.

In view of the considerable literature now available on day care it is not easy to choose a few representative studies. However, those outlined below give an indication of some of the more important questions to which research has been addressed and the kinds of answers that have typically been found.

Research findings

(1) SUMMARIES

Rubenstein, J. L. and Howes, C. 1983: Social-emotional development of toddlers in day care. Advances in Early Education and Day Care, 3, 13–45.

This paper summarizes a series of studies by these authors designed to compare the experiences and development of very young children reared exclusively at home with those in group day care. The sample consisted of 30 middle-class toddlers between 17 and 20 months of age, half of whom had been attending day care for an average of just under 5 months when first seen. Home-reared and day-care children were carefully matched on a range of social and personal variables.

Each child was observed for a total of 5 hours, during which time the behaviour of caretakers interacting with the child was recorded as well as the children's own behaviour. On the whole, the similarities for the two groups turned out to be more impressive than the differences. Thus, verbal and cognitive stimulation experienced by the children in the two settings was largely comparable, as was the adults' responsiveness to the children's social behaviour. Neither group could therefore be said to be in a more 'stimulating' or more 'responsive' environment. The degree of sophistication of the children's social behaviour during play episodes with others was also similar for the two groups. There was, however, a difference in the developmental level of the children's play with toys, in so far as that in the day-care sample was found to be higher. This appeared to have something to do with the presence of other children: when the home-reared children too were observed while playing with a peer, their behaviour with toys also became more sophisticated and mature.

The children were seen again when they were between 3½ and 4 years old. Assessment was based on a variety of observation procedures, interviews and tests, all administered in the child's home. Apart from the fact that the day-care children were found to be less compliant to their mothers, the measures do not point to any global impairment of social or emotional development in this group. Indeed, on language tests, as well as on measures of spontaneous speech, the day-care children were found to be superior.

Thus, for this particular sample, coming from middle-class homes and attending 'good' day-care centres, there was clearly no reason for concern about the effects of group care.

Kagan, J., Kearsley, J. B. and Zelazo, P. R. 1978: Infancy: its place in human development. *Cambridge, Mass.: Harvard University Press.*

These investigators specially set up a day-care centre in order carefully to monitor the progress of the children attending it. Here too the quality of care provided was of a high standard, but the children were drawn from working-class as well as middle-class families and included ethnic minority (Chinese) children. All began to attend the centre as early as 4 months and were followed up to the age of 2½ years. During this time the 33 children were assessed periodically and compared with a group of 67 children reared at home from whom the same measures were obtained. These were derived from a large battery of tests and observations and dealt with such characteristics as attentiveness, excitability, reactivity to others, attachment, language, perceptual analysis and memory. In addition, more general tests of development and intelligence were also administered.

The results can be summarized briefly, for they are quite unequivocal: no consistent differences between day-care and home-reared children were found on any of the numerous measures obtained from the eight occasions that assessment was carried out during the 2 years of the investigation. Thus, there were no suggestions that the emotional bond to the mother was adversely affected by the experience of day care, that intellectual development was retarded or that any specific cognitive function was in any way held back. While the quality of care provided in the centre was such that it makes it difficult to generalize to groups raised under less favourable circumstances, this study, in conjunction with the previous one summarized, does show that day care at the very least *need* not have adverse effects.

Cochran, M. M. 1977: A comparison of group day and family child-rearing patterns in Sweden. Child Development, 48, 702–7.

This study is useful not only because, unlike most others, it was carried out in a country other than the United States, but also because it is based on a comparison of group day-care children with two other samples, namely children looked after by their parents at home throughout the day and children cared for in the home of a child-minder with no more than one or two other children. The numbers in these three samples were 60, 34 and 26 respectively, matched with each other at three age levels, i.e. 12, 15 and 18 months. Observational and developmental data were gathered, the observations including the behaviour of the care givers and the kinds of experiences they offered to the children in their charge.

Most of the experiences were common to all three groups. Where differences occurred, the children in their own homes or the homes of child-minders were able to explore their surroundings more and were able to interact more frequently with adults in stimulating situations than the day-care-centre children. The Griffiths Mental Development Scale showed no significant differences at any of the three ages between the groups, with the exception of one subscale (hearing-and-speech) that showed the home groups to be superior at 12 months – a finding not repeated at 15 or at 18 months. Observations of the children in a semi-structured separation situation set up in each child's own home gave no indication of differences in behaviour with the mother.

Once again, as the authors themselves point out, the findings indicate more similarities than differences across groups. There are no suggestions that one environment is necessarily superior to any other.

Ramey, C. T., Dorval, B. and Baker-Ward, L. 1983: Group day care and socially disadvantaged families: effects on the child and the family. In S. Kilmer (ed.), Advances in Early Education and Day Care, Vol. 3. *Greenwich, Connecticut: JAI Press.*

One aim of day care is to make it possible for mothers to go out to work, and another is to advance children's social and intellectual development. The latter applies in particular to schemes designed to provide supplementary care to children from disadvantaged families. This report evaluates the effectiveness of one such scheme which is described here in detail.

The children on which this project is based were drawn from poor, ill-educated, disadvantaged families and were considered as a result of their social background to be a high risk for failure at school. The findings reported here refer to a group of 54 children, half of whom were randomly assigned to a day-care group, the remainder forming a control group where the children stayed at home throughout the period of investigation. Admission to day care was as early as 6 weeks for some and by age 3 months nearly all children had entered the programme, where they were able to re-main right through the child's pre-school years. As well as providing a carefully planned curriculum for the children the centre also made available medical and social welfare services for the families.

A variety of tests, experimental procedures and observations were employed in order periodically to monitor the progress of both groups. In particular, intellectual assessment was carried out by means of standardized developmental and intelligence tests at 12, 24, 36, 48 and 60 months. At 12 months there was no difference between the two groups, but at each assessment thereafter the groups differed significantly. This was primarily because of the de-cline of the control group, suggesting that the day-care programme was effective because it was preventing developmental retardation from setting in among this high-risk sample of disadvantaged chil-dren. In the absence of an early intervention programme, progressive IQ decline seemed inevitable – a conclusion borne out by finding that the IQs of the home-reared older siblings of the day-care chil-dren were deteriorating with age. As further tests of particular cognitive functions showed, certain specific psychological processes were most likely to be affected by the ameliorative action taken. Thus, at 42 months the day-care children were superior to their controls on scales dealing with verbal, perceptual, quantitative and memory functioning but not on a test of motor development. It was concluded that early compensatory education appears to improve disadvantaged children's ability to attend to structured tasks, to comprehend verbal instructions and to carry out abstract and complex tasks.

Data were also gathered about the children's social development. In infancy those who attended day care were assessed as being more socially confident and more goal-directed than the control children. They were also found to be just as interested in peers and as friendly and co-operative as middle-class age mates. Contrary to the findings of some other research workers, the present sample of day-care attenders was neither more aggressive nor more selfish as a result of sharing the attention of one teacher with several other children.

Thus, the results of this study as a whole paint a largely optimistic picture as to the effectiveness of early intervention: they suggest that day care does not have the deleterious consequences for children's social behaviour that some have feared, and the study emphasizes that by applying a cognitively and linguistically oriented curriculum during the pre-school years it is possible to prevent the intellectual deterioration that might otherwise set in.

McCartney, M., Scarr, S. Phillips, D., Grajek, S. and Schwarz, J. C. 1982: Environmental differences among day care centres and their effects on children's development. In E. F. Zigler and E. W. Gordon (eds), Day Care: Scientific and Social Policy Issues. *Boston: Auburn House.*

In this report attention is given to the effect that the *quality* of day care has on children's development. Thus, instead of comparing a group of children in day care with a group of children at home, the approach taken here is to compare different centres distinguished by a number of quality indices and ascertain the implications that such variation has for children's development. It should be stressed that the report is a preliminary one; however, it does have the advantage of providing an overall picture of the investigation. It can best be read in conjunction with later publications by the same investigators (McCartney, 1984; Phillips et al., 1987), though these deal with rather more specific aspects.

The study was carried out in Bermuda, where something like 90 per cent of children are in some form of substitute care during the day by the time they reach their second year of life. All children aged between 3 to 5½ years who had attended one of ten centres were included in the study; the eventual sample was 156. Assessments were made both of the children's development and of the nature of the day-care environment. For the former a range of standardized and experimental tests was used, together with care-giver and parental ratings, referring to various aspects of cognitive, linguistic and social competence. The latter were derived from several hours of observation and from staff and investigator ratings, giving information about such features as the nature of personal care, the amount of creative activities offered and the type of furnishings found. In addition, details were also collected about such aspects as staff–child ratios, amount and variety of play equipment and the experience and training of staff.

In the data analysis various precautions were adopted to guard against the possible influence on the results of such variables as the age when children first began to attend the centres and the amount of time spent there, as well as of possible genetic, social-class and cultural differences. In this way the uncontaminated effect of day-care quality could be examined. The findings show that measures of quality were indeed closely related to a considerable number of children's characteristics: intellectual functioning as measured by verbal tests, various aspects of language development and communicative competence, the children's sociability and considerateness to others, their task orientation and their overall social competence. All these functions were more highly developed in centres judged to be of a good standard according to the particular quality indices used. A specially significant role was played by the amount of verbal interaction that customarily took place between staff and children. Emotional adjustment, on the other hand, turned out not to be related to the quality measures used; it may well be that different aspects of the day-care environment would need to be assessed for this purpose.

In general, the authors conclude that differences in the quality of the type of day care offered in different centres can have important effects on a number of aspects of children's development, and that the identification of the features that make up 'good quality' is therefore essential for social-policy and training purposes.

Howes, C. 1988: Relations between early child care and schooling.
Developmental Psychology, 24, 53–7.

Here too the focus is principally on the quality of children's experiences in day care, but instead of asking about the immediate effects of varying degrees of quality the project investigated longer-term effects, with particular reference to adjustment to school.

Eighty-seven children participated in the research. They were first seen in a university nursery which they entered around 4 years of age, but most had previously been in some form of group care for varying periods of time. The sample was mixed with regard to ethnicity, level of parental education, maternal employment and family status (one or two parents at home). Information was obtained from the parents about various features of the children's nursery experience, such as the child's age at entry, the number of different nurseries attended in the past and whether the child attended on a full- or part-time basis. At the same time, the quality of care received was rated on the basis of 5 dimensions i.e. teacher training, group size, adult-child ratio, adequacy of physical space and educational programme.

Three years later children were seen again in order to assess their adjustment to elementary school. Ratings were obtained from teachers about the children's academic progress and also about various school skills (group participation, independence, and so on). In addition, parents were asked to complete questionnaires regarding behaviour problems shown by the children.

The results indicate those aspects of children's experience that matter and those that appear not to matter when it comes to future adjustment at school. Among the former are the quality and the stability of care provided in pre-school settings: though the pattern differs slightly for boys and for girls and also according to what aspect of school adjustment is examined, in general one can conclude that, even after 3 years in elementary school, children who had been in high-quality nursery centres and who had experienced the fewest number of changes in their care arrangements were the most likely to be functioning well socially, emotionally and academically. Whether the pre-school experience had been of a full- or a part-time nature did not affect the outcome, nor did such family characteristics as single parenthood and maternal employment.

It therefore appears that enrolment in pre-school nurseries *per se* is not as important as the quality and stability of the care provided. There was also some indication that the earlier children had entered nurseries (and therefore the longer their pre-school experience had been), the more positive was the outcome as far as later school adjustment was concerned. Group care is thus not a unitary influence; it needs to be unpacked and the effects of its constituents separately investigated if one is to understand its consequences for children's development.

(2)   COMMENTS ON RESEARCH

There is in general an impressive degree of consensus among research workers who have examined the effects of day care on young children. The great majority of studies do *not* find such an experience to be harmful, and many have pointed to the positive gains that children can make as a result of day-care attendance. A great many different outcome measures have been employed to arrive at this conclusion, including various aspects of intellectual functioning, sociability with other children, the relationship with the mother, emotional stability, confidence, the development of language skills, and so forth. This diversity may sometimes make it difficult to compare studies that have used different measures, but at the same time the wide range of developmental functions examined gives one all the more confidence in the conclusions reached and makes agreement all the more impressive. Let us hastily add that the consensus is by no means complete: thus, some studies have produced results suggesting that day care in the first year may not be advisable, but this has not been confirmed by others; there is a measure of disagreement as to the effects on certain specific functions such as aggressiveness and concentration; and the optimistic results about fostering language development obtained by some investigators are not borne out by others. In addition, there is still uncertainty about the long-term implications of day care – largely because of the considerable methodological difficulties involved in carrying out such research. No doubt further work will in due course clarify such problems, but in the mean time, the consensus on the major question is welcome.

This means that research need no longer be obsessed with the good-or-bad issue and can move on to examine how to maximize the advantages to be gained from day-care experience. The last two abstracts presented above are an example of this approach: instead of comparing children who are in day care with children who are not, the research design involves a comparison of different kinds of care centres, aiming thereby to pin-point those aspects of care that can be designated as 'good-quality' indicators. In the past there has been a tendency to make sweeping generalizations about day care as a whole; this has turned out to be misleading – for what applies to one kind of centre may not apply to another. In so far as most of the early research was carried out on high-quality centres, the results were not always representative: what these studies showed was what *can* be done rather than what generally *is* done. Casting the nets more widely to include centres that seem less satisfactory in what they offer makes it necessary to face the question of what actually goes on during children's everyday life when away from home. Thus, research is moving away from a concern with *outcome* to a concern with *process*: the good-or-bad question is being replaced with attempts to investigate the precise circumstances under which day care exerts its influence and the kinds of children on whom it is likely to have the most beneficial impact.

Implications for practice

The issue of day care has given rise to more emotion in recent years than almost any other aspect of child rearing – partly, of course, because of the concern about possible effects on children, and partly also because implicated in this debate are questions about the nature of the family and the role of women. There are still many who remain convinced that the tradition must be upheld whereby children, for their first years at least, remain at home with their mothers and who, as Selma Fraiberg (1977) in her influential book *Every Child's Birthright: In Defence of Mothering* put it, worry about babies and small children being delivered like packages to neighbours, strangers and 'storage houses'. Yet, as we have noted, the demand for day care is considerable, especially from working women, and by no means all of it can be met by means of shared parenting or willing relatives. Group-care arrangements are a fact of life, and for some parents a necessity. Such parents in particular want reassurance that they are not putting their children at risk.

As we have seen, that reassurance can be given, though with some important qualifications. In general, it appears, one can safely assume that an arrangement other than full-time care at home is not necessarily inferior, even for children under 3 – on the contrary, given the necessary safeguards, such an arrangement might well form a most useful supplement to children's socialization, and especially so in those cases where the home cannot, for one reason or another, satisfactorily cater for all of the child's needs.

The safeguards that one needs to look for refer above all to the consistency and the quality of the substitute care arrangements. Consistency is largely an organizational matter: it involves ensuring that day-care children are not looked after indiscriminately by any one of a number of caretakers but that instead, each child is assigned to some specific individual who is more or less constantly available and feels responsible for that child. Consistency in routine, in physical environment and in the composition of the group to which a child belongs are further considerations. Quality of care is more difficult to define. It has been assessed by such indices as the availability of suitable toys and of sufficient playspace, the amount of training received by staff and the ratio of adults to children; but important though these are, it is the specific nature of the adults' interaction with the children that matters most. The amount of verbal interaction, particularly in one-to-one conversations, has emerged as one essential ingredient of high-quality care; another must surely be the extent to which regimentation of children is avoided and each child's individuality catered for. Regimentation is probably the greatest danger in any form of group care; it is unfortunately so much easier to relate to the group as a whole than to its individual members, each with his or her own peculiarities and requirements. The ability of staff to do justice to specific children, and the organization of the centre to enable this to happen, ought to be recognized as one of the most important criteria to be used in the assessment of day-care services.

The message from research that day care has considerable potential in fostering the development of children has unfortunately still not reached many policy makers, administrators and members of the general public, including parents. In part this reflects the continuing prejudice that mothers ought not to share the care of their children, that mothering should be a full-time task. In part, however, this is also because the quality of day care can sometimes be appallingly bad, and those who have had unfortunate experiences in this respect are unlikely to view favourably the idea of day care in general. Yet wholesale condemnation from such limited examples is unjustified; instead, such instances show that an enormous effort is still required to raise standards by means of greater resources, improved staff training and constant review of organizational structures.

Most attention has, of course, been given to the effects that day care has on the child. Let us also bear in mind, however, the implications for the family as a whole. Does the fact that the child's upbringing is shared with other, professionally trained individuals in any way diminish the parents' feelings of adequacy or responsibility? There are no indications that this is so but the evidence is almost wholly anecdotal. Does the fact that the child may be exposed to a different set of expectations, values and disciplinary techniques when away from home cause difficulties for parents or, for that matter, bring confusion to the child? Again we do not know, for the fact that a shared care arrangement means the child spending its days in two separate worlds has not as yet been properly acknowledged. It is, however, significant that the most successful compensatory schemes for young children have been those which did not merely remove the child from home for part of the day in order to provide something enriching in another environment, but instead also directed considerable effort at the parents in an attempt to have them understand and, if at all possible, themselves adopt the aims of the day-care personnel. There is, of course, great danger in imposing a new set of values on any family, however unsatisfactorily that family may seem to be functioning and however good the intention of the professionals, and this is a situation that clearly needs to be handled with care and sensitivity. In general, however, the way in which home and nursery become interlinked is only now becoming recognized as of crucial importance (as seen, for example, in the launching of various parent-involvement schemes), and no doubt this is an area to which a great deal more attention will need to be given.

Thus, day care, having previously been viewed almost entirely in a negative light, and indeed seen by some as no more than an evil necessity, should now be recognized as holding out opportunities for positive advancement – not only for children but for the family as a whole. Far from disrupting the family by taking over some of its child-rearing functions, day-care services ought to be seen as providing experiences that complement those obtained at home, with corresponding advantages for children's development. And far from supplanting parents, they are in a position to support them, thus adopting a role which, in view of the woefully inadequate standard of parental competence often found, is now badly in need of further definition and refinement.

Further reading

Belsky, J. 1988: Infant day care and socio-emotional development: the United States. *Journal of Child Psychology and Psychiatry*, 29, 397–406.

Belsky, J. 1984: Two waves of day care research: developmental effects and conditions of quality. In R. Ainslie (ed.), *The Child and the Daycare Setting*. New York: Praeger.

Clarke-Stewart, A. 1982: *Daycare*. London: Fontana; Cambridge, Mass.: Harvard University Press.

Clarke-Stewart, A. 1989: Infant day care: maligned or malignant? *American Psychologist*, 44, 266–73.

Rutter, M. 1981: Social-emotional consequences of day care for preschool children. *American Journal of Orthopsychiatry*, 51, 4–28.

Issue: Are children harmed by their parents' divorce?

Background

Divorce has become a major social phenomenon in many countries, and there are indications that the sharp increase witnessed over the last few decades may continue for some time yet. For those personally involved it usually signals a major life change, with all sorts of social, psychological and economic implications. Of particular concern is the fact that children are so frequently involved: it has, for example, been estimated that 40 per cent of all children born in the 1980s in the United States will experience their parents' divorce, and included among these are many of pre-school age. To a child, parental divorce not only means witnessing the disintegration of the relationship between mother and father; in many cases it also means a break in the child's own relationship with one of the parents, usually the father – fathers do not merely move out of the family home but, in a disturbingly large proportion of cases, lose touch altogether with their children.

Given the emotional turmoil that usually accompanies divorce, it is hardly surprising that so much concern has been expressed about the effects on children's psychological health. Thus, there have been suggestions that parental divorce is one of the best predictors for psychiatric referral of children. Equally, it has been stated that experiencing the dissolution of the family is likely to leave the child with permanent scars that will affect all of its future relationships, as an adult as well as during childhood. No wonder questions are urgently being asked as to how this situation should be handled so as to minimize the emotional trauma for children, and parents caught up in a conflict-ridden marriage indeed often wonder whether they ought not to stay together for the sake of the children rather than follow their personal inclination and separate.

Research on this topic has ben somewhat slow to get off the ground, and much of the earlier work tended to be of poor quality: impressionistic in nature, lacking proper controls and based on such biased samples as clinic referrals. Conclusions from these studies were sometimes alarmist and often quite unjustified; for instance, statements would be made about the occurrence of behaviour problems without first ascertaining the incidence of these problems in the population as a whole. However, in recent years a number of much more sophisticated research projects have yielded results of greater credibility and provided a picture of reasonable coherence, and as a result we now know rather more about both the short-term and the long-term impact of this experience on children's development, as well as being able to identify some of the factors that determine the considerable variability in response to parental divorce.

The number of questions and practical problems that divorce raises with respect to the children caught up therein is considerable, involving issues such as the preparation of children for their parents' separation, the choice of the custodial parent, the amount and nature of access by the non-custodial parent, the transition from two-parent to single-parent family life, the formation of a step-parent family, and so on. Here our concern will primarily be with the overall impact of parental divorce on children's emotional adjustment and the extent to which that impact varies according to age, sex, the passage of time, family relations and other possible influences which studies such as those summarized below have examined.

Research findings

(1) SUMMARIES

Wallerstein, J. S., Corbin, S. B. and Lewis, J. M. 1988: Children of divorce: a 10-year study. In E. M. Hetherington and J. D. Arasteh (eds), Impact of Divorce, Single Parenting, and Stepparenting on Children. Hillsdale, New Jersey: Erlbaum.

Wallerstein and her colleagues were among the first to recognize that divorce is 'not a single circumscribed event but a multistage process of radically changing family relationships', and that research into its effects must therefore take a longitudinal form. The present paper provides a summary of the various more specific reports that have been published by this group, giving the results of their investigation.

Some 131 children from 60 families, together with their parents, were studied intensively near the time of the marital separation, and then followed up 18 months, 5 years and 10 years later. The families were mostly middle-class, well-educated and white; the couples had been married for an average period of 11 years; and the children ranged in age from pre-school to adolescence at the time of the divorce. At each follow-up point, intensive interviews were held with each family member, and young children were seen for extended play sessions. Information was also obtained about each child from schools.

The nature of children's response to their parents' separation depended primarily on the child's age. Among the pre-school children there was profound upset, a high incidence of regression and acute separation anxiety. At the 18-months follow-up, a marked sex difference was apparent: many of the boys were still troubled whereas most girls appeared recovered. At the 5-year mark these sex differences were no longer significant; instead, there was a strong connection between the children's psychological adjustment and the overall quality of life within the post-divorce or remarried family. Ten years after divorce this group of children had few conscious memories of the original family or of the marital rupture, though half continued to have reconciliation fantasies. Most were performing adequately at school, and this group generally appeared to be considerably less burdened in later years than children older at the time of the divorce.

Initial reactions among older children were also marked. They included feelings of powerlessness in the face of the marital rupture, intense anger at one or both parents, acute depression, social withdrawal and a severe drop in school work. These symptoms applied equally to both sexes; 18 months later, however, many of the girls seemed to be well on the way to recovery while a large proportion of boys still appeared troubled. As with the pre-school children, psychological adjustment at the 5-year follow-up depended primarily on the overall quality of life within the post-divorce or remarried family. However, even at the 10-year mark clinical assessment still detected various after-effects, in that some of the young people were burdened with vivid memories of the stressful events surrounding the divorce and showed apprehension about repeating their parents' unhappy marriage during their own adulthood.

In general, therefore, initial reactions at all ages tended to be severe in many cases, and though these abated within the next 2 years or so, long-term sequelae were by no means uncommon. The authors believe, however, that these were not so much due to the divorce as such as to the disrupted parenting and diminished quality of life that so often follow marital rupture.

Hetherington, E. M., Cox, M. and Cox, R. 1979: Play and social interaction in children following divorce. Journal of Social Issues. 35, 26–49.

This paper is among a number of reports derived from one of the best-known and most soundly designed investigations in this area. In the course of a longitudinal study these research workers too found distress and parent–child disturbance to be most marked in the year following divorce but to improve dramatically in the second year. In this paper, however, atttention is given to behaviour outside the family, with particular reference to play and relationships with other children in the school setting.

The group studied consisted of 48 boys and girls from middle-class families in which the mother had custody following a divorce. The children were studied 2 months, 1 year and 2 years after the divorce and compared with a control group of children from non-divorced families. Their average age at the beginning of the project was just under 4 years. Various methods were used to obtain the data, including observational measures of free play and social interaction at nursery school, teacher ratings of behaviour and a number of measures obtained from other children in the school situation.

The pattern of results parallels the findings for behaviour in the family. Play tended to be less mature, intellectually and socially, in the children from divorced families during the first year following the divorce. For boys, but not for girls, some of these immature play patterns continued into the second year. The divorce-group children were also initially found to be more anxious, guilty and apathetic than the control-group children; and again, these differences had disappeared for girls but were still present among boys, though in much less marked form. The same applied to social behaviour: in their interactions with other children, the divorce-group sample showed various immature, ineffective and negative reactions, including dependency, attention seeking and aggressiveness. These effects rapidly disappeared for girls, so that 2 years after the divorce there was no difference in this respect between them and their controls. In boys the effects decreased, but some differences were still present 2 years later, when these children were found to be unpopular with other boys, to have difficulty in gaining access to play groups and to spend more time playing with girls and younger children.

Thus, the impact of divorce extended beyond the family to the children's school behaviour. Although this was initially very marked, an adjustment process gradually set in, which appeared to be easier for girls than for boys.

Hetherington, E. M., Cox, M. and Cox, R. 1985: Long-term effects of divorce and remarriage on the adjustment of children. Journal of the American Academy of Child Psychiatry, 24, 518–30.

The children reported on in the previous paper were seen again 6 years after the divorce (though the sample size described here had been enlarged to 124 families, including non-divorced controls). Again, a large number of measures were obtained, including home observations, rating scales completed by teachers, parents and the children themselves, and peer assessments. On average, the children were just over 10 years old by this time.

The sex difference noted previously in the children's adjustment still held 6 years later. In those families where the mother had not remarried, the girls were very similar in their general adjustment to girls from non-divorced families. Boys, on the other hand, tended to be somewhat more aggressive and rather less socially competent than their controls. However, the picture that emerges for those children whose custodial parent had married again is rather different. Where the marriage was less than 2 years old, both boys and girls were found to have more behavioural problems than children in non-divorced families. Where the remarriage had occurred more than 2 years ago, the boys showed no difference when compared with their controls; girls, on the other hand, were less well adjusted.

It therefore appears that long-term effects depend both on the child's sex and the mother's remarriage: in single-parent families boys continued to show more adverse reactions than girls; however, when the mother marries again and a stepfather joins the family, an increase in behaviour problems is found in girls but there is a decrease in boys. Yet it seems that even these girls gradually adjust to their new family set-up, for those whose mothers had remarried more than 2 years ago were on the whole said to be in better psychological condition than those in families in the early stages of remarriage.

However, as further reports by Hetherington (1987, 1988) make clear, long-term effects on children depend on various other factors too: the mother's own adjustment, the marital relationship in a new stepfamily, the stepfather's attitude to and treatment of the child, the support available from sources outside the family, and so forth. In addition, as far as the effects themselves are concerned, the impact of divorce (and of remarriage) is a widely pervasive one which affects, for example, the child's relationships with siblings, in that these tend to mirror the extent to which a sound parent–child relationship has been maintained. Largely, however, they are more often problematic in divorced than in non-divorced families.

Guidubaldi, J., Cleminshaw, H. K., Perry, J. D., Nastasi, B. K. and Lightel, J. 1986: The role of selected family environment factors in children's post-divorce adjustment. Family Relations, 35, 141–51.

A rather different approach to obtaining information is taken by this investigation. Instead of examining intensively a relatively small number of families, a large national sample was collected and studied at two points in time. The families were contacted through school psychologists in 38 states of the USA, each psychologist randomly selecting two children from grade 1, grade 3 and grade 5. Sufficient data were available on 699 children, of whom 341 came from divorced families. Two years later 123 children were seen again, including 46 from the divorced group. Data were obtained from ratings by the psychologists and by the children's teachers, from interviews with parents and the children themselves and also from various standardized tests.

In general, the children from divorced families did not come out as well as other children on most measures of social and academic adjustment – a trend found more consistently for boys than for girls. The authors emphasize, however, that not all children in divorced families suffer poor adjustment, and a major focus of their enquiry is therefore the idenification of those factors in the home that contribute to healthy development. Amongst the factors they single out is the quality of the child's relationships – not only with the custodial but also with the non-custodial parent, this being closely related to children's adjustment on both occasions when assessment took place. For boys in particular a good relationship with the father (usually the non-custodial parent) seemed important for school performance. Also important, and again especially so for boys, was a reduction of parental conflict in the period following the divorce. Another factor related to children's adjustment was the particular style of child rearing adopted by the custodial parent: where this assumed an authoritarian form, the children (and once more, curiously, the boys in particular) did not do as well as under more relaxed regimes. In addition, the parent's ability to maintain regular routines for television viewing, bedtime, and so forth had a bearing on the children's psychological welfare.

The report illustrates well the usefulness of not only comparing divorced with non-divorced families but also examining the variations that commonly occur within the divorced group. If one can thereby pin-point the factors that make for good adjustment in children in the period following divorce, one is clearly in a position to provide help and advice to families aimed at fostering these factors.

Kulka, R. A. and Weingarten, H. 1979: The long term effects of parental divorce in childhood on adult adjustment. Journal of Social Issues, 35, 50–78.

Most attention has been paid to effects in childhood, but this study examines the psychological functioning and general adjustment of *adults* who had experienced their parents' divorce at some point during childhood. Data from two cross-sectional surveys, conducted in the United States in 1957 and in 1976, were used for this purpose, each including well over 2,000 adults. The information was obtained in the course of 90-minute structured interviews, when questions were asked about the intactness of the subjects' family of origin and various measures were taken of psychological adjustment and of perceptions and evaluations of marital and parental roles.

The findings indicate that for all measures of psychological adjustment examined in both survey years, the long-term effects of coming from a home broken by divorce appear to be limited or at least potentially modifiable. Various symptoms, such as a high level of anxiety and poor physical health, were reported more frequently by those from a divorced background, but in both survey years this difference occurred only among the younger adults, suggesting that these effects tend to diminish over time. There were no apparent differences between those from divorced and those from non-divorced backgrounds in their evaluation of marital happiness, even though the divorce-group individuals were somewhat more likely to report having themselves experienced marital problems. Although there was a tendency for the adults from this group to have gone though divorce or separation from their marital partner to a greater extent, comparison with the adults from non-disrupted backgrounds showed the difference to be statistically significant ony for the earlier survey and then only for women. In addition, while men from divorced families appear to value marriage at least as much as other men, women from such backgrounds were somewhat less oriented towards putting all their eggs into the marital basket: they were more likely to put greater stress on their role as mother or as worker than as wife. As regards parenting, no differences between those from parentally divorced and those from intact families were found in general satisfaction with parenthood, in their perceived adequacy as parents or in the incidence of problems reported in raising their children.

Given the admittedly exclusive reliance of this study on self-report, the authors nevertheless feel that there is compelling evidence to suggest that the childhood experiences examined have, at most, a modest effect on adult adjustment. What differences there are according to family background are never very large statistically, and those that do exist appear to have weakened over the two decades separating the surveys.

Block, J. H., Block, J. and Gjerde, P. F. 1986: The personality of children prior to divorce: a prospective study. Child Development, 57, 827–40.

The studies we have described so far were all concerned with documenting the extent and kind of effects of parental divorce. This report aims instead to shed some light on the processes responsible for these effects. The present study is an unusual one in that children were investigated some considerable time *before* the divorce took place as well as subsequently; this makes it particularly valuable in sorting out the contribution of various factors to the eventual outcome.

The subjects were 128 children who participated in a longitudinal investigation beginning at age 3 and continuing through to adolescence. At 14 years 101 children were still available for study, and of these 41 had experienced parental divorce or separation at various earlier ages. They were compared with the remaining 60 children on various measures, in particular on a personality scale completed by teachers and consisting of 100 items referring to a wide range of social and intellectual characteristics.

The most striking finding refers to the fact that the divorce-group children differed in many respects from the others well before their parents actually separated – sometimes many years before. Thus, at the age of 3, boys who eventually experienced divorce were already found to be restless, stubborn and emotionally labile. When assessed at 7, they were described as aggressive, impulsive and uncooperative, going to pieces under stress more easily than their controls, and this pattern was also found in adolescence. What was remarkable was that such behaviour could be evident so many years prior to the dissolution of the parents' marriage. For girls the differences between the two groups were not as clear-cut. They were not at all apparent at age 3; at age 4 girls in families that eventually went through divorce were described in more negative terms (for example, not eager to please, not able to get along with other children and to be emotionally labile). These differences also appeared at subsequent ages but were accompanied by many positive features which they shared with children whose parents did not subsequently divorce.

One must conclude that the so-called effects of parental divorce can already be found a long time before the separation actually takes place. The operative factor is therefore not so much the break in the relationship brought about by the dissolution of the marriage; it is rather the atmosphere of conflict that existed when the parents were still together. This is supported by a further analysis by Block et al. (1988) of their data, in which they show that as much as 11 years before the event, parents who eventually divorce disagree more among themselves about child-rearing methods than other parents. They are also significantly less supportive of and oriented towards their children and display various signs of tension both in the marital and the parent–child relationship. In addition, the fact that the mothers in the eventually divorcing families often described themselves in terms indicating low self-esteem (presumably as a result of their marital problems) no doubt imposed yet another source of strain on the children, who thus were brought up in a very different atmosphere than children whose families remained intact.

(2)   COMMENTS ON RESEARCH

A number of points have become clear from the work carried out in this area, and it may be as well to list those where there is general agreement:

1   Divorce should not be thought of as a single event happening at one particular point in time. As far as the families involved are concerned, the moment of legal separation is just part of a long

drawn-out process that begins with disagreements and arguments at home and extends many years beyond the actual breakup of the marriage and the departure of one of the spouses. A longitudinal perspective is thus essential if one is to understand the impact on children. To study this by merely lumping together all children from divorced families irrespective of the stage of family dissolution is meaningless – hence, the sometimes misleading results of earlier studies. As Hetherington and others have shown, the effects found depend entirely on when in the course of the total sequence the family is studied.

2 Once such a longitudinal perspective is adopted, it becomes apparent that the nature and severity of effects vary from one stage to another. They are most evident early on, in particular during the first year following the separation, but with time a gradual readjustment takes place and whatever behaviour problems originally existed tend to abate. The notion that parental divorce is an experience that will continue to reverberate throughout childhood needs to be treated with scepticism: once again we can point to the recuperative powers of children, given favourable circumstances. There is, however, still considerable uncertainty as far as very long-term effects are concerned: the relatively optimistic conclusions by Kulka and Weingarten, quoted above, regarding the adjustment of adults who had experienced parental divorce in childhood are not borne out by the results of some other studies (for example, Glenn and Kramer, 1985). It seems at least conceivable that the effects of this experience can surface again in adulthood, and until further research clarifies this question one has to keep an open mind as to this possibility.

3 A whole configuration of factors influences the process of adjustment: the child's age, child's sex, the nature of previous relationships with each of the parents, the arrangements made for custody and access, the quality of life in the single-parent family, the parents' remarriage, and so on. No wonder there is such great variability in outcome within any one sample!

4 One factor that is worth singling out for special mention is the child's sex. In keeping with many other findings on children's reactions to stress, boys have been found to be more vulnerable to the divorce experience than girls. The effect on them at the time is greater and their eventual readjustment is generally slower than is the case with girls. Only in response to the mother's

remarriage is this effect apparently reversed: girls are more likely to be adversely affected by this event whereas on boys it may produce beneficial effects.

5 Probably the most important finding to come out of this research refers to the all-powerful effect of the quality of family relationships, both before the divorce and after it. It is by no means easy to sort out the influence which the various constituents of the whole divorce experience have on children: the atmosphere of conflict, the separation from one of the parents, the changes in life-style once the parents have parted, the impact on the custodial parent and consequently her altered capacity to provide care, and so on. Yet several of the studies summarized above point unequivocally to the presence of conflict in the home as the most powerful influence on children's adjustment – a point borne out by other research which has shown, for instance, that later psychological health is much more closely related to the presence of conflict in the home than to parental divorce. Not that the other factors are unimportant, but the study by Block et al. in particular makes it very clear that many of the effects ascribed to divorce are already apparent in children long before the parents' separation. Research on divorce, that is, points to the same conclusions as the research considered in previous sections dealing with children's separation from their families: any such event must be seen in the wider context of children's experience of family life, and the nature of that family life can attenuate or exacerbate the consequences of that event, be it hospitalization, admission to care or parental divorce.

Implications for practice

The fact that parental conflict has a more pervasive and destructive influence on children than the separation itself needs to be taken particularly seriously. Parents sometimes ask whether they should stay together for the sake of the children – a question to which one cannot possibly give a dogmatic answer, for so much depends on the unique circumstances of each individual case. Nevertheless, it does appear that separation may sometimes be the better alternative if staying together means raising the child in an atmosphere of continuing conflict and tension. That separation is hurtful, sometimes deeply so, to children at all ages cannot, of course, be denied, yet from a long-term point of view this course may well be the lesser of two evils. One research finding that is pertinent in this connection is that children in conflict-free single-parent families show fewer behaviour problems than children in intact but unhappy families, and though in view of the great variability that exists from one family situation to the next one must beware of making sweeping generalizations, it follows that divorce must sometimes be seen as a positive solution – one that brings gains for children as well as losses. Any psychological disturbance found in children of divorced parents may well have resulted from the period when the family was still together rather than from the legal dissolution of the marriage and the consequent loss of close contact with one of the parents.

Nevertheless, in the short run at any rate, divorce does constitute a high-risk situation for children which can give rise to considerable upset and bewilderment. Above all, parents need to be made aware of the strong association between conflict and children's behaviour problems; efforts to minimize any direct involvement of children in conflict are especially important. It is not always easy for parents, caught up in their own turmoil, to bear in mind that children badly need psychological support in such a situation, and even if they are aware of it they may find it difficult under the circumstances to provide such support. Relatives and friends may then be needed to fill this role until the parents have, as it were, psychological space available once more to devote to the child. Certainly the most stressed children, it has been demonstrated, are those who themselves become objects in their parents' acrimonious personal and legal battles, centring on issues of access and custody. Under such conditions, mediation by professional workers with mental health qualifications ought to be implemented as a matter of urgency, with the principal aim of shortening the experience of conflict for children as much as is possible.

The situation most conducive to children's welfare is one where there is only minimal overt conflict between the parents and maximal agreement as to methods of child rearing, and where both parents continue to remain easily accessible and properly involved. That some fathers disappear altogether after divorce may well be less a reflection of parental irresponsibility and more a reaction to an intolerably painful and frustrating situation for these men. Becoming a subsidiary parent, with access available for only limited periods and often under artificial conditions, is not conducive to maintaining a relaxed relationship with the child. Yet, for boys especially, frequent contact with the father has been found to be associated with positive adjustment. Equally, the longing for the absent parent is a poignant theme in a great many accounts provided by children from divorced families. Maintaining contact with *both* parents ought therefore to be a matter of priority for all those responsible for arranging these children's lives. The more continuity is preserved, the less difficult the transition will be – a consideration that ought also to apply to other circumstances which often follow a divorce such as moving house, changing school and living in financially reduced circumstances. As far as practically possible, breaks in continuity ought to be kept at a minimum, or at least staggered over time. Children may be adaptable, but there is a limit to the number of adaptations that a young child can make all at one.

Further reading

Emery, R. E. 1982: Interparental conflict and the children of discord and divorce. *Psychological Bulletin*, 92, 310–30.

Emery, R. E., Hetherington, E. M. and Dilalla, L. F. 1984: Divorce, children and social policy. In H. W. Stevenson and A. E. Siegel (eds), *Child Development Research and Social Policy*. Chicago: University of Chicago Press.

Hetherington, E. M., Stanley-Hagan, M. and Anderson E. R. 1989: Marital transitions: a child's perspective. *American Psychologist*, 44, 303–12.

Kitson, G. C. and Raschke, H. J. 1981: Divorce research: what we know, what we need to know. *Journal of Divorce*, 4, 1–37.

Issue: Can children form love relationships to new parent-figures?

Background

At birth children become members of a particular family group, and it is within that group that they form their first love relationships. Subsequently, however, a substantial number go through the trauma of family disintegration – because of divorce or death or removal from home as a result of parental abuse or neglect. In such cases children must first of all cope with all the emotional implications of severing established relationships. In addition, however, many subsequently have to face a further challenge, namely the need to become a member of a new family and to form relationships to new individuals: step-parents, foster parents, adoptive parents or parent substitutes in residential homes. Are children capable of forming 'proper' relationships with such individuals? Can these later relationships provide the same love and security as primary ones, or are they no more than a poor substitute? For that matter, are children who are reared by new parents thereby put at a disadvantage so that their later psychological functioning is in some way inferior to that of other children?

Such doubts may arise because of the common belief in the all-encompassing role of the child's initial bond with the mother or other primary attachment figure. If (as has often been suggested) this sets the tone for all later relationships, then substitute parents would indeed have a difficult task on their hands; expecting children to treat them as 'real' parents might well be asking for the impossible. Yet a large number of chilren are expected to make this adjustment: divorce, for example, is followed in a high proportion of cases by remarriage, whereupon the child finds itself as a member of a reconstituted family with a new mother or father. Some divorced parents with custody of their children may indeed hesitate in marrying again for fear of the difficulties that such adjustments might entail for the child – a fear no doubt fuelled by the popular stereotype (expressed in many a fairy tale) of the wicked step-parent: an individual with no emotional commitment to the child whom he or she might well see as a rival for the affection of the new spouse. No wonder that early research on this topic was based on the assumption that any new parent–child relationship is bound to be fraught with severe difficulties and will inevitably give rise to lasting problems, and no wonder that investigators then reported finding nothing but negative consequences that bore out their expectations.

More recent research has rid itself of such blinkers and adopted a more balanced stance. Unfortunately, the total amount of research available on this topic is still limited. There are a lot of questions to which, ideally, one would like conclusive answers – questions concerned with such matters as the precise manner in which children of various ages come to adjust to a new parent-figure, the factors that promote or impede adjustment, the desirability of maintaining contact with original parents (for example, a divorced non-custodial parent, or the biological parents of a child placed in foster care), the way in which 'new' families function, the long-term consequences for children of various kinds of family rearrangments, and so forth. However, research in this area has only recently got under way and is still only able to provide some tentative indications with respect to most of these questions. Yet the issue is so important that it is worth drawing attention to the information that does exist. As most of the better work on substitute relationships has been done on step-parents, it is studies on this topic with which we shall primarily be concerned.

Research findings

(1) SUMMARIES

Ferri, E. 1984: Step Children: a national study. *Windsor: NFER-Nelson.*

This report is based on a large-scale survey, taking the form of a follow-up by the National Children's Bureau of the 17,000 or so children born in Britain during 1 week in 1958. Amongst this cohort, investigated periodically throughout childhood, 5.1 per cent were found to be members of a step-family at the age of 16, the original family having broken up as a result of either divorce or parental death. More than three times as many children were living-with stepfathers as with stepmothers.

The data collected cover a great many aspects of the children's lives. They show, amongst other things, that on the material side children with stepfathers were somewhat worse off than either chil-ren with stepmothers or those with both natural parents – a finding possibly due to the fact that stepfather families contained rather more children. Even so, the longitudinal analysis demonstrated that for many children who had previously been cared for by a lone mother, the acquisition of a stepfather had meant a definite im-provement in their material circumstances. When the 16-year olds were asked to rate how well they got on with each of their parents (natural and step), the majority in step-families gave positive ratings, but unsatisfactory relationships were reported rather more frequent-ly with step-parents than with parents in unbroken homes. This applied in particular to the relationship between girls and step-mothers; to a lesser extent it was also seen in boys' relationship to the stepmother. Both boys and girls reported that on the whole they got on well with stepfathers, though here too there was a minority with less satisfactory relationships that was somewhat greater than that found in unbroken families. It was notable that in both types of step-families poor relationships were found to be much more com-mon when the original family had been broken by divorce than by a parent's death. Social class also exerted some influence: the differ-ence between unbroken and step-families tended to be more pro-nounced among the manual social-class group. There was no indica-tion, however, that children in step-families had a negative view of their relationship with the natural parent with whom they were living: on the contrary, especially those who had stayed with their father had a particularly close relationship with him.

In general, as far as most of the stepchildren were concerned there was little to distinguish them from other children. Teachers reported them to get on just as well with peers, and tests of educational attainment also indicated no difference at age 16. On the other hand, more parents in both types of step-families saw their sons and daughters as exhibiting behaviour problems than did parents in unbroken homes. It may well be, however, that this reflects the attitudes and perceptions of the parents themselves, for it is perti-nent in this respect that such differences did not emerge from teachers' reports, leading the author to speculate that parents in step-families tend to be more anxious, even hypersensitive, about their children's development and hence more likely to report problems. Again, this tended to occur more in cases of divorce than bereavement. Thus, a number of differences between step- and other children emerged across all areas examined. These differences were, however, rarely dramatic in magnitude and any indication of real developmental difficulties concerned only a small minority of children – though a minority to whom special attention needs to be given.

Furstenberg, F. F. 1987: The new extended family: the experience of parents and children after remarriage. In K. Pasley and M. Ihinger-Tallman (eds), Remarriage and Stepparenting. New York: Guildford.

Here too the information was obtained by means of a large-scale enquiry, namely the National Survey of Children which was first carried out in the United States in 1976 and involved a representative sample of 2,279 children between the ages of 7 and 11. Five years later all children from divorced families were seen again, together with a random subsample of children from non-divorced families. Data were collected by interviewing the children and their parents and from mailed questionnaries filled in by teachers.

When the children who were living in step-families at the second contact were asked to rate various aspects of their family life (indicating such qualities as closeness, tension, sharing, and so on), the majority provided a positive portrait. Admittedly, their descriptions were not quite as favourable as those found among children from nuclear families, but the difference turned out to be largely due to stepmother families. In those families, rather more negative ratings were given, whereas children in households with stepfathers gave an almost identical picture to that provided by children living with two biological parents. This is confirmed by the parents' ratings: those in first-married families gave a more positive description but the difference was small and statistically insignificant, and the great majority of step-parents portrayed the quality of their family life in relatively rosy terms. In addition, when asked for information about family routines and practices (such as the amount of joint activities by parents and children concerned with games, sport, shopping, going to the movies, and so on), it emerged that the daily character of step-family life was no different from that seen in other households.

In interviews, most parents acknowledged that there had been some difficulty in assuming the step-parent role. This applied in particular to giving love and affection and to disciplining. The children's reports mirrored this picture, in that they indicated less intimacy with step-parents than with biological parents. Nevertheless, the majority of both parents and children in step-families do have fairly or very positive relations, with most children expressing benign, if not lavishly positive sentiments. It was clear, however, that relations between children and stepmothers tended to be more stressful than relations between children and stepfathers. It was also found that children were just as attached to the stepfather when they continued to see the biological father on a regular basis. On the other hand, they appeared to have more difficulty in simultaneously handling relationships with two mothers.

The author concludes that a mixed picture emerges from his investigation: children frequently do experience problems in forming relationships with step-parents, but given sufficient time most do establish relatively close ties, especially to their stepfathers. A sizeable minority, however, report troubled relations with step-parents in adolescence.

Santrock, J. W., Sitterle, K. A. and Warshak, R. A. 1988: Parent–child relationships in stepfather families. In P. Bronstein and C. P. Cowan (eds), Contemporary Fathers. *New York: Wiley.*

The interest of these investigators focused primarily on an analysis of a much more limited number of step-parent families and a much closer look at the way in which they function, with particular reference to their interpersonal relationships. In order to provide a comprehensive picture, data were obtained from every member of each family and by means of a variety of assessment techniques.

Sixty-nine families took part in this study: 26 stepfather families (with which the present report is primarily concerned), 18 stepmother families and 25 control (never-divorced) families. All were white and middle class, living in Texas, with children between 7 and 11 years old. The step-families had lived together for at least 1 year and on average for 3 years. All biological parents as well as the step-parents were interviewed and asked to fill in a battery of questionnaires, and children were also interviewed and given various paper-and-pencil tests. In addition, observational material was obtained about the children's interactions with each parent and step-parent and also with other children.

Among the considerable amount of data gathered, the following findings are of particular interest. The majority of stepfathers reported themselves to be involved in the care and supervision of their stepchildren, and most stepchildren expressed positive feelings about their stepfathers. Little could be found to differentiate the overall descriptions of family life offered by members of stepfamilies and members of never-divorced families. However, many of the stepfathers acknowledged one or more areas of difficulty in assuming the parental role, with discipline especially presenting problems. The importance of assuming that role slowly and gradually, and the danger of expecting too much to begin with, emerged frequently from these reports. Overall, there was no difference between never-divorced families and remarried families in the quality of relationships between children and their biological parents with whom they were living. On the other hand, there were disparities in how children felt about their natural fathers and their stepfathers, with the latter being seen as less involved than fathers in intact families.

Nevertheless, the majority of children from step-families appeared to be functioning well. On a variety of measures of competence in physical, social and cognitive skills, children in stepfater families fared about as well as did children living with both biological parents. Teachers also perceived children with stepfathers as being just as good academically and as well-accepted by peers as children from never-divorced families. This was confirmed by direct observations of the children's behaviour in playgroups. There was also no difference in the incidence of behaviour problems; on the other hand there were some indications that stepchildren had a rather more negative view of themselves than other children (though whether this was related to their status as a stepchild or to their previous experience in a divorcing family cannot be ascertained).

One further finding from this study is worth stressing. The children's mothers reported that their remarriage had had a positive and stabilizing effect on their relationships with their children. This presumably reflects the change from single parenthood, when as the custodial parent these women had to deal with task overload, personal disorganization and problematic relationships with their children. The stepfathers thus had an indirect effect on the children's adjustment, which improved as the mother's own mental status improved.

Santrock, J. W. and Sitterle, K. A. 1987: Parent–child relationships in stepmother families. In K. Pasley and M. Ihinger–Tallman (eds), Remarriage and Stepparenting. *New York: Guilford.*

This report is derived from the same investigation as the one summarized above, but instead of dealing with stepfathers it is mainly concerned with stepmothers – a much rarer phenomenon as custody of children is only infrequently awarded to fathers in divorce cases. Eighteen such families were investigated by Santrock and his colleagues; the methods used are as described above.

There were many signs of the stepmothers' efforts to establish a good relationship with their stepchildren, but the children tended to take a somewhat negative view of their new parent, seeing her as rather detached and unsupportive. Not surprisingly, the stepmothers themselves therefore described the relationship in similar terms: compared with mothers from intact families they felt themselves to be less close to and less involved with their stepchildren. On the whole, these women were rather more confident in their parental role with stepdaughters than with stepsons, taking a somewhat more active role in the moral training of the girls than of the boys. The main source of security for the children was without doubt the father, who was seen as much more nurturant and close than the stepmother – a finding paralleled by the observation in stepfather families regarding the child's closeness to the mother. It seems that the constant relationship with the biological custodial parent (whether mother or father) is the key ingredient in helping the child through the disrupting experiences of divorce and remarriage.

Various other factors were found to influence the process of adjustment. Thus, children fared better in a stepmother family when only their own father brought children from the previous marriage; if the child also had to cope with new stepsibling relationships the task was a much more difficult one. Similarly, adjustment often received a set-back when a new child was produced by the remarried father and the stepmother: the usual occurrence of jealousy was then exaggerated by the insecurity left by the child's previous experiences of stress and disequilibrium, with adverse effects on the developing relationship between stepmother and stepchild. In general, the total number of children living in the household, irrespective of their origin, played a part: the greater that number, the more likely were reports of an increase in conflict following remarriage.

Hetherington, E. M., Cox, M. and Cox, R. 1982: *Effects of divorce on parents and children. In M. E. Lamb (ed.),* Nontraditional Families. *Hillsdale, New Jersey: Erlbaum.*

Hetherington, E. M. 1988: *Parents, children and siblings: six years after divorce. In R. A. Hinde and J. Stevenson–Hinde (eds),* Relationships Within Families: mutual influences. *Oxford: Clarendon Press.*

We shall deal with these two reports together, for they refer to the same body of findings. The study has already been mentioned in our discussion of divorce, and in so far as it took a longitudinal form the investigators were able not only to plot the consequences of the divorce itself but also to observe the effects on children and adults of remarriage. Six years after the divorce, 70 per cent of the women and 80 per cent of the men had remarried, and in these two papers a general summary is given of the findings regarding the impact of this new transition on parents and children.

As in the study by Santrock, the beneficial effects of remarriage are frequently referred to by the parents – effects from which not only they profit but also, indirectly, their children. Loneliness, anxiety, economic concerns and household disorganization all diminished and higher ratings of happiness were reported. Much depended, of course, on the kind of relationship established with the new spouse: remarried mothers of sons in particular benefited from a warm, supportive relationship with the stepfather. It was also found, however, that continued involvement with the child by the divorced, non-custodial father, even after 6 years, led to positive outcomes for the children.

Interviews and observations showed that the relationship between stepfather and stepchild differed in certain respects from that of biological fathers and children. Many of the stepfathers tended to adopt one of two extremes: either they were highly involved with their stepchildren (though often in a rather restrictive manner) or, more commonly, they tended to be emotionally 'disengaged', being somewhat distant and inattentive and giving the mother little support in child rearing. This might well have been in response to the child's attitude, for in the early stages of remarriage many children saw the stepfather as an intruder and rival. Girls in particular were often reported as adopting a sulky, hostile manner, rejecting the stepfather no matter how hard he tried.

Over time this situation improved somewhat in the case of boys; some of the young boys especially formed intense attachments and warm, companionate relationships with the stepfather. In cases where remarriage did not occur till the child was 9 or 10 years of age, acceptance and a positive relationship were on the whole more difficult to achieve. Otherwise, in longer remarried families boys were sometimes very close to the stepfather, enjoying his company and seeking his advice and support. In the case of girls, however, the relationship often deteriorated: on the one hand, stepdaughters viewed the stepfather as hostile, punitive and unreasonable; on the other, the fathers became increasingly impatient with the girls' difficult behaviour and saw them in a more negative light than was evident in the descriptions given by biological fathers of their daughters.

In this study, too, adjustment was found to be affected by the composition of the stepfamily, in that significantly more problems were reported when the stepfather had also brought children from a previous marriage into the new household. Again, it appears that the more complex the new blended family is, the greater the difficulties. Thus, both parents were more likely to refer to conflicts and disagreements about child rearing in those families in which the set-up was complicated by the existence of multiple relationships and the consequent need to make a whole series of new adjustments.

(2)   COMMENTS ON RESEARCH

The amount of research relevant to the issue of new relationships is on the whole still very limited. This applies particularly to children taken away from home and placed in foster homes or institutions, where they may then be in the care of new parent-figures for lengthy periods of time. We know something about the factors associated with breakdown of relationships in such settings, especially in foster homes, but little about the way in which relationships to new parent-figures can initially be built up and subsequently maintained. Somewhat more research is available on step-parents, for the increasing prevalence of remarriage has ensured that questions concerning this issue are now being investigated with rather greater urgency. Here too, however, the number of systematic studies is as yet limited and caution in arriving at generalizations from such a slender base is therefore essential.

This is especially important because much of the earlier work in this area (as in so many of the others examined here) has been plagued by methodological inadequacies that make their conclusions doubtful. Thus, clinical reports on step-parent relationships, of which there have been many, may have been useful in simply drawing attention to this phenomenon, but their reliance on just a few, mostly atypical cases has given rise to some very misleading ideas. More recent work, such as the studies quoted above, shows greater sophistication. Such research has, for instance, generally taken the essential precaution of including control groups of non-divorced families: to find, let us say, that a certain proportion of adolescent boys have difficulties with their stepfathers is of little significance if it emerges that the same is true of a similar proportion of adolescent boys in the population at large. Equally essential is the need to rely not merely on self-reports. However useful these may be, no one method can provide a complete picture, and assessment by such other and more objective means as observations, tests and teachers' reports ought therefore to be added to the use of interviews and questionnaires. Similarly with the number of family members investigated: reliance on reports from just one individual may, at best, come up with only a partial picture, and all relevant members of the family ought therefore to be included. And one other feature that must be considered essential is the adoption of a longitudinal approach. As we saw in discussing the effects of divorce, investigating a family at only one point may tell us little about their reactions at other points – a step-relationship is after all a developing one and may go through many phases before it settles down.

The inclusion of such methodological features in more recent studies provides one with greater confidence in their findings. Even so, generalizations are still hazardous in view of the very many variables that can affect the particular results obtained. Thus, it has become apparent that the outcome depends on such factors as the sex of the stepchild, the sex of the step-parent, the structural complexity of the new family and the total number of its members, the child's continuing relationship with the non-custodial parent and the length of time that the family has been together. In addition, there are the usual dangers of generalizing from highly specific samples: for instance, Santrock and his colleagues investigated white, middle-class American families living in Texas, but given the very many cultural factors that may influence divorce, remarriage and the functioning of families generally, it is clearly necessary to consider carefully whether conclusions from specific studies can be applied to other populations.

What is significant, however, is that results from different investigations have shown a fairly substantial congruence in their findings. Not only have they pin-pointed the influence of variables such as those just mentioned and indicated that adjustment of children is easier under some conditions than under others; they have also swung the emphasis away from the negative, problem-focused view of the step-relationship and drawn attention to some of its more positive features, showing that in many instances such a relationship can be a force to the good. The essential comparisons that one needs to make in order to demonstrate this point are, first, with divorced single-parent families and, second, with non-divorced but conflict-ridden families, and there is now sufficient data available to indicate that life in a step-family may well be easier for most children (as well as parents) than in either of these two alternative settings.

Implications for practice

That children are capable of forming attachments to parent-figures in the later years of childhood has already emerged from our discussion of late adoption. There, however, the evidence came from children who had never had the chance of forming emotional bonds before; here we are concerned with children whose original bond with a parent had become severed (or at least loosened) and who were subsequently provided with a substitute for that parent. Such children have experienced all the problems associated with the break-up of their original family and with life subsequently in a one-parent household; they do not therefore come unscathed to the new relationship, and any difficulties that may occur in its formation may well reflect those previous experiences. What is clear is that children *can* form proper relationships; there is nothing in human nature to prevent this occurring. Under optimal conditions these can be close and satisfying; the fact that in a certain proportion of cases they fall short of this ideal makes it all the more important to search for the factors that prevent this occurring, as only then can appropriate action be taken.

Step-parents do not have an easy task and they deserve help and understanding. Unlike biological parents they do not grow up with the child and thus have no chance of learning on the job. The child comes to them already half-formed and in many respects the demands on their parenting skills are thus all the greater. Every step-parent also has to resolve a role conflict, i.e. the conflict between being a newcomer and being a 'real' parent: how much to get involved, how much affection to display, to what extent to participate in discipline – these are just some of the questions which present no problem to other parents but which often leave step-parents puzzled and undecided. Access to counselling and family-therapy services for such individuals is therefore highly desirable. However, there are difficulties for stepchildren too, especially as membership of a step-family is usually thrust upon them following a period of living in a single-parent family where they had the custodial parent all to themselves. Having to share that parent now with someone else calls for considerable readjustment and may not always be received with much enthusiasm.

Yet the research on step-families suggests that, on the whole, there is some cause for optimism. Admittedly, the likelihood of interpersonal difficulties is greater than in unbroken families, but this applies only to a minority made vulnerable by a combination of past and present circumstances. What is clear is that the stigma popularly attached to the step-relationship is an undeserved one: most step-parents work hard at winning the child's love and affection, many stepchildren in time develop a genuine attachment to the new parent, and improvement frequently takes place in the psychological state of the remarried parent that in turn favourably affects the child. Not to consider marrying again because of fear of the effects of such a move on the child appears therefore to be unjustified.

While the majority of children make the transition successfully, some do react adversely. Research has indicated at least some of the circumstances under which this may occur, thus alerting us to possible problems. Certain combinations of factors are rather more likely to give rise to difficulties and define who is most vulnerable – for instance, teenagers (especially girls) in stepmother families whose original family broke up through divorce and who are no longer in contact with the non-custodial parent. Girls in general appear to find assimilation in a new family more difficult to cope with than boys. Similarly the stepmother relationship has been found by several investigators to be a more problematic one than the stepfather relationship. A lot also depends, of course, on the support that the step-parent is willing to offer the natural parent. Given the fact that most children regard the enduring relationship with the latter (whether mother or father) as their main source of security, the willingness of the new parent to bolster this feeling is likely to be crucial. And all along, patience is clearly required on the part of the step-parent: suspicion, bewilderment and resentment at the start of the new household are almost bound to occur; a new love relationship will not spring up all at once but is likely to develop only slowly and with many hesitations. Too much too soon cannot be expected, and the more one can convey this caution to new step-parents, the better.

What may seem surprising is the suggestion from some of the research that children adjust better to the step-family if they have a continuing relationship with the non-custodial parent. The fear of divided loyalties is understandable and has sometimes been used as a reason for breaking off all contact. It seems, however, that children are much more capable of sorting out the roles of the various individuals in their lives and sustaining relationships with all of them than they have been given credit for. This certainly applies to children's relationships with stepfathers and biological fathers; the ability simultaneously to sustain meaningful contact with two mother-figures is perhaps more questionable. A great deal obviously hangs on the goodwill of the different parties and the extent to which they are prepared to co-operate in not undermining the child's trust in the others: in cases of divorce, adults' jealousies unfortunately only too often swamp the child's efforts at understanding and adjustment. We need a lot more research on this important point; what there is, however, gives no support to the idea that a clean break with the non-custodial parent is an essential pre-condition for establishing a good relationship with the step-parent, nor need one fear that the new relationship will inevitably destroy the old one. On the contrary, it seems there is every reason why the non-custodial parent should continue to remain in regular contact with the child even after the remarriage of his or her former spouse. The idea of a child with three parents may seem strange, even unnatural, but it does appear that there are circumstances where children can cope with such a situation – given, let us re-emphasize, the goodwill of all those concerned.

In certain respects the findings regarding step-parents may well be relevant to children's relationships with such other substitute figures as foster parents. This includes such considerations as the greater difficulty older children and girls have in putting their trust in a new care giver, the time necessary with a child to win its confidence, the reverberating effects of previous scarring experiences, the extent to which success is dependent on the actions of the substitute parent, and the ability of all children but the very youngest to maintain an orientation to non-resident parents even when an affectionate bond develops with substitutes. The analogy can, however, be taken too far: the step-parent relationship is meant to be a permanent one whereas the placement of a child with foster parents is mostly a temporary measure, and even in those cases where the stay is a long-term one, a restoration to the original family is still the eventual aim in most instances. Under such circumstances the partners involved, foster parent and child, are unlikely to show the same commitment to the relationship; knowing its temporary nature they will not 'work' on it as much as those brought together for good.

Further reading

Ganong, L. H. and Coleman, M. 1984: The effects of remarriage on children: a review of the empirical literature. *Family Relations*, 33, 389–406.

Pasley, K. and Ihinger-Tallman, M. (eds) 1984: Remarriage and step-parenting. Special issue of *Family Relations*, 33, no. 3.

Spanier, G. B. and Furstenberg, F. F. 1987: Remarriage and reconstituted families. In M. B. Sussman and S.K. Steinmetz (eds), *Handbook of Marriage and the Family*. New York: Plenum.

Issue: Is the traditional nuclear family essential to the development of psychological health?

Background

The belief that the traditional nuclear family is essential to the raising of psychologically healthy children is a very common one indeed. The word 'family' is, after all, one of the most emotive words we have in our vocabulary. It is associated by most people with 'good things': with love and affection, warmth, security, comfort and shelter. It is frequently referred to as the foundation of society, and such ills as delinquency, violence and addiction, especially among the young, are automatically ascribed to the failure of certain families to adhere to conventional values and behaviour patterns. Strengthening the family is thus regarded as the ultimate goal of many social-welfare policies and the solution to a wide range of problems besetting society.

Traditional families are those where there are two parents, one of each sex, living as a separate unit, and where family tasks are strictly divided between the parents, the father being the bread-winner and the mother taking responsibility for home and children. Most of our understanding of children's socialization is based on this kind of family, and yet statistics derived from national surveys carried out in many countries have repeatedly shown that increasing numbers of children are now being reared in other, non-traditional settings: single-parent families, reconstituted families following divorce and remarriage, families where the mother is employed outside the home and shares the child's care with others, families where the father has prime responsibility for the children, families that do not live on their own but form part of communal groups, and so forth. Deviations from the norm can thus take many forms, but though at least some of these have become much more common in recent years they still tend to be met with prejudice and disapproval and also with the genuine fear that such deviations from the customary arrangement will be harmful to children. For example, the absence of a father-figure (as in the majority of single-parent families) has been said to produce disturbances in the sex-role development of children, especially of boys; perhaps paradoxically, the same is said of those cases where the father reverses roles with the mother and becomes the main care giver – an arrangement which many fear produces confusion in chidren's ideas about masculinity and femininity. Similarly, as we saw previously, there are apprehensions about employed mothers' daily absences from home and their effects on the security and adjustment of children; for that matter, any form of shared care and multiple mothering has for long been widely disapproved of because of its presumed deleterious consequences for the child's primary social relationship.

We have already touched on several of such deviations from the accepted norm and considered their implications for children's development, and we have seen enough to cast doubt on the justification for many of these fears. Here we will bring this issue into focus by looking at some of the work done on children brought up in a variety of non-traditional families and seeing how they compare with those reared in the conventional nuclear family.

Research findings

(1) SUMMARIES

Eiduson, B. T., Kornfein, M., Zimmerman, I. L. and Weisner, T. S. 1982: Comparative socialization practices in traditional and alternative families. In M. Lamb (ed.), Non-Traditional Families: Parenting and Child Development. *Hillsdale, New Jersey: Erlbaum.*

In this study 200 children from four different backgrounds were investigated: (1) 50 from single-mother families, including a group of unmarried mothers who had consciously chosen to become pregnant without marriage; (2) 50 from 'social-contract' couples, where the parents, though living together, had decided for one reason or another to remain unmarried; (3) 50 from families forming part of communal living groups which they had joined in order to share their lives with other like-minded people; and (4) 50 from tradition-al two-parent nuclear families. All lived in California, were white and from middle-class backgrounds, and were followed up from the mother's pregnancy onward.

Data were obtained by means of a variety of techniques, including parental interviews and questionnaires, home observations, standar-dized tests and experimental situations. The data were used to in-vestigate how children's development and their socialization were related to family life-style, and they also yielded detailed descriptions of how the different families conducted themselves and of the values to which they adhered. The present report deals with the children's first three years of life; the findings referring to the effects on their development are those of principal interest to us.

The children from the four groups started off similarly, in that at birth there were no differences between them in terms of obstetric and neurological indices. Observations at the age of 6 months of a range of affective and social-behaviour patterns revealed no differ-ence; the Bayley Scales of Infant Development administered at 8 and again at 12 months found the children from all the groups to be on the whole well within the average range. A 'Strange Situation' test at 1 year, designed to highlight children's attachment security with their mothers, found negligible differences, with the majority of children from all family types being classified as secure. A parent-report measure of the children's developmental progress, obtained both at 18 months and at 2 years, again found no group differences. This also applied to an IQ test and a vocabulary test at age 3, as well as to assessments of the children's creativity, persistence and social maturity. Because of the anti-authoritarian stance of some of the alternative families, special attention was paid to the children's aggression, failure to co-operate and tolerance for frustration; once again no significant group differences were found. When social, intellectual and emotional competence scores were summarized for each child's performance on all 3-year tests, differences again failed to emerge.

The project is a continuing one and reports on the children at older ages will be made available. For the first 3 years, however, it is clear that the kind of life-style adopted by the families had not systematic effects whatsoever on any of the wide range of behaviour patterns and abilities assessed in these children.

Radin, N. 1982: Primary caregiving and role-sharing fathers. In M. Lamb (ed.), Non-Traditional Families: Parenting and Child Development. Hillsdale, New Jersey: Erlbaum.

One kind of non-traditional family occurs when husband and wife reverse roles, the former staying at home to take on responsibility for housework and child care, the latter going out to a job and becoming the principal wage earner. What happens to the children under such circumstances, and in particular how is their sex-role development affected by the father assuming a traditionally feminine role?

This study set out to throw light on these questions (as well as on the personal characteristics and socialization experiences of the men and women that led them to adopt this style of family life). The sample consisted of 59 middle-class, American families, each with a child of between 3 and 6 years of age. On the basis of the parents' answers to detailed questions about the respective responsibilities of the mother and the father for a range of specified child-care activities, the families were divided into three groups: one where the father was the primary care giver, another where the mother was primary care giver, and an intermediate group. Global estimates for the percentage of time that fathers had primary responsibility for their chidren were 58 per cent, 22 per cent and 40 per cent respectively. The degree of paternal involvement was then related to various measures obtained from tests administered to the children.

The main findings pertinent here refer to the children's development of sexual orientation. In particular, it emerged from the data that the children's perceptions of their own masculinity or femininity was in no way affected by the extent of the father's involvement in their care. Perhaps this is not surprising, for when the fathers themselves were tested for sex-role orientation, those in the high-involvement group turned out to be just as masculine as those in the other groups. It seems that the activities that the children saw their fathers engage in (cooking, washing, cleaning, and so forth) were of far less importance than the personality traits (such as assertiveness and forcefulness) that characterized the fathers. What is more, children in the high-involvement group described their fathers in more markedly masculine terms than was the case with other children – presumably because a constantly present father is in a better position to impress his children with his 'manliness' than one comparatively seldom at home. One other finding also worth quoting is that the children from the high-involvement group scored higher on verbal intelligence tests, the most likely reason being that these children's fathers spent more time in attempts to stimulate the children's cognitive growth than did other fathers. For some reason this occurred particularly so with daughters.

It therefore appears that parental role reversal does not affect children's sexual identities and that it may have some beneficial effects on their intellectual development. To quote the author's cautious conclusion: 'As a whole, the evidence should not discourage other families from considering this alternative family style.'

Sagi, A. 1982: Antecedents and consequences of various degrees of paternal involvement in child rearing: the Israeli project. In M. Lamb (ed.), Non-Traditional Families: Parenting and Child Development. Hillsdale, New Jersey: Erlbaum.

This study deals with the same problem as the previous one, i.e. the implications for children of fathers assuming primary responsibility for child care. However, it is also worth quoting because it deals with a different kind of sample and uses somewhat different assessment techniques. The sample is an Israeli one, consisting of 60 urban, middle-class families, in some of which the father was the primary caretaker while in others the mother was so classified. On the basis of the same questionnaire used by Radin with her American families, designed to indicate the role the father plays in the family, three groups of 20 each were constructed: a high-involvement, an intermediate and a low-involvement group. Each of the families had a child between 3 and 6 years old from whom measures were obtained with regard to a variety of domains of psychological functions.

As in Radin's study, the findings give no grounds for concern that the development of children's sexual orientation will be adversely affected when the father assumes the conventional mothering role. In the high-involvement group, children's gender development proceeded as normally as in the other two groups, in that the boys exhibited predominantly male-oriented and the girls female-oriented behaviour. Yet the extent of fathers' involvement did have an influence, in so far as the daughters of primary-care fathers tended to show certain masculine characteristics to a greater extent than their counterparts in the other groups. This is interpreted as showing that involved fathers do not eliminate the feminine tendencies of their daughters but instead add to their sex role orientation a masculine perspective. Children with constantly available fathers are, of course, more likely to imitate them, and certainly these children had a different perception of their fathers, describing them as more dominant and powerful, and yet also as warmer, than children who had less frequent contact with their fathers. One further finding was that the highly involved fathers appeared to exert more pressure on their children: they expected them to be more independent and more achievement oriented, and they also aimed to provide their children with intellectual stimulation to a greater extent than other fathers.

The author believes that the general pattern of findings contradicts the notion that men feel uncomfortable when they are deeply involved in child care. He also suggests that fathers who are prepared to adopt such a non-traditional role are in a good position to affect their children's development for the better.

Levy-Shiff, R. 1983: Adaptation and competence in early childhood: communally raised kibbutz children versus family raised children in the city. Child Development, 54, 1606–14.

The Israeli kibbutz system affords the opportunity of looking at another kind of non-conventional family set-up, in that here the usual experiences children obtain within the family are supplemented and partially replaced by what other socializing agents offer. In the Israeli kibbutz, children from the beginning experience two parallel systems: the family, where they spend only a small part of their time, and the children's house, where they are reared together with other children by a professional care giver (the *metapelet*). Thus, the major part of their socialization is delegated to someone other than their parents, and multiple mothering, together with the peer group, plays a significant part right through childhood.

In this study a group of 44 kibbutz children was compared with a group of 42 family-raised children, all around 3 years old. The parents were roughly comparable in age, education and ethnic origin. All family-raised chidren attended nursery school. Amongst the areas examined were the children's attachment to their mothers and fathers, their independence in carrying out routine tasks, their ability to adapt to unfamiliar settings, their responsiveness to strangers and ability to co-operate with them, the children's behaviour during problem solving and the extent of any developmental disturbance.

The results do not bear out the expectation that reduced mother–child interaction among the kibbutz children is detrimental to their development – nor, for that matter, that this kind of upbringing makes them necessarily more competent. In certain respects the two groups differed, but in most they were alike. Thus, despite the metapelet's dominant role, the kibbutz children were as strongly attached to their parents as were children reared in conventional families. They also did not differ in their general developmental status or behavioural adjustment, nor were there any differences in their ability to cope with nursery school. The kibbutz children were found to be somewhat ahead in independence and self-reliance, but on the other hand they were judged to be less effective in structured problem-solving tasks. They were also less responsive to adult strangers.

It therefore appears that the two systems of child rearing differ not so much in terms of one being 'better' than the other but that each enhances some kinds of competence in the child while being detrimental for others. In any case the similarities between the effects they produce on children's development are more marked than any difference.

Leiderman, P. H. and Leiderman, G. F. 1974: Affective and cognitive consequences of polymatric infant care in the East African Highlands. In A. D. Pick (ed.), Minnesota Symposia on Child Psychology, Vol. 8. *Minneapolis: University of Minnesota Press.*

What is conventional in one culture may not be so regarded in another, and it is therefore useful to examine how children fare in societies where families may function differently in one way or another compared with Western norms. However, direct comparisons with Western families may be misleading because of the simultaneous existence of so many other differences. The present study is therefore especially useful because it allows us to compare families within the same culture. Like that dealing with the Israeli kibbutz system, it is concerned with examining what happens when the mother does not have sole responsibility for the care of her children in infancy but shares it with others.

The investigation was carried out in a Kikuyu village in Kenya. In this particular community some babies are raised primarily by their mothers while others have two principal caretakers, namely the mother and an older girl (who may be the child's sister). In the latter case the mother gradually reduces her participation in child rearing in order to work in the fields, so that from about 5 months onwards the infant is being looked after for about half the day by the substitute caretaker. Most of the physical routines remain the mother's responsibility, whereas the child's social stimulation comes mainly from the older girl.

Detailed and extensive anthropological observations were carried out on the 67 families included in this study, with a view to plotting the child-rearing practices of the single-mothering and multi-mothering families. In addition, social and cognitive aspects of the children's development were assessed during the latter half of their first year. These included the infant's reaction to the departure and brief absence of the mother and (in the multi-mothering group) of the other caretaker, the child's reaction to a stranger and perform-ance on the Bayley Test of Infant Development. As shown both by the strength of their positive behaviour towards the mother and the way in which they reacted to separation from her, the infants of both groups were clearly attached to their mothers and appeared to be so to a similar extent, though the multi-mothered children reacted somewhat more strongly to her absence. By the end of the first year these children also showed a similar degree of attachment to the caretaker as to the mother. The major effect of multiple mothering, however, was on cognitive development as revealed by the infant test scores: these children, and in particular those from families of lower economic status, showed a more advanced developmental level than the children reared by a single mother-figure. It therefore seems that the presence of alternate caretakers has the effect of improving the children's test performance, presumably because the extra social stimulation provided helped in enlarging the behaviour repertoire of the children. Otherwise there were no indications that one kind of family functioning was in any way 'better' than the other.

(2) COMMENTS ON RESEARCH

A great variety of non-traditional families exist, some of which we have referred to under other Issues. These include single-parent families, step-families, same-sex couples and their children and fami-lies with working mothers, and the research on these needs to be taken in conjunction with that summarized here. There may be some danger in lumping all of them together and making sweeping gener-alizations about the way in which all affect children's development. Fortunately, the message from this diversity is a fairly unanimous one, namely that there is no indication that departures from the conventional norm of family structure are necessarily harmful to children and that that norm must be considered a *sine qua non* to the development of psychologically healthy personalities. Some of the problems associated with various kinds of non-traditional families may give rise to difficulties, such as the greater likelihood of poverty that occurs in single-parent families or the poor-quality substitute care sometimes found among the children of working mothers, but these are secondary effects and are not inherent in these kinds of families as such.

There are, however, some cautions to be borne in mind. One refers to the usual constraint regarding the specific samples investigated and the danger of generalizing from them to an undue extent. In certain countries, such as Sweden and Israel, and in certain parts of the USA such as California, there is a greater readiness to depart from conventional forms of family life and to evolve various alternate styles. The tolerance shown in these societies to those choosing such alternatives is likely to be far greater than would be found in more conservative communities where respect for traditional forms of living is still a potent force and where a by-product of growing up in a non-conventional family might well be a certain degree of ostracism that in turn would have implications for the children's psychological health. Thus, caution in generalizing from findings obtained in particular societies is essential.

In addition, there are reservations regarding the methods of assessment used in some of the studies. As we have seen, the development of children's sex roles has been of particular interest to those investigating the effects of role reversal among parents. There is a considerable literature on sex-role acquisition, i.e. on the way in which children assume behavioural patterns and psychological characteristics commonly associated with one sex in contrast with the other. However, not only has this turned out to be a highly complex developmental process but the concept of sex role itself is in many respects an elusive one that is by no means easy to measure. Some studies (for example, those by Radin and Sagi summarized above) employ only one particular test – in their case the IT-scale which requires children to make choices among sex-typed toys such as dolls and guns. This may be much too crude as a reliable indication of a child's masculinity or femininity and again calls for caution in accepting the relevant findings.

Over and above this, however, there is also the question of the values that one attaches to the development of a definitely masculine or definitely feminine personality. Until quite recently, these were considered in terms of rigid dichotomies, and any deviation, as found in an effeminate boy or a tomboyish girl, were regarded as undesirable and even an indication of psychological ill-health. As mentioned before, the dichotomy is nowhere near as rigid now: the advantages of rather more mixed (androgynous) personalities are more widely accepted these days as social conventions with respect to the differential roles of men and women have undergone drastic change. This in turn means redefining what we mean by psychological health – a concept that is by no means an absolute one but instead is relative to the values currently prevalent in particular societies.

Fortunately, other aspects of children's development do not present quite the same difficulties and the methods used in their assessment are somewhat more robust. Findings derived from these provide one with a rather firmer base for conclusions, and especially so when, as in the study by Eiduson and her colleagues, they are obtained from examining a variety of different family life-styles, cover a wide range of psychological functions and follow up the subjects over a period of years. It is studies such as this which give one grounds for confidence in the assertion that non-conventional family settings need not by any means be regarded as harmful to children's development.

Implications for practice

Surely the most important implication is the need for tolerance of a wide variety of family life-styles. Despite the many changes that have taken place in the nature of the family in the course of the last few decades, there is still the prevalent belief that the conventional nuclear family is the only suitable environment for children to grow up in and that any deviation from this norm is bound to put children at a disadvantage. Yet the proportion of households that fit this idealized image of an enduring unit containing a bread-winning father, a homemaking mother and the children of this couple has become comparatively small, and increasingly it is necessary to do justice to the many children who experience other kinds of family environments. That drastic changes in life-style associated with such events as divorce and remarriage do affect many children adversely cannot, of course, be doubted; this does not mean to say, however, that all children living in single-parent families following divorce or in reconstituted families following remarriage are inevitably conde-mned to misery and that divorce is therefore to be discouraged at all costs. Similarly with parental role reversal and shared care: the message from enquiries into all such arrangements is that sound parent–child relationships can exist in a wide variety of social con-texts that sometimes differ markedly from the traditional nuclear family.

It is in fact the nature of children's interpersonal relationships that is the key factor in influencing the course of psychological develop-ment rather than family structure as such. As we have seen, families apparently intact and conforming to all the usual requirements of convention may in reality be so conflict-ridden that they are utterly destructive to the children's welfare; divorce in such circumstances may in the long run serve to alleviate this situation. A mother sitting at home may be so depressed and frustrated that her relationship with the child is adversely affected; obtaining outside employment and arranging for good substitute care can then only improve their life together. Parents leading an isolated existence in their own home may feel themselves trapped and lonely, with adverse consequences for the atmosphere in that home; joining a community, where they share household tasks and child care, could in some cases mean fulfilment and a marked improvement in their mental state. In every case it is the quality of interpersonal relationships that matters and these can flourish in many different kinds of family settings. Action concerned with prevention and with preserving or improving chil-dren's psychological health ought accordingly to be aimed in the first place at the nature of the child's relationships with its caretakers and take into account the type of family setting as only a secondary consideration.

Convention does, of course, exert a powerful influence on people's thinking, and the tradition that only one narrowly defined family type is suitable for children will not be easily shaken. Let us refer back to the Issue asking whether women make better parents than men. One of the studies summarized there describes how teachers, social workers and others made less favourable judgements about children when told they came from single-parent families (especially those headed by a father) than when told they were from intact two-parent families. It is such prejudices and negative expectations that are probably the greatest handicap for members of non-conventional families, and it is the need to counter these that is the most pressing requirement and that is most likely to be of help to the children concerned. The family is not a closed, static system utterly impervious to outside events. On the contrary, over the centuries it has adapted itself in all sorts of respects to social, economic and technological changes in society, and the respective roles of men and women and the way in which parents define their responsibility towards their children are particularly good examples of such adaptation. The danger of sticking to some particular stereotype of the family, regarding it as the norm to which all must conform, needs to be avoided even more nowadays when changes in society are so much more profound and come at such a greater rate than in previous times.

Further reading

Birns, B. and Hay, D. F. (eds) 1988: *The Different Faces of Motherhood.* New York: Plenum.

Humphrey, M. and Humphrey, H. 1988: *Families with a Difference: varieties of surrogate parenthood.* London: Routledge.

Parke, R. D. (ed.) 1984: *The Family: review of child development research, Vol. 7.* Chicago: University of Chicago Press.

Issue: Do early problems continue into later life?

Background

Behavioural problems in early childhood are by no means uncommon. They may already be found immediately after birth, stemming from pre- or perinatal complications of one kind or another. They may appear in infancy, taking the form of feeding or sleeping disturbances or excessive crying; or they may emerge sometime during the pre-school years, affecting any of a variety of emotional and social functions such as aggression, fears, excessive temper tantrums or shyness, or they may show themselves as conduct disorders like hyperactivity or poor concentration. In each case they are likely to give rise to concern among parents and a lot of effort may be spent in attempting to deal with them as problems in their own right.

Over and above such concern, however, there is the worry as to whether these early problems are of significance with respect to the future. Some people no doubt wonder whether their presence might not indicate a fundamental 'weakness' in the child which will persist and continue to give rise to psychological difficulties at later stages. Does a child's early status predict its later condition? Is there a link betwen childhood disturbance and adult maladjustment? Once a worry always a worry? Or are behavioural problems that occur in the early stages of development mostly of a transient nature and of no predictive significance?

The amount of information we have on this issue is as yet patchy. This is not surprising in view of the methodological difficulties. Longitudinal studies are required to provide credible results, and such studies are time-consuming and expensive and therefore relatively rare. In addition, anything to do with the continuity or discontinuity of human development will almost certainly turn out to be highly complex to interpret. Thus, problems do not necessarily persist but may reappear, possibly in different form – in which case they could be new problems rather than linked in some way to the previous ones. Furthermore, what applies to one kind of psychological disturbance may not apply to another: different symptoms may have different predictive significance and each ought therefore to be studied separately. And finally age at onset, the ameliorative action taken at the time, the nature and stability of the environment in which the child is reared – all these and other variables will affect the results obtained and need to be taken into account. It is thus not surprising that our knowledge is less complete than one might wish.

Yet the implications for the provision of services are so considerable that it does seem justified to examine some of the relevant work in order to see what has been found out so far. If, say, early problems are not generally transient but do have predictive significance, then they need to be taken much more seriously, for intervention at an early stage may well be effective in preventing subsequent trouble. It also then becomes important to identify the kinds of problems that are more likely to persist and the types of conditions that are conducive to maintaining them, as one is able to target interventionist action more effectively as a result of such knowledge. In addition, however, at a more fundamental level questions concerning this topic raise issues regarding children's capacity for flexibility and adaptability and thus provide us with essential information regarding the basic nature of human personality development.

Research findings

(1) SUMMARIES

Richman, N., Stevenson, J. and Graham, P. J. 1982: Preschool to School: a behavioural study. *London: Academic Press.*

In this investigation the continuity of behaviour problems from age 3 to age 8 was investigated. At the 3-year point the subjects comprised 705 families, these representing a one in four random sample drawn from a London borough. The information was obtained from the mothers by means of interviews and a standardized behaviour-screening questionnaire. This showed that, given certain specified criteria for disturbance, approximately 7 per cent of the 3-year olds could be said to be moderately or severely disturbed and a further

15 per cent mildly disturbed. Sex, social class and the mother's employment status showed little relation to these figures.

The follow-up was based primarily on a group of 94 problem and 91 non-problem (control) children. The mothers were again interviewed and again a standardized questionnaire was used for screening purposes. It was found that 61 per cent of problematic 3-year olds still had significant difficulties 5 years later. Comparison of the problem group with the control group showed the former to have a continued higher level of disturbance at age 8. Continuity was found mainly with respect to certain types of symptoms: thus, restlessness and high activity in particular were signs of poor outcome, leading to antisocial behaviour at the older age, and similarly, early fearfulness was associated with later neurotic difficulties. In general, boys' problems were more likely to persist than those of girls, and children with moderate or severe problems had a greater persistence rate than those with mild problems. It was also found that the problem group had to cope with more external stress during the follow-up period than the controls. In addition, the mothers of the problem children had themselves higher rates of psychological disturbance throughout the 5 years and the parents had more marital difficulties and more physical ill-health.

The authors conclude that the degree of continuity of behaviour problems from the pre-school to the early school period is fairly high: 'Once a child's behaviour is established in a maladaptive pattern it does not readily change .... Even minor disturbance in young children predisposes to later difficulties in some degree.' At the same time they warn that despite the high level of continuity, screening in the pre-school years will not detect all children who will be disturbed at the age of 8 and that continuous monitoring is therefore necessary.

Fischer, M., Rolf, J. E., Hasazi, J. E. and Cummings, L. 1984: Follow-up of a preschool epidemiological sample. Child Development, 55, 137–50.

One of the conclusions of the Richman et al. study is that continuity varies according to *type* of behavioural disturbance. This is underlined by the findings of the present investigation, which focuses on two kinds of psychological maladjustment referred to as 'internalizing' and 'externalizing' dimensions. Internalizing relates to behaviour characterized by inhibition, withdrawal and problems within the self; externalizing encompasses aggression, hostility and acting out against the environment or society. Others have referred to these as neurotic and antisocial tendencies respectively, and there is considerable evidence to indicate the usefulness of distinguishing between these two clusters.

The study is based on 541 children who were first seen when they were between 2 and 6 years of age and then again 7 years later. At both ages, parents were asked to complete a behaviour check-list, comprising about 100 items dealing with the frequency with which specific kinds of behaviour occurred and indicating the presence and severity of problems, with particular reference to those falling into the internalizing and externalizing categories.

Of these two, the externalizing dimension appears to be the more stable. For both sexes externalizing symptoms found during the pre-school period showed a significant continuity with externalizing symptoms 7 years later. No such stability over age was found for internalizing behaviour. The same conclusion emerged when a clinically disturbed group was selected from the total sample on the basis of their deviant score on either of the two dimensions: the results show that pre-school children with severe internalizing symptoms are no more likely still to be showing such severe shy, withdrawing behaviour 7 years later than are other children. On the other hand children with severe behaviour problems of the externalizing kind early on are much more likely to persist with the same kind of disturbance after this long interval.

Continuity thus varies according to type of symptomatology; sweeping generalizations about behavioural disturbance in general cannot be made. It is important to emphasize, however, that even for the externalizing type continuity, though statistically significant, was modest. An early intervention programme would therefore be wasted on some children, who would subsequently outgrow their problems, as well as miss some initially 'normal' children who would later show disturbance. As far as these authors are concerned, 'what impresses one about these results is the flexibility and plasticity of development that they seem to imply, such that discontinuity rather than significant continuity in behavioural expression . . . seems to be the norm.'

Jenkins, S., Owen, C., Bax, M. and Hart, H. 1984: Continuities of common behaviour problems in preschool children. Journal of Child Psychology and Psychiatry, 25, 75–89.

This study takes the issue of continuity further back into infancy, in that it is based on a follow-up investigation of children from birth to age 5. The specific points at which data were obtained about the children were at ages 6 months, 1 year, 18 months, 2 years, 3 years and 4½ years. The sample of 361 children (subsequently somewhat reduced by loss of subjects for various reasons) consisted of all children of the relevant age living within a particular area of North London. Data were obtained by interview with parents using a standard questionnaire.

The prevalence rates for behaviour problems as reported by parents increased with age, being only 3 per cent at 6 months and going up to 15 per cent at 3 years and 13 per cent at 4½ years. Continuity turned out to be a highly complex issue, in that its extent varied considerably according to the specific problem and the age range examined. To give some examples: for poor appetite the continuity rate from 18 months to 2 years was 23 per cent, and from 2 years to 3 years it was 65 per cent. For food faddiness the respective rates for these two age ranges were 25 per cent and 31 per cent. In the case of night waking a 44 per cent rate was found between 6 months and 1 year, 41 per cent between 1 year and 18 months, 54 per cent between 18 months and 2 years, 25 per cent between 2 and 3 years, and 14 per cent between 3 and 4½ years. Of children reported as having frequent temper tantrums at age 2, almost half (45 per cent) were still having frequent tantrums at 3; between 3 and 4½ the persistence rate was 34 per cent.

These figures give some indication of the considerable variability to be found in even the short-term persistence of specific symptoms. The findings of the study as a whole demonstrate that, while for many children behaviour problems are short-lived, for others the difficulties can persist over rather longer periods of time during the pre-school years.

Thomas, A. and Chess, S. 1984: Genesis and evolution of behavioral disorders: from infancy to early adult life. American Journal of Psychiatry, 141, 1–9.

The New York Longitudinal Study, directed by Thomas and Chess, is a widely known and respected attempt to trace the behavioural development of a group of children from early infancy into adult life. It has generated knowledge about a variety of topics, including material relevant to the present issue.

Data on the sample of 133 children were obtained periodically throughout childhood. A wide variety of assessment tools were used to describe the children's behaviour at home, at school and in standard psychometric test situations, and at the same time information was gathered about the parents' attitudes and child-rearing practices. Given the fact that the two principal investigators are child psychiatrists it is not surprising that special attention was given to the systematic clinical investigation of all children presenting any evidence of behaviour disorder. This was done primarily by means of interviews with the parents and play sessions and interviews with the children.

A group of 45 children was thus identified as showing clinical problems. The great majority of these, i.e. 41, were diagnosed as having adjustment disorders, 26 being considered mild, ten moderate and five severe. Most of these first appeared in the 3–5 year age period. By adolescence the majority (25) had recovered and two others had improved, while three were unchanged and 11 worse. In early adult life the number recovered had increased to 29, with five others improved from adolescence; those who did not recover or improve tended to grow worse rather than retain the same degree of disturbance. In addition, 12 new clinical cases appeared between 13 and 16 years, none of these having shown any sign of disorder before then.

Thus, in many cases of behavioural disorder arising in childhood the outcome was favourable. Nevertheless, a significant number did not improve, some even getting worse. According to this study it was thus by no means easy to predict the developmental course of any clinical disorder identified early on.

Werner, E. E. and Smith, R. S. 1979: An epidemiologic perspective on some antecedents and consequences of childhood mental health problems and learning disabilities. Journal of the American Academy of Child Psychiatry, *18, 292–306.*

Here we have another well known, ambitious longitudinal investigation with findings relevant to the present issue. It is based on an extensive examination of a multiracial cohort of 660 children, born in 1955 on the island of Kauai, Hawaii. The follow-up investigation began during the mother's pregnancy and continued throughout childhood, with special data collection points at ages 2, 10 and 18 years. Attrition rates were unusually low, 88 per cent of subjects being still available for study at age 18. A very large amount of data was gathered by means of a considerable array of assessment techniques, covering the children's physical, medical, intellectual and social functioning, as well as their experience within the family and in other significant settings.

One aspect to which special attention was given were the behavioural and neurological problems which children manifested at the very start of life as a result of perinatal stress, due to complications arising during the pre-natal, labour, delivery and neonatal periods. Of the total sample, 31 per cent were judged to have experienced mild stress, 10 per cent moderate and 3 per cent serious stress. This classification was found to relate to the subsequent development of mental health problems (for example, schizoid, paranoid or obsessive behaviour): at the age of 18 years, 9 per cent of those with moderate perinatal stress symptoms and 14.5 per cent of those with severe symptoms showed such problems, as compared with 3 per cent in the cohort as a whole. However, the likelihood of these very early difficulties leading to later psychological difficulties depended very much on the nature of the family in which the child was reared: indeed, the family variables on the whole exerted a more powerful effect in this respect than the residual effect of perinatal stress. To give an instance, for those who at birth were diagnosed as having some form of pathology, the likelihood of developing serious mental-health problems at age 10 was increased sevenfold if they had mothers rated as low in the provision of emotional support and ninefold in the case of mothers' inadequate educational stimulation.

Another part of the analysis involved those children who, at the age of 10, were identified as having behaviour problems severe enough to require at least 6 months of help from the mental health services. Looking back at their history indicated that 20 per cent of this group showed moderate to severe perinatal stress symptoms as compared with 8 per cent in control cases; at age 2 these children were more often characterized as 'inhibited', 'frustrated' and 'serious'; and the mothers were more often rated as 'matter of fact', 'ambivalent' and 'hostile' in their relationship to their toddlers. Only one in three of these children was judged to have improved by the age of 18. However, the prognosis was much more favourable for those children who, at age 10, had been considered to be in need of only a limited amount of help from mental health services. There were no differences between them and controls in the incidence of perinatal complications, and their symptoms of anxiety or nervous habits appeared to be only temporary reactions to environmental stress, though painful at the time.

Thus, looking back from the end of childhood it was apparent that those behaviour disorders that persisted were frequently associated with biological factors evident at birth. However, it was the combination of early biological stress and early family instability that led to the greatest risk of developing serious and persistent psychological problems.

(2) COMMENTS ON RESEARCH

The conclusions from the research done so far on this issue are by no means clear-cut, and it is apparent that a lot more work still needs to be done before we properly understand the nature of continuity. The study by Richman and her colleagues appears to present the least ambiguous results: 61 per cent of 3-year-old children with behaviour problems still present problems 5 years later, indicating a high degree of continuity. Yet even these authors are careful to point out the difficulties involved in predicting from one age to another, and when we turn to other studies, that difficulty is highlighted. The results overall give some indication of how complex the task of prediction can be, for continuity may be affected by a large number of influential conditions. One of these is the age range within which one is attempting to trace continuity: for example, what applies to the 3–8-year range may not apply to the 8–13 range, and in so far as different studies have examined different age ranges as well as different lengths of period it is hardly surprising to find that there is no unanimity of findings. Another aspect to take into account refers to variation among symptoms and clinical conditions: here too it has become apparent that one cannot make generalizations, for the developmental course of some behaviour problems may be very different to that of others, with particular reference to the extent to which they persist or lead into other clinical conditions. Given the different ways in which the notion of 'behaviour problems' has been defined by the various research workers; add to that the different methods used for their assessment (parental interviews, standardized questionnaires, direct observation, and so forth); together with, of course, the difference in the social and cultural composition of the samples examined, and it comes as no surprise to find that sweeping generalizations about the question of continuity cannot possibly be made.

What is clear from a research point of view is that one can only provide an answer to this question by employing prospective longitudinal investigations, however time-consuming these may be. The various studies we have quoted above all took this form and the credibility of their findings is accordingly enhanced. Research of this type is essential not only to investigate the extent of continuity but also to pinpoint the factors in child and environment responsible for continuity, for without knowledge about the latter any findings about the former have only limited use.

Implications for practice

However complex the picture may be, there are enough indications to suggest that a certain degree of continuity does exist. Children, that is, who show behaviour problems early in life are rather more likely to manifest problems in later years, whether these are a continuation of former symptoms or a manifestation of new kinds of pathology. In other words, such children are an 'at-risk' group; therapeutic intervention could therefore be justified at this early stage not merely for the sake of providing help at the time but also in order to forestall subsequent trouble. It is true that an intervention programme aimed at all such children would be wasting its efforts on those who will grow out of their problems unaided (as well as missing those children who are initially problem-free but develop behavioural disturbance subsequently). It will clearly be necessary to define the at-risk group much more precisely, but until we have the knowledge to be in a position to do so, one can argue (as Thomas and Chess have done) that just because it is by no means easy to predict the developmental course of a disorder after its diagnosis early on one ought to be prepared to intervene in *all* such cases. Therapeutic help provided at an early stage may well enable one to deal with the factors responsible for otherwise maintaining the disturbance – factors such as family discord which might persist and adversely affect the child at all levels of development if left untreated. In such a case, by improving the child's environmental conditions one can cut through the vicious circle that might otherwise make the disturbed young child into a disturbed adolescent and adult.

However, in order to intervene effectively and thereby prevent later pathology, one needs to know the identity of the factors responsible for the continuity of psychological disturbance. Unfortunately, our ignorance in this respect is considerable. What is certain is that the explanation lies rarely just within the child itself, the exception being endogenous disorders such as mental handicap or psychosis which tend to persist and where environmental influences have limited effect. Otherwise, the notion that behaviour problems are an indication of some fundamental 'weakness' in the child which will continue to manifest itself at all ages cannot be supported. The answer is more likely to lie in a combination of such internal factors as the child's temperament and such external factors as the family situation. It is in this connection that Thomas and Chess found the idea of 'goodness of fit' so useful, this being a concept which expresses the consonance between the child's characteristics on the one hand and the demands made by the environment (parents in particular) on the other. When such consonance is present, optimal development is possible; when there is dissonance or poorness of fit, distorted development and maladaptive functioning are likely to occur. Thus, it is in the combination of a particular child in a particular rearing environment that one must search for the factors responsible for producing desirable or undesirable outcomes.

While those with early pathology may as a group be at risk for later pathology, the degree of continuity found so far by the various longitudinal studies is by no means so great that one can make predictive statements about individual children. At present we cannot be sure that any given child with some form of behaviour difficulty in the early years will suffer from a clinical condition in the later years too. Many such difficulties turn out to be purely temporary developmental disorders or short-term reactions to specific stresses, with no significance for long-term outcome. There is thus no need to cause alarm among parents: isolated symptoms, when occurring in the context of a generally satisfactory family situation, need not be taken as an indication of troubles ahead. But for that matter, not all those who succumb at later stages were disturbed earlier on: some clinical conditions arise out of the blue with no obvious prior warning.

Generally speaking, the notion of continuity has been the focus of much interest among all those wanting to understand the process of human development. The idea that one can trace later personality characteristics back to early behavioural manifestations and events, that the child is father to the man, has a certain intuitive plausibility and gained a lot of apparent scientific respectability through the writings of Freud. In fact, it has become increasingly apparent that the developmental process is far too complex to allow simplistic statements about continuity. Few would doubt that some sort of thread runs right through the course of development, that links exist between one age and another. Yet discontinuities, sometimes brought about by radical shifts in the child's environment and sometimes by ill-understood internal forces, do exist and make prediction from earlier to later stages hazardous. The clinician in particular may like to know whether treatment of early manifestations of deviance will prevent later trouble (motivated perhaps also by the quite unsupported idea that the younger the patient, the easier the treatment). At the present state of knowledge, no such definite assurance can be given. What one can assert is that children showing problems early on are somewhat more likely to show problems in their later years and can justifiably be regarded therefore as an at-risk group.

Further reading

Brim, O. F. and Kagan, J. (eds) 1980: *Constancy and Change in Human Development*. Cambridge, Mass.: Harvard University Press.

Chess, S. and Thomas, A. 1984: *Origins and Evolution of Behavior Disorders*. New York: Brunner/Mazel.

Clarke, A. D. B. and Clarke, A. M. 1984: Consistency and change in the growth of human characteristics. *Journal of Child Psychology and Psychiatry*, 25, 191–210.

Rutter, M. 1987: Continuities and discontinuities from infancy. In J. D. Osofsky (ed.), *Handbook of Infant Development*, 2nd edn. New York: Wiley.

Issue: Who are the vulnerable children?

Background

There is great variability in response to stress. In the face of apparently identical circumstances, some individuals are completely bowled over while others emerge relatively unscathed. This applies to children every bit as much as it does to adults, and so the question arises: what makes for vulnerability?

In fact, this question has in recent years been turned round to: What makes for *in*vulnerability? At one time our attention focused exclusively on victims – those children who succumbed to deprivation, maltreatment, neglect and other such stresses. This is hardly surprising, for these children were obviously in urgent need of help. What is more, it was their plight that drew the attention of society to the fact that exposure to certain kinds of experience could produce harmful effects, thereby highlighting the need to take appropriate preventive action. Thus, once it was realized, for example, that maternal deprivation can under certain conditions produce severe, perhaps even permanent effects on children's personality development, relevant action could be taken with a view to amelioration and prevention, based initially on the assumption that such an experience is bound to affect all children undergoing it.

More recently, it has become clear, however, that some children may encounter considerable trauma and yet come through apparently unharmed. Thus, not every maternally deprived child becomes an affectionless character; it is rather that the *probability* of psychological pathology in such children is greater than in those reared in families. This, of course, parallels the situation that exists with respect to any pathogenic factor. Not every heavy smoker develops lung cancer; the established association between smoking and disease rests rather on the much greater incidence of cancer among smokers than among non-smokers. Such a statistical link provides sufficient justification for society to take the necessary action regarding tobacco consumption. At the level of the individual, however, we cannot predict with certainty that a particular person will develop lung cancer merely from knowledge of his or her smoking habits. Other factors play a part and these need to be added to the predictive formula before one can understand who will succumb and who will survive.

It is the search for these other factors that is now increasingly occupying those concerned with children's reactions to stresses of various kinds, and it is with their efforts that we will be dealing here. There are on the one hand vulnerability factors that make some individuals more susceptible, and on the other hand there are buffering influences that serve a protective function. They may either be 'inside' the child (temperament, sex, birth condition, and so forth) or 'outside' (for example, poverty, unsettled life-style, family discord). Whatever their nature, being able to isolate such influences means that one can increasingly get away from generalizations like 'deprivation is harmful' and attend to the precise circumstances under which deprivation produces particular effects. Instead of being unduly swayed by the reactions of the majority and by group averages, we can also attend to the exceptions – those who, perhaps against all the odds, do manage to survive intact and who do cope with adversity without undue cost. Understanding the reasons for such individual variability in stress resistance may then also help in our efforts at prevention.

Research findings

(1)   SUMMARIES

Werner, E. E. and Smith, R. S. 1982: Vulnerable but Invincible: a longitudinal study of resilient children and youth. *New York: McGraw Hill.*

We have already referred to Werner and Smith's important study on the island of Kauai, Hawaii, in discussing the issue of continuity of early behaviour problems. Just to recap: their investigation involved the follow-up of 600 children from before birth into early adulthood, data being collected primarily at ages 2, 10 and 18 years. A great deal of information was obtained about all aspects of these children's development, as well as about their families and other significant environmental influences.

A substantial number of these children were reared under conditions of considerable adversity: poverty, reproductive risk, family instability, parental mental illness, and so forth. It is therefore not surprising to find that many developed behaviour problems of some kind. What is pertinent here is the further finding that other children, equally exposed to such adversities, apparently remained unscathed. Given the amount of information available about each child the authors took the opportunity to track down the factors that accounted for such resilience.

One factor to which others have also drawn attention concerns children's sex: boys on the whole tend to be less resilient than girls in the face of a wide variety of physiological and psychosocial stresses. Thus, among Werner and Smith's children, more boys than girls experienced moderate or marked perinatal difficulties, and of those with the most serious complications a greater proportion of boys died in infancy. This sex difference in vulnerability continued to show itself in a wide variety of functions throughout the first decade of life: more boys than girls had serious learning and behaviour problems, necessitating remedial services or special-class placements; more boys than girls were exposed to serious physical defects of illness requiring medical care; and more boys than girls reacted adversely to the effects of poverty, family instability and lack of educational stimulation in the home by developing problems that called for long-term remedial education, mental-health-service care or attention from delinquency services. However, in the second decade this pattern changed: more boys than girls had *improved* by age 18, and *new* problems appeared more frequently among the girls than the boys. Nevertheless, females overall in the course of childhood appeared to cope rather more successfully with stress associated with reproductive risk, chronic poverty or family distress than did males.

Taking the first 2 years of life, a number of psychological characteristics were found to distinguish resilient from vulnerable children. These applied in particular to temperamental features: resilient infants, for instance, were perceived by their caretakers as very active and socially responsive and as both eliciting and receiving a great deal of attention. These characteristics continued into the second year, when they became skilled in participating in positive social interaction, displayed a great deal of independence and were quick and facile in tasks requiring information processing. They were thus more likely to be involved in supportive and stimulating interactions with parents, having evolved coping patterns that combined the ability to provide their own ideas with the ability to ask for support when needed.

These early characteristics of resilience were predictive of resilience in later years as well. Nevertheless, there was some change in the factors associated with children's response to stress. Whereas in infancy these factors primarily involved health and temperament, in mid-childhood they stemmed mainly from family structure and functioning (for example, quality of relationships with parents, consistency of discipline and amount of emotional support). Finally, in adolescence they increasingly took an intra-personal form, concerning in particular the individual's self-esteem. Even then, however, the social environment continued to play a part, in that resilient adolescents were found to be those who tended to experience fewer cumulative stresses within the family.

It was in general a combination of biological and social factors that was most successful in differentiating children according to vulnerability. Thus, for instance, birth complications were consistently related to later impaired physical and psychological development *only* when combined with persistently poor environmental circumstances. The authors also stress, however, that one should not underestimate the self-righting tendencies of children which produced normal development in all but the most persistent adverse circumstances.

Barron, A. P. and Earls, F. 1984: The relation of temperament and social factors to behaviour problems in three-year-old children. Journal of Child Psychology and Psychiatry, 25, 23–33.

This is another study based on a total population, namely all 3-year-old children living on Martha's Vineyard, an island community off the Massachusetts coastline. Out of 110 families contacted, 100 were available for study. Some information was collected directly from the children but most was derived from interviews with the parents. These interviews provided data about such family stresses as marital discord and number of moves that the child had experienced, and they also provided data relevant to an assessment of the parents' psychiatric status. In addition, parents completed the Behaviour Screening Questionnaire, a device for assessing the child's current behaviour and emotional adjustment, as well as a standardized questionnaire designed to measure the child's temperament. After each interview the quality of the parent–child interaction was rated on the basis of all information obtained.

The basic question the authors attempted to answer was: What sort of children are most likely to develop behaviour problems? They found that several factors were related to the incidence of problems. First, children with the most adverse scores on the Behaviour Screening Questionnaire tended to be characterized by particular temperamental qualities, especially inflexibility in response to changing environmental circumstances, high intensity of energy level and low adaptability to others' demands. In addition, behaviour problems were also most likely in children with poor relationships with their parents and among those who had encountered a relatively large number of stresses. All in all, the best prediction of behaviour problems was provided by a *combination* of factors, in particular an inflexible temperament in the child, a poor parent–child relationship and high family stress.

Wolkind, S. N. and De Salis, W. 1982: Infant temperament, maternal mental state and child behaviour problems. In R. Porter and G. Collins (eds). Temperamental Differences in Infants and Young Children. Ciba Foundation Symposium 89. London: Pitman.

This study is also concerned with the question: What children are most likely to succumb to behavioural difficulties and what children will avoid them?; and it also examines temperamental qualities in order to provide an answer. However, it adds the further important point that some children, by virtue of their personal characteristics, may have such an adverse effect on those caring for them that to all intents and purposes they create their own stressful environment to which they then respond adversely in turn.

Information was obtained from a group of 106 mothers, who were followed up from pregnancy onwards and interviewed at length at 4, 14, 27 and 42 months after the child's birth. At each age, questions were asked about the mother's child-rearing practices and attitudes, and a psychiatric assessment was made of her mental state. In addition, a measure of the child's temperamental qualities was obtained at 4 months, based on established temperament scales. At 42 months, the Behavioural Screening Questionnaire was included in the interview in order to assess the nature and extent of the child's psychological adjustment.

The results show a significant association between children's type of temperament at 4 months of age and the degree to which they had developed behavioural problems at 42 months. Those with the most problems at the older age had been assessed as 'difficult' in infancy, in that they tended to be predominantly negative in mood (as shown, for instance, by a great deal of crying) and to be resistant to their mothers' efforts at establishing regular routines in feeding and sleeping. However, the toddlers most severely affected were those who not only had a 'difficult' temperament but also had a mother with psychiatric symptoms (mostly depression, with associated anxiety). It seems that the *combination* of these two factors, i.e. a vulnerable disposition and an environmental stress, is most likely to give rise to problem behaviour – a point well illustrated by the fact that children of an 'easy' temperamental disposition appeared to be strikingly unaffected by depression in their mothers. It also seems, however, that maternal depression was, to some extent at least, affected by the child: those women who had difficult infants were most likely at the 14-months interview to report that they were physically tired, and it was these women who were most likely subsequently to develop psychiatric symptoms. The authors thus speculate that 'difficult' children make their own contribution to environmental stress, possibly through the loss of the mother's self-esteem caused by looking after a difficult baby, this contributing to the development of the psychiatric condition in the mother which in turn adversely affects the child.

Block, J. H., Block, J. and Morrison, A. 1981: Parental agreement–disagreement on child-rearing orientation and gender-related personality correlates in children. Child Development, 52, 965–74.

Parental discord is known to be especially stressful for children. This study highlights the extent to which boys and girls respond differently to such a stress.

One hundred families, approximately half with a son and half with a daughter, were followed up longitudinally. Each child's personality and adjustment were assessed by teachers in nurseries and schools when the children were aged 3, 4 and 7. Parental discord was measured here in terms of the extent to which mother and father disagreed about methods of child rearing, and accordingly, each parent was asked independently to complete a report detailing his or her practices and values in bringing up the child.

When the findings were broken down according to the child's sex, it emerged that boys reacted more strongly to parental disagreement than girls. Thus, at the age of 3 those boys whose parents showed marked disagreement were characterized by more immature social relations, poorer impulse control and less effective ability to cope independently than boys where there was little disagreement among parents. Similarly, at the age of 4 a number of psychological functions (verbal facility, task orientation, formation of open and direct interpersonal relationships, and so on) were adversely affected by parental discord in boys. By contrast, girls showed no such pattern: parental disagreement did not exert so notable an effect on their adjustment.

These sex differences were replicated in another study with a sample of older children and a different outcome measure. Parents of 14- and 15-year-old children were asked independently to complete a report on child-rearing values. In the case of boys, a relationship between parental disagreement and the child's IQ was found; in girls, however, there was no indication of such an adverse effect. According to the authors, the results from these studies thus suggest that the quality of parental interactions has greater impact on the psychological functioning of sons than of daughters. They believe that this is because boys, being inherently more vulnerable, need a more structured and predictable environment and will therefore be more affected when this is not provided.

Wolkind, S. and Rutter, M. 1973: Children who have been 'in care' – an epidemiological study. Journal of Child Psychology and Psychiatry, *14, 97–106.*

This report is also about sex differences. The data come from two epidemiological studies of children aged 10 and 11, one carried out on the Isle of Wight and the other in an inner-London borough. A proportion of both groups of children had been admitted to residential care for at least 1 week at some time in their lives, and these children were compared with others in a randomly selected control group.

The adjustment of all children was assessed by means of a teacher questionnaire, and in addition, a psychiatric diagnosis was derived from information obtained during parental interviews. In this way a deviant group was identified, i.e. children who were found to function adversely in relation to a particular cut-off point. It was found that a substantially higher proportion of these deviant children had been in care compared with the control children (13 per cent vs. 2 per cent on the Isle of Wight, 10 per cent vs. 1 per cent in London). Moreover, most of the deviant children who had had a care experience were boys (85 per cent and only 15 per cent girls). Generally, the deviance took the form of antisocial behaviour.

It therefore seems that the majority of boys who had been in care later developed behaviour problems, whereas very few girls did so. It should be stressed, however, that this applies mainly to short-term periods in care, for other findings suggest that long-term care affects both sexes equally. In addition, the adverse effect noted in this study may not stem from the care experience as such but rather from the family discord to which most of these children had been exposed even before their admission to care and which may very well have been responsible for the child temporarily having to leave home.

(2) COMMENTS ON RESEARCH

The main accomplishments of the research on vulnerability undertaken so far are, first, to make us aware of the considerable differences that exist even among very young children in responsiveness to stress and in the proclivity to develop behaviour problems; second, to point to some of the factors that account for these differences; and third, to show that rarely if ever does any one of these factors operate in isolation and that combinations of characteristics need to be considered instead.

As to the existence of variability in response to stress, this has now been amply demonstrated by the research literature. Even in the face of considerable trauma there are survivors as well as victims, and we can learn as much from studying the former as the latter. Vulnerability, is however, not necessarily a unitary characteristic; there are hints in research findings that responsiveness may vary from one situation to another, depending on the kind of stress to which the child is exposed. This is just one area where a great deal more work needs to be done.

As far as the identification of factors accounting for vulnerability is concerned, a useful start has been made but here too far more needs to be done. Among the factors 'inside' the child investigated so far, sex and temperament are the main ones to have been singled out. Sex in particular has been confirmed as playing a part across a wide range of different kinds of stress: for instance, the greater vulnerability of boys to their parents' divorce has already been pointed out, and on the physical side infant mortality rate, perinatal complications and susceptibility to early infection all show males to be the weaker sex. No satisfactory explanations exist for this; in any case, it is important to bear in mind that it usually takes very large samples before the distinction becomes evident, for the overlap of the two sexes in this respect is more marked than any difference.

The notion that temperamental qualities play a role in vulnerability is probably acceptable as sheer common sense. Yet it has not proved easy to define and distinguish specific temperamental qualities, nor to measure them and to establish their stability over age. Such conceptual and assessment problems obviously make it difficult to arrive at a consensus among research workers as to the precise way in which temperament affects responsiveness to stress. Nevertheless, the proposal that infants can be classified into 'easy' and 'difficult' (these terms being tied to precise behavioural descriptions) and that these qualities continue in some form into later childhood has found wide acceptance and been shown to predict, to some extent at least, who is likely to succumb and who is likely to survive.

Turning to 'outside' influences that may account for children's vulnerability, a considerable number of those that have been put forward can be summarized under one concept, namely social class. It is true that social class is merely an umbrella term for a great variety of characteristics concerned with education, financial resources, housing, health and occupation, but it has repeatedly emerged as a useful predictor of children's welfare and developmental progress. There is, of course, far more social mobility these days than in former times and the concept of social class has accordingly become more fluid. Even so, many studies concur that children reared in socially disadvantaged families are far more likely to be exposed to stresses of many kinds that will adversely affect their development than children higher up the socio-economic scale. In this sense, a child's social-class membership does provide some indication of the extent to which it is vulnerable to or protected from adverse circumstances.

Yet neither 'inside' nor 'outside' influences alone are sufficient (with rare exceptions) to explain individual variability. An analogy has been made with the conditions that produce earthquakes: it takes both a fault line in the earth and an external strain to produce tremors. In the same way, a combination of factors is required before the psychological equivalent of an earthquake, i.e. some form of breakdown in mental functioning, will occur. As Wolkind and De Salis have shown in the study summarized above, a mother's psychiatric disturbance (the external strain) may lead to behaviour problems in the child but only if that child is of a particular temperament (the fault line). Similarly, Werner and Smith's findings illustrate the fact that complications at birth lead to undesirable consequences only if the child is reared in a stressful family environment: a harmonious family will attenuate the early disadvantage and protect the child from ill-effects. Much effort is currently going into attempts to isolate protective factors, and as one example we may refer back to the study by Dowdney et al. that was described in our discussion of the long-term damage brought about maternal deprivation. In that study it was shown that women who had spent a period in care during their childhood were protected from the consequences of that experience if they had been capable of good academic achievement at school, had later on made a good marriage and above all original-ly came from a harmonious home to which they returned after the period in care. That a supportive family milieu affords the best protection against a wide range of childhood stresses is perhaps not surprising; it has certainly been demonstrated repeatedly by different studies.

Implications for practice

It is obviously right and proper to pay serious attention to those circumstances that have been found capable of producing disorder and unhappiness in children and to take all possible preventive and ameliorative steps in dealing with them. At the same time, however, one ought not to overestimate either the extent of the damage produced or the irreversibility of that damage. Certain children at least show a surprising amount of resilience, whether by virtue of their own make-up or because of the supportive environment in which they live, and even among those who are badly affected a kind of self-righting tendency can often be seen, in that the child spontaneously recovers after a disturbed period and regains mental poise. Thus, a sense of balance is required in dealing with the effects of stress on children: on the one hand, one must be prepared to provide help and support as far as one is able, and on the other hand one ought not to underrate children's ability to recover from even quite severe trauma. Stray too far in one direction and one is in danger of remaining passive when action is required; stray too far in the other direction and one might well squander resources on those not in need. There is no simple formula to guide one here, but at least we need to be aware of the range of individual variability in the face of stressful circumstances and of the factors that, according to research findings, appear to determine such variability.

In arriving at definitions of those most at risk, the need to take into account *combinations* of factors must again be stressed. It is, for example, meaningless to consider all boys to be at risk, even though statistically speaking they are more vulnerable than girls. It is also not very meaningful to state that all children who had been subjected to complications at birth are at risk, for a very large percentage develop perfectly normally – though admittedly the proportion who do not is greater than among children born without complications. Further, it is, of course, of little use to regard every child of a family from the lower end of the socio-economic spectrum as vulnerable on the basis of social-class membership alone: the majority after all develop into perfectly competent individuals. It is only when we combine perinatal complications, sex and social class that we arrive at a group of far greater vulnerability which indeed justifies the label 'at risk' and whatever action may then follow from that designation. Even in this group there will be many who show no sign of any deviance, indicating the need to add yet further vulnerability factors before we can arrive at a much tighter definition of the target group and consequently a much more economic use of resources.

One reservation needs to be borne in mind. Invulnerability is a relative term – indeed, *resilience* is now preferred by some because it expresses more easily the notion that resistance to stress is a matter of degree. Children cannot be neatly divided into the vulnerable and the invulnerable; all shades in between these two extremes can be found. For that matter it is at least conceivable that vulnerability – invulnerability does not refer to a unitary characteristic but varies with a child's age and with the nature of the stressful circumstances impinging on the child. There is at present no evidence bearing on this point, though experience suggests that variations do exist. Thus, a child found resistant to stress under one set of conditions may not necessarily show resistance under all other conditions right through childhood, just as apparently vulnerable children may sometimes show surprising strengths in certain situations. Labelling children as 'vulnerable' or 'invulnerable' without qualification is therefore hazardous; nature does not contain dichotomies as neat as those provided by language. One also needs to consider the possibility that apparent survivors may not in fact be wholly unmarked; some effects may be latent and only emerge, say, in marriage and parenthood. And one other generalization needs to be avoided: children are not necessarily most vulnerable in the early years and become less so as they grow older. Rather, it is that at every phase certain kinds of conditions may be upsetting; what changes with age is the nature of these conditions, not children's vulnerability in general.

Further reading

Compas, B. E. 1987: Coping with stress during childhood and adolescence. *Psychological Bulletin*, 101, 393–403.

Garmezy, N. and Rutter, M. (eds) 1988: *Stress, Coping and Development in Children*. Baltimore: Johns Hopkins University Press.

Murphy, L. B. and Moriarty, A. E. 1976: *Vulnerability, Coping and Growth*. New Haven: Yale University Press.

Rutter, M. 1985: Resilience in the face of adversity: protective factors and resistance to psychiatric disorder. *British Journal of Psychiatry*, 147, 598–611.

Part 3

A view of childhood

Child development research can provide information of the kind that enables us to answer specific factual questions and to choose between alternative courses. That kind of information, as it relates to various practical issues, was examined in Part 2. In addition, however, research also contributes certain overarching statements about the general nature of children, about their development and about the conditions under which that development ought to take place. Thus, in the course of research there gradually arises a particular view of childhood – a view which will need to be modified from time to time as new findings are uncovered but which is not dependent on any one specific study or set of studies and instead reflects the general thrust of knowledge currently available about children's development generally. There are, that is, certain generalizations which arise over and above the level of specific findings – generalizations whch concern the very nature of children and consequently also of their caretakers' task.

Whether implicitly or explicitly, we probably all have certain preconceptions about children – about what it is that makes a child different from an adult, about the forces that propel a child into maturity and about the role which parents ought to play in the child's life. It would indeed be difficult to avoid having such preconceptions, for we were all children ourselves once and what transpired during those years will inevitably colour our notions of childhood and our theories of child rearing. The influence may be subtle, even unconscious, but it does not follow that the resulting ideas are necessarily rigid and unchangeable. Later personal experience (say of bringing up one's own children) may well modify the assumptions originally held about children, parents and family relationships. And by the same token, exposure to new knowledge, of the kind produced by child-development research, can help in bringing about changes in how we think about children and how we define for ourselves their capabilities and requirements. Clearly, the more one is concerned with children in a professional capacity, the more important it becomes to make one's assumptions explicit. Their influence on decision-making is likely to be profound and ought therefore to be accessible and communicable. It also helps if different practitioners hold identical, or at least similar, sets of assumptions, so that a common framework exists within which action with respect to individual cases can be decided upon.

Some general themes

The propositions that arise from research are generally explicit and communicable and can therefore be examined, discussed and shared. Those presented below are conclusions that have emerged from recent work; they are overall themes indicated by a wide range of studies including (but not confined to) those to which we have already referred. They do not by any means constitute a finite list but are the principal ones relevant to working with young children and their families.

(1)   *Children's experience of interpersonal relationships*
      is crucial to their psychological adjustment
The centrality of interpersonal relationships is a recurrent theme in any overview of children's development. In attempting to explain the course of that development, all sorts of possible influences have been examined: social class, family structure, birth order, ethnicity, stresses such as separation from home, schooling, television, physical-care practices (for example, breast or bottle feeding, early or late toilet training) and so forth. Again and again, however, one is brought back to what children actually experience in the course of their interactions with other people as the essential ingredient to which one must attend.

Take social class. A great body of research shows class to be a pervasive factor that is related in diverse ways to the nature of children's development (see Hess, 1970). Social class is, however, an abstraction: children's behaviour is not formed by class as such but by the attitudes, expectations and experiences that are associated with class differences. A mother bringing up her children in conditions of poverty, unemployment and ill-health will provide a very different kind of personal environment from a mother who does not have to cope with the strain of such an existence. It is the mother's behaviour and the type of relationship between her and the child that transmit whatever effects follow from differences in the socio-economic status of individuals.

Alternatively, take family structure. As we have seen, both when discussing single-parent families and the differences between traditional and non-traditional families, the type of family to which children belong bears little relation to their adjustment. Psychological deviance is far from inevitable just because a child is part of a set-up other than the conventional two-parent family: children in single-parent families, for example, function more adequately than children in intact but conflict-ridden homes; children in lesbian households do not appear to be adversely affected; father absence *per se* does not inevitably produce distortions in the development of sex-role identity; and parental role reversal, where the father acts as the child's main caretaker, has not been shown to produce undesirable consequences. In every case, it is the quality of relationships prevailing in the home that is the principal factor to take into account, and good interpersonal relationships (or, for that matter, bad interpersonal relationships) are not the monopoly of any one kind of family set-up. On the contrary, they occur whether the mother and father are the child's biological parents or not, whether the mother goes out to work or not, whether it is the father that does the mothering, whether the parents are married or not, and so forth (see Lamb, 1982, for a résumé of the evidence). Psychologically healthy personalities can develop, it appears, in the context of a great variety of social groupings – as long as the relationships in which they are enmeshed and which form the nitty-gritty of their daily experience are of a satisfactory nature.

The same general principle applies to other possible determinants of personality development: their influence too is predominantly channelled through the child's interactions with other people. Birth order, for example, has attracted a lot of attention (Ernst and Angst, 1983, provide a useful summary), but it is generally agreed now that it asserts its effects primarily through differences in parental treatment of first-born and later-born children (as illustrated by Dunn and Kendrick, 1982). Even television as an agent of children's socialization turns out to depend heavily for its effects upon the parent–child relationship: both amount of viewing and programme preference have been found to be affected by such characteristics as parent–child conflict, parental insensitivity and lack of warmth in the parent–child relationship, in that the poorer the relationship, the more time children spend watching television and the greater are preferences for programmes containing violence (Tangney, 1988). And as far as effects of stresses such as separation from home are concerned, it is now clear that the extent of harm produced depends very much on whether the relationship with the parents can act as a modifying influence: where that relationship was sound both before-hand and subsequently, it will constitute a buffer and prevent the pathology that may emerge after the same experience in children from less satisfactory family backgrounds (Rutter, 1981).

To assert that the quality of interpersonal relationships is impor-tant may be easy; to define that quality presents considerable dif-ficulties. Much effort is being spent on attempts to pin-point the necessary ingredients. What one can confidently maintain is that quality does not imply quantity: good parenting is not defined by the number of hours spent with the child but by the kind of interac-tions that go on when parent and child are together.

(2)   *Child rearing is a joint enterprise involving children as well as parents*

The emphasis on interpersonal relationships is not on what parents (and other caring adults) do *to* children but on what they do *with* children. What transpires between adult and child is not simply dependent on the adult's wishes and intentions; children's indi-viduality must also be taken into account. Throughout our previous discussion of issues the theme of individual variability was brought up repeatedly: in the face of identical circumstances children re-spond differently. To understand a child's behaviour one must look 'inside' the child as well as 'outside': what happens to a child is determined by its own characteristics and not only by external events such as treatment by other people.

The notion that children's psychological development can be en-tirely explained in terms of parental upbringing is unfortunately a common one. Child rearing, that is, is seen as a kind of clay moulding: the child is thought of as coming into the world like a formless blob of clay, and parents and other adults then proceed to mould that blob into any shape that they regard as right and proper.

In due course that shape will set, its characteristics having been wholly determined by the parents. It would follow that any mishap in the child's development must be due to adult action, and it is therefore to the adults that one turns in order to find the responsible factors.

Yet as any parent with more than one child can testify, the notion of children as lacking all individuality and being entirely at the mercy of their caretakers is nonsense. What may have worked with one child does not necessarily work with another, for from the very beginning children have certain characteristics of their own which play a crucial part in shaping their development – characteristics to which the parents respond and which affect their treatment of any particular child. In that sense, bringing up a child is a joint enterprise involving both adult and child: the parent does not act unilaterally on a passive being; each child's individuality needs to be taken into account in determining what is appropriate treatment (for a more detailed discussion see Schaffer, 1984).

An extreme example of the need to consider child as well as parental characteristics comes from the study of child abuse. There are indications that certain kinds of children, by virtue of being more difficult to rear as a result of congenital disorders, early health problems, low birth weight or perinatal problems, are more likely to fall victim to abuse (Sameroff and Chandler, 1975; Starr, 1988). Such a child may well be the only one in a family containing several siblings to be singled out for abusive treatment: the child, that is, unwittingly contributes to its own fate. Any attempt to provide a full explanation of the circumstances surrounding the case cannot therefore be confined to examining the parents but must also include the child's individuality. At a more general level Chess et al. (1967), the authors of the New York Longitudinal Study to which we have previously referred, have stressed how mistaken the prevalent assumption is that a child's behaviour problem must inevitably be due to unhealthy parental influences – an assumption reflected in the slogan 'To meet Johnny's mother is to understand his problem.' Such a view results in a mistaken preoccupation with the supposed pathogenic influence of the mother – a view which is substituted for a study of the many complex factors that produced the child's disturbed development of which parental influences are in fact only one.

Parent–child interaction is a two-way affair; what the parent does is as much affected by the child as vice versa. It is for this reason that Thomas and Chess (1984) proposed their concept of 'goodness of fit', for they found that the development of children's behavioural problems could not be predicted from a knowledge of the parents alone or, for that matter, of the child alone, but rather from the fit or lack of fit of the characteristics of both parties. To take an example: some infants dislike being cuddled and will resist all attempts by the mother to provide close physical contact by struggling and crying. However, it has been shown (by Schaffer and Emerson, 1964) that these are usually highly active infants and that their protest stems from being held still and confined rather than from contact as such. Most mothers quickly recognize this and adapt their behaviour accordingly by providing other forms of contact. If, on the other hand, a mother fails to do so and continues to offer a manifestly unsuitable kind of stimulation, thereby disregarding the infant's individuality, lack of fit will occur and developmental problems may emerge. The explanation for these problems, however, lies in the interaction of mother and child and not in the characteristics of one or the other partner alone.

Children's individuality thus needs to be respected by those responsible for their care and taken into account by anyone attempting to understand the course of their development. The nature of that individuality, as shown by the diversity of children's reactions to any given experience, is as yet obscure, though ongoing research on inborn temperamental qualities (for example, Rothbart and Goldsmith, 1985) will no doubt enable us eventually to pin-point more precisely what it is that makes one child different from another from the early weeks of life onwards. Even without that knowledge, however, the general point must be accepted: children's development cannot be explained solely in terms of their environment and what other people do to them. Instead, we must consider how such experiences impinge on and are absorbed by particular kinds of individuals. Assessment requires knowledge of the child as well as of parents.

(3) *Sensitivity to children's individuality is an essential ingredient of competent parenting*

Another conclusion to emerge from recent child-development research follows directly from the last. If bringing up children is to be seen as a joint enterprise of both parent and child and if successful development depends on the 'fit' of the two sets of characteristics, then parents need to be attuned to their child's individuality in order to help bring about that fit. As we saw in the example of infants' dislike of cuddling, sensitivity to each child's peculiarities and requirements has to be shown by the parent in order to ensure the smoothness of the relationship.

There have been many attempts to analyse mothering (and fathering) in order to determine just what is involved in this so familiar and yet so elusive function (for a more detailed account, see Schaffer, 1977). Generally, these attempts have as yet met with only limited success, the problem being largely the sheer complexity of this human activity. We may agree that to assess parents merely in terms of 'good' and 'bad' is totally inadequate and that we require more precise and less evaluative terms. So far we are still a long way from identifying all the diverse constituents of parenting, but some aspects have emerged as pertinent, and of these sensitivity has been singled out by a large number of studies (summarized by Schaffer and Collis, 1986) as a fundamental aspect with apparently considerable implications for children's development.

In everyday language there is a tendency to talk in terms of dichotomies and one is therefore tempted to divide people simply into the sensitive and the insensitive. In fact, sensitivity is a continuum, with most parents likely to fall somewhere between the two extremes – showing, for example, moderate degrees of sensitivity or, for that matter, being inconsistently sensitive. In assessing individuals one must thus allow for variation from one situation to another (from toilet training, say, to mutual play) and from one period of time to another (for example, the new and unsure mother with her first baby may become much more competent with growing acquaintance of the child). Putting labels on individuals on the basis of limited information can therefore be grossly misleading.

At the heart of sensitivity lies the ability to see things from the other person's point of view. Thus, the sensitive parent is tuned in to the child's signals and communications and will respond to them promptly and appropriately. In contrast, parents at the other end of the continuum will not appreciate the child in its own right but interpret all communications in the light of their own wishes. One can well appreciate that in the latter case there could be pathological consequences for the child, and there is indeed evidence to this effect. Thus, there are suggestions that insensitive mothering produces emotional insecurity in children, shown particularly in the relationship with the mother, and likewise, there is evidence linking insensitive treatment to delayed development in functions such as learning to talk.

If parental sensitivity is so important it becomes essential to find out why people differ in this respect and in particular why some parents appear to be lacking in this quality. There are some possible influences that can be discounted, and of these the parent's sex is one: as we have already seen, there is no indication that men are inevitably less responsive to children by virtue of their inborn make-up than women. On the other hand, the parent's own upbringing and experience in childhood may well be a determinant: deprived children, it has been suggested, become depriving parents. This may be an over-simplification: as Quinton and Rutter (1988) have shown, such one-to-one correspondence is not inevitable; given the right conditions people can break out of this vicious circle. Nevertheless, prolonged experience of disturbed parenting does have to be considered as a predisposing factor, in that such individuals are more likely to have difficulty in tuning in to their own children. It would be a mistake, however, to look for explanations solely within the parent. Parental effectiveness also depends on the child – the complementary point to our previous assertion that a child's development depends as much on the child as on the parent. As has been shown repeatedly (see Schaffer and Collis, 1986), some children are more difficult to bring up than others: neurologically damaged children, premature infants in the early months, children with mental or physical handicap and any others whose behaviour may be so disorganized that it is difficult to 'read' them. In such cases an extra burden is placed on the parent: the usual norms and expectations one has of a child no longer apply, the child's signals and communications may be ambiguous and therefore the chances of inappropriate treatment will be much increased (Goldberg and Marcovitch, 1986, give examples). Thus, parental sensitivity is not just some immutable characteristic of an individual's personality make-up; it is, rather, a feature describing a *relationship* of a particular parent and a particular child.

(4)   *Children require consistency of care*
We all need a reasonably predictable environment, but young children especially so, for in the early years the ability to cope with drastic change is limited.

We have touched on this theme repeatedly, so let us draw the different threads together. In discussing the effects of separation from home, for instance, it became apparent that the extent of adverse reactions is largely dependent on the degree to which one can sustain continuity for the child. The more existing relationships can be preserved (through parental visiting or by siblings remaining together), the more familiar routines can be maintained; and the more the new environment resembles the old, the less likely it is that the child will be severely affected. The traumatic nature of hospitalization, for example, as described by so many studies, was in the past largely due to the very drastic change in just about every aspect of child's life. A similar picture emerges from the research on the effects of parental divorce, in that this experience too can bring about a whole network of changes: loss of contact with a parent, move to a new neighbourhood, a change of school, the need to make new friends, a different life-style because of reduced financial circumstances, and so on. On their own, some of these changes matter little; coming together they may add up to more than a child can easily cope with. To take one more example: consistency in day-care arrangements has been found to be essential for children's adjustment to out-of home care. As long as the child remains with the same adults in the day-care setting, as long as there is reasonable stability in the peer group to which the child belongs and as long as routines and environments are consistent, the child will benefit rather than be harmed by this experience.

There is, of course, an optimal balance between sameness and change – a balance that probably varies according to age and children's increasing capacity to adjust to new experiences. Both extremes, total sameness and constant change, are likely to be harmful: the former because it prevents children from acquiring skills for dealing with a variety of different circumstances and people; the latter because it exceeds the child's capacity to take in new information and will therefore produce confusion and bewilderment – and as we saw in the study by Wolkind and Kruk (1985) (p. 123), an unsettled childhood resulting from family disruption and admission to care may well be a precursor to an unsettled life-style in adulthood.

Consistency of care depends largely on the child's caretakers. Its lack can be due to a multiplicity of such individuals: in her research on institutionalized children, Tizard (1977) found that by the age of 4½ years the paricular group investigated by her had been looked after at one time or another by an average of 50 different individuals (see p. 39 above). This is the hazard that faces children admitted to public care: not only do they experience changes in physical environment as they move from one institution or foster home to another but, more importantly, they may also be exposed to a large and ever-changing number of so-called parent substitutes, each with ways of relating to the child that may be quite distinct from those of other caretakers. This indeed makes for an unsettled childhood! Yet the child need never leave home to experience inconsistency: differences between the two parents in child-rearing practices and values have been found by Block et al. (1981) to be a potent force in bringing about maladjustment in children, and for that matter one and the same parent may be highly inconsistent in his or her demands on the child, leaving it confused as to what is acceptable and what is not. Consistency of behaviour, we can conclude, appears to be another parental characteristic that is vital to children's sound development.

As a general aim, when making arrangements for children, consistency of experience is clearly of great importance. Thus, Goldstein et al. (1973) were right in stressing that continuity of a child's relationships ought to be considered a primary criterion for placement decisions in divorce cases – though by the same token they were surely wrong in also proposing that the custodial parent should have the right to prevent the child from having a continuing relationship with the non-custodial parent. There are unfortunately circumstances where it is not possible or advisable to maintain continuity, such as in cases of parental death or in some instances of child abuse where a break with the past is necessary. It is worth bearing in mind, however, that children do have considerable recuperative powers and that they are capable of forming new relationships. A break may leave a child vulnerable; it need not by itself produce lasting pathology. *Continuing* disruption, on the other hand, of the kind investigated by Wolkind and Kruk and by Tizard, represents a far more serious hazard. It is when a large part of childhood is thus unsettled that the outlook becomes much more serious.

(5)   *One of the most destructive influences on children is family discord*

In some respects the experience of conflict within the family represents the opposite side of the coin to the need for good-quality interpersonal relationships. More often than not the conflict is between husband and wife, with the child as a bystander and only indirectly involved. Nevertheless, what the child witnesses is the disintegration of a relationship between two people to both of whom a strong emotional attachment has usually been formed. It is this dual loyalty which makes parental strife such a painful experience, as amply illustrated by children's own accounts (Mitchell, 1985).

There is plenty of evidence (reviewed by Emery, 1982) that interparental conflict is one of the most destructive experiences as far as children's mental health is concerned. As shown so strikingly in the study by Block et al. (1986, 1988), summarized in our discussion of the effects of parental divorce (p. 162), it is not so much the event of the parents' separation as such that brings about adverse consequences for children as the tension and hostility that precede separtion. If the children from these families are already disturbed years before the divorce, one must conclude that it is less the dissolution of the parents' marriage and more than atmosphere in the home when the parents were still together that is the operative factor in bringing about the children's disorder. This is confirmed by comparisons of children who have lost a parent through death with children who have lost a parent through divorce, of children whose parents conducted their separation in a reasonably amicable fashion with those where divorce was part of a long drawn-out saga of conflict, and of children from broken but conflict-free homes with children from unbroken but conflict-ridden homes (Emery, 1982). In every case we find that it is the presence of conflict that accounts for maladjustment and unhappiness.

A similar conclusion comes from studies in which parent–child separation comes about through the *child's* removal from home (see Rutter, 1981). It has become apparent that the effects of such separation depend to a considerable extent on the cause for the child leaving home: when separation is due to holidays or illness, the outlook is far better than when it is brought about by family disruption or deviance. Likewise, the nature of the family to which the child is restored will affect outcome: a harmonious home can in due course alleviate whatever traumatic effects the separation brought about at the time, whereas return to a non-harmonious family is more likely to maintain and aggravate the disturbance.

Once we accept that there is an association between family discord and child pathology, various other questions need to be asked. Some of these involve attempts to understand just precisely what it is in such families that brings about ill-effects for children: is it that unhappy parents are less emotionally available to their children, or that their tension spills over into conflict with the child as well, or that they attempt to compensate for an unloving marital relationship by investing too much feeling in the relationship with the child? There are no doubt many other possibilities, and these need to be investigated if one is to help such families. Still other questions concern the precise nature of the effects on the child. Preliminary indications suggest, however, that these usually take the form of conduct disorders, i.e. acting out by being aggressive, disobedient and antisocial, rather than of disorders characterized by internalizing the problem and then developing neurotic states and anxiety.

For all forms of pathologies the favourite explanation put forward at one time was the broken home. If by broken home we mean one in which the two parents no longer live together, then we must conclude that we are looking at the wrong level of family functioning. As previously emphasized, it is the nature of children's interpersonal relationships that are the key influences on psychological development and not family structure as such. In terms of social action, priority ought therefore to be given to straightening out these relationships rather than ensuring that the family conforms to some stereotype as far as its composition is concerned. Such action becomes especially important in so far as individuals with a history of family discord during childhood may be at risk for deviant parental behaviour in adulthood (the evidence has been reveiwed by Rutter, 1979). Thus, those brought up in unhappy or disrupted homes are more likely to have illegitimate children, become pregnant as teenagers, make unhappy and brief marriages and behave neglectfully, insensitively or abusively to their own children. Intergenerational cycles, though far from inevitable, occur often enough to consider prolonged experience of family discord during childhood as a serious risk factor.

(6)　*Enduring adversity rather than specific stress leads to psychopathology*

One reason why family discord is so potent an influence is that it tends to be enduring. All families have their moments of conflict; some families, however, remain more or less continuously in a state of tension and discord, creating an atmosphere which becomes a constant part of growing up for the children involved. It is the sheer continuity, the fact that these influences form part of the child's experience all day and every day, that makes them in the long run so potent a force in shaping personality development.

It has become clear that it is not so much isolated events, however traumatic they may be at the time, that are responsible for serious behaviour problems in children, but, rather, enduring adversity. This goes against popular belief, which tends to fasten on to specific experiences of a stressful nature as causes – if for no other reason than that such experiences are generally well remembered just because they are so different from the rest of the individual's life. Yet we have seen, for instance, that a child's separation from home, while producing great distress at the time, is unlikely by itself to produce lasting psychopathology if it is confined in time and if it takes place against a background of an otherwise settled family life. The same applies to other drastic and sudden changes. Take a parent leaving home. As the divorce literature shows, children for the most part do settle down eventually following such an event, provided it does not lead to any enduring crisis in the family's affairs. Similarly with parental death: there is no convincing evidence that on its own such an experience during childhood is necessarily associated with behavioural deviance in later years (Rutter, 1981). This even holds for so traumatic an event as the suicide of a parent: according to findings by Shepherd and Barraclough (1976), children seen several years later were not inevitably disturbed, and those that were had had to cope with continuing family instability. Once again we see that it is the enduring nature of stress that constitutes the cruicial factor in producing long-term consequences – a conclusion reinforced by one other set of studies, namely those concerned with the effects on children of experiencing natural disasters (earthquakes, floods, cyclones, bushfires, and so on). These reports (for example, Burke et al., 1982; McFarlane et al., 1987) show, for one thing, that only some children are found to be psychologically affected in subsequent months or years and, for another, that any long-term effects tend to occur when families have to cope with lasting consequences of the disaster such as loss of livelihood or of home.

Isolated crises, it appears, need not lead to later disorder. Specific stresses are only of long-term significance if they are the first link in a chain of unfortunate events. Thus, a child's removal from home may lead to a series of placements in unfavourable institutions and foster homes, each one adding to the child's insecurity and lack of identity and all helping eventually to bring about a disturbed personality. If one then looks back, it is difficult indeed to single out one specific link in the chain as responsible for the final outcome. It is the totality of experience as it impinges on the child throughout the formative years rather than some specific event occurring at one particular point of time that accounts for the end result.

Not that this is any reason to take isolated stresses lightly! For one thing, they produce suffering at the time, and minimizing that is alone plenty of justification for action; and for another, intervention at this point may prevent the formation of a chain of undesirable events that would otherwise follow on in an apparently relentless sequence. Nevertheless, we do need to bear in mind that when attempting to understand the development of psychopathology, one must attend to the full course of the individual's life and not ascribe everything to some isolated trauma, however vivid its memory.

(7)   *The effects of adverse experience in the early years are not irreversible*

Another popular belief is that anything which happens to children in their first few years is likely to leave permanent effects. The notion that early experience is more important than later experience as far as personality development is concerned is based on the idea of the very young child as a highly impressionable being, one who will bear the marks of its encounters permanently, whether for good or for ill. The younger the child, the greater the degree of susceptibility, and if experience at that time happens to be adverse, then little can subsequently be done to help the child.

This belief is wrong. There is now plenty of evidence to show that the effects of early experience are reversible, given the right conditions. As we saw previously, children are not permanently incapacitated in their ability to form attachments to others just because they were brought up without parents in their early years. Equally, severance of already established bonds with parents through separation does not necessarily produce lasting consequences for young children – indeed, episodes of any kind of deprivation, neglect and abuse need not, in and by themselves, constitute a permanent handicap just because they occurred early in a child's life.

Some striking examples have been published to illustrate this point. One is a report by Dennis (1973) on the effects of early deprivation of a most gross nature. Children admitted soon after birth to a highly unstimulating institution, where they were provided with a bare minimum of care, developed in the course of their early years a degreee of mental retardation so marked that they were functioning at the level of children only half their age. However, those among the children who were subsequently transferred to another, far more stimulating institution or who were adopted into ordinary homes were able to recover from their early experience and make such good progress that eventually they were able to function well within the normal range. A similar finding comes from a study by Koluchova (1976) on a pair of twins who had been shut away by their stepmother for a large part of their first 6 years in a small closet where they grew up in almost total isolation. When discovered, the children were grossly incapacitated in a wide range of intellectual and social functions and emotionally highly disturbed, yet when subsequently placed in a foster home and provided with a great deal of love and attention, their development began to accelerate markedly until eventually the children appeared to have made a full recovery.

Such reports illustrate well the danger of over-estimating the power of the past. However horrific early experience may have been, people are not inevitably trapped thereby. The eventual outcome depends not just on what happened early on but also on subsequent events, this being one major reason for the great diversity of consequences seen in individuals who have gone through apparently identical experiences. To regard the early years as a critical period, i.e. as a time when children are so vulnerable that they will be permanently affected by whatever happens to them, is dangerous for two reasons: first, because it may lead to the belief that children who have encountered early adversity are beyond help, and second, because one may think that children in later years are not vulnerable. Neither proposition is true: subsequent experience can counter the effects of early adversity, and children at all ages are vulnerable in one way or another.

There is no doubt that the ability of children to recover from adversity has been underestimated in the past. However, as a result of the research mentioned above, it is now apparent that all is not lost by any means if the early years are deficient in some way and that children do have considerable rallying powers. There is certainly no particular cut-off point (after the first 2 years, or 5 years, or whatever) when intervention is too late. It does appear that with increasing age, it gradually becomes more difficult to reverse ill-effects and that the capacity for change is not infinite. However, to provide age limits beyond which plasticity can no longer be taken for granted is impossible at the present state of knowledge and will in any case vary according to a great many different conditions. In the mean time, therefore, it is perhaps best to go on the assumption that it is never too late.

How people escape early adversity is not as yet well understood. The reports on deprived children show that this can be accomplished through a major change of environment, as happens when a child leaves an unsatisfactory institution and is adopted or transferred to some other more caring environment. Much therefore depends on the transition points which individuals reach – not only in childhood but as adults too. As the research by Quinton and Rutter (1988) shows, women who had spent parts of their childhood in care were apparently saved from the worst after-effects by making a successful marriage. There are various such turning-points – leaving home, getting a job, marriage, pregnancy, and so on; and how these are negotiated and how successful the path is which the individual chooses may make an enormous difference to the final outcome (for a more extended discussion see Rutter, 1989). Some choices, say a dead-end job or an unsatisfactory marriage, will merely reinforce early adversity; others, such as a fulfilling occupation or a supportive spouse, will break the chain and allow the individual to escape.

(8) *Single-cause explanations are rarely appropriate for
     psychological events; multiple causation is the rule*
We have repeatedly seen that the effects of particular experiences on children depend not just on the experience itself but also on the context in which it occurs. Does loss of father produce serious consequences? Well, it all depends – on, for instance, the reason for such loss (for example, death or divorce), the mother's reaction, the financial and other practical consequences for the family, the support of relatives and friends, and so on. What impact does separation from home have on children? Again, it depends on a large number of other considerations: on the reason for the separation, on preceding family relationships, on the familiarity or otherwise of substitute caretakers, on continuing contact with siblings, on the disruption of routines and on the home atmosphere to which the child returns. Similarly with the effects of the mother going out to work: these depend on such factors as the reasons for working, the satisfaction the mother obtains from doing so, the father's support and the kind of arrangements made for the child's care during the mother's absence. And similarly also with other explanations: paren-

tal incompetence and child abuse cannot simply be ascribed to 'bonding failure' resulting from mother having insufficient contact with her new-born baby; the effects of early adversity on children do not merely depend on how early and how adverse the experience was; and how a child survives the parents' divorce is affected by much more than the divorce itself.

Most people, understandably, want simple and clear-cut answers to questions about psychosocial conditions. Should mothers go out to work or not? Is day care beneficial or harmful? Is being brought up in a single-parent family a handicap? It may be frustrating and annoying when social scientists do not come up with straightforward yes–no, good–bad, always–never replies to such questions, yet it is amply apparent from the research available to us that so often, simple answers are in fact simplistic answers which overlook the complexities of real life. Nearly always a combination of factors has to be considered; simple cause-and-effect models are rarely of use in explaining human behaviour; events occur in contexts and the conditions defining these contexts can exercise a powerful modulating effect on the eventual outcome. There is, for example, no one-to-one relationship between parental alcoholism and the development of psychopathology in children (see the review by West and Prinz, 1987). It is true that in families with an alcoholic parent there is a heightened incidence of disturbed children, but neither all nor even a major portion of children are doomed to psychological disorder. Additional factors operate that make some individuals vulnerable while protecting others. Thus, care needs to be taken about making sweeping generalizations and advancing global solutions. 'It all depends' may be an annoying phrase and it does not make good headlines, but it accurately reflects reality.

Not that social scientists themselves have always appreciated this point. Indeed, the history of research with respect to most of the examples we have listed has proceeded from a disregard of context and a belief in single-cause models to the realization that context does matter, that its analysis is vital and that more complex models need to be adopted if one is to understand human behaviour. Various schemes have been advanced for this purpose (see Bronfenbrenner, 1979; Minushin, 1985); what they have in common is an emphasis on the need to see the child not in isolation but as an integral part of a wider system composed of the interpersonal relationships in which the child is embedded, the family group within which relationships are first experienced, the social network (containing friends, relations and neighbours) of which the family is a part and the culture to which all such individuals and groups belong. A complete explanation of, say, a separation experience would require one to consider all these levels. Thus, at the relationship level, a mother's lack of competence with her child may have been implicated in bringing about the separation; that lack may in turn have been affected by the atmosphere and cohesiveness of the family as a whole; this could have been influenced by the support received from others outside the family such as relatives; and the extent to which the extended family, acts as a supportive force in turn depends on cultural values currently operating. In practice, it may be neither possible nor feasible to take absolutely everything into account, but it is as well to appreciate that there is an arbitrary element involved in excluding certain levels.

Thus, there is no such thing as a 'pure' experience, operating in isolation and producing uniform effects on all children. Not only do the children themselves differ in age, sex, temperament, and so forth, but each experience takes place against a background of contextual factors that help to account for the outcome. Thus, how a father reacts to his wife taking a job may have considerable implications for the child's reaction: it may well be this rather than the mother's daily absence that accounts for the effects on the child. To concentrate merely on what goes on between mother and child in such a case might well miss a crucial influence: a wider perspective is needed.

(9) *Human nature is flexible and can satisfactorily develop under a wide range of differing conditions*

One further lesson we have now learned is that there are far fewer constraints on healthy, well-adjusted development than was thought at one time. According to previous opinion, events must happen at prticular ages and in particular settings if development is to proceed normally; any child missing out on the 'right' events at the 'right' time, or brought up under family circumstances that do not conform to particular, narrowly defined limits, is likely to be penalized, What is apparent now, however, is that there is far greater latitude in the requirements for healthy psychological development than had previously been realized.

Take the notion that there are critical ages when children must be exposed to particular experiences: if they miss out on these at that time they will be unable to make up subsequently, never mind how much of that experience they later obtain. The example that we looked at was the formation of a child's first attachment – a development that normally takes place sometime in the latter half of the first year of life and that is dependent on a permanent parent-figure being available. However, as the findings from studies of late-adopted children show, a child deprived of parental care at that time and kept emotionally 'on ice' well beyond the ciritical period need not be written off as permanently damaged in its capacity to form emotionally meaningful interpersonal relationships. It appears that even after a delay of several years, this capacity has not atrophied but, given the right conditions, can be mobilized and for the first time be overtly expressed. It is true that there may be a price to pay for the child's previous history of deprivation in terms of other aspects of behaviour; it is also true that the limits cannot be stretched indefinitely and that at some stage (which cannot be defined at the present state of knowledge) irreversible damage is brought about. Nevertheless, the notion that there is only one right age and that children missing out on that cannot make up subsequently is clearly mistaken.

The same applies to many other aspects of children's development: the beginnings of language, of various motor skills and of educational competencies may normally take place within a specified age range but can be delayed for considerable periods without long-term harm. For that matter, the notion that everything has to happen at a particular time is also inappropriate with respect to parental functions. As we saw in the case of maternal bonding, there is no support for the idea that a mother's competence is crucially dependent on events confined to a few days, even though they may be the very first few days of her life with a new baby. Again, there is plenty of evidence that nature has arranged matters far more flexibly, that the parent–child relationship is not irretrievably affected by particular events (or non-events) at specific points of time and that far more latitude exists in human nature.

That latitude is found in other respects too. Most children are brought up by their biological parents, but those who are not are by no means necessarily handicapped thereby: the blood bond is not an essential condition for successful rearing. Likewise, children who are brought up by a father rather than a mother do not miss out on some essential ingredient of early experience. Despite cultural pressures to confine child care to females, there is no reason to believe that males cannot perform this task just as competently. The nature of the family setting in general can take all sorts of different forms without threat to children's mental health: the idea that only a conventional family (a permanent unit composed of father, mother and children, with strict role segregation between the parents) can successfully bring up children cannot be sustained in the light of the evidence. Various non-traditional arrangements have been found to be perfectly capable of providing all the love and security children require, and if children from such settings are sometimes more vulnerable to emotional difficulties, then extraneous factors are usually responsible, such as the financial difficulties that single-parent families often encounter or the social disapproval that role reversal of husband and wife may give rise to. The precise nature of the particular family set-up is of far less account.

Notions such as critical age periods and rigid parental role segregation arose originally from studies of animals, where the limits for the rearing of the young tend to be much more tightly stipulated. It is however, a hallmark of the human species that it has to a considerable extent been able to free itself from such biological 'musts'. There are, of course, certain essentials that do need to be met if one is to ensure children's healthy psychological development, but these exist primarily at the level of interpersonal relationships, to do with such qualities as harmony, consistency, affection, firmness, warmth and sensitivity. An environment providing these requirements can take many forms, and that includes some that may not meet current social conventions. Thus, a considerable degree of flexibility, with respect to both the timing and the conditions under which development occurs, appears to be a basic characteristic of human childhood.

A concluding note of optimism

The general thrust of many of the trends we have listed is towards a much more positive, hopeful picture of childhood. This is in marked contrast to views that prevailed in earlier decades. At that time the urgency of attention to the victims of deprivation and trauma was still uppermost; there was preoccupation with what can go wrong with development, with stress and with the pathological consequences that were assumed inevitably to follow stress; there was widespread belief in the fixed nature of human development, with its critical periods when certain things must happen and its total dependence on events in the earliest years; and there was insistence that acceptable child rearing could only occur under certain narrowly defined limits of family environment and by means of only the 'right' methods of child care.

We now know that there are survivors as well as victims, that children who miss out on particular experiences at the usual time may well make up subsequently, that healthy development can occur in a great range of different family environments and that there are many 'right' ways of bringing up a child. We also know that the effects of stressful experiences can be minimized by suitable action, that isolated traumatic events need not leave harmful consequences and that an individual's personality does not for ever more have to be at the mercy of past experience. We have even learned that stress, under certain circumstances, can produce beneficial results.

As a consequence, a less distorted picture of child development has emerged. The focus on deprivation, neglect and abuse was, of course, correct in drawing attention to the fact that children can be seriously harmed by certain life conditions. It is only recently, however, that we have begun to ask why some children, undergoing the same adverse experiences, are not harmed thereby, or at any rate are subsequently able to recover. The resilience of children has thus been highlighted; and at the same time there has been a growing realization that positive action can be taken to help children cope with the consequences of even quite considerable adversity and that no child need be regarded as condemned by the circumstances of its life. There are limits to any child's adaptability and these need to be respected; however, the fact of adaptability remains.

References

Block, J., Block, J. H. and Gjerde, P. F. 1988: Parental functioning and the home environment in families of divorce: prospective concurrent analyses. *Journal of the American Academy of Child and Adolescent Psychiatry*, 27, 207–13.

Block, J. H., Block, J. and Morrison, A. 1981: Parental agreement–disagreement on child rearing orientation and gender-related personality correlates in children. *Child Development*, 52, 965–74.

Bowlby, J. 1951: *Maternal Care and Mental Health*. Geneva: World Health Organization.

Bronfenbrenner, U. 1979: *The Ecology of Human Development*. Cambridge, Mass.: Harvard University Press.

Burke, J. D., Borus, J. F., Burns, B. J., Millsten, K. H. and Beasley, M. C. 1982: Changes in children's behaviour after a natural disaster. *American Journal of Psychiatry*, 139, 1010–14.

Chess, S., Thomas, A. and Birch, H. G. 1967: Behaviour problems revisited: findings of an anterospective study. *Journal of the American Academy of Child Psychiatry*, 6, 321–31.

de Mause, L. (ed.) 1974: *The History of Childhood*. New York: Psychohistory Press.

Dennis, W. 1973: *Children of the Creche*. New York: Appleton-Century-Crofts.

Dunn, J. and Kendrick, C. 1982: *Siblings: love, envy and understanding*. Cambridge, Mass.: Harvard University Press.

Emery, R. E. 1982: Interpersonal conflict and the children of discord and divorce. *Psychological Bulletin*, 92, 310–30.

Ernst, C. and Angst, J. 1983: *Birth Order: its effects on personality*. New York: Springer.

Fraiberg, S. 1977: *Every Child's Birthright: in defence of mothering*. New York: Basic Books.

Freeman, M. 1988: Time to stop hitting our children. *Childright*, 51, 5–8.

Glenn, N. D. and Kramer, K. B. 1985: The psychological well-being of adult children of divorce. *Journal of Marriage and the Family*, 47, 905–12.

Goldberg, S. and Marcovitch, S. 1986: Nurturing under stress: the care of preterm infants and developmentally delayed preschoolers. In A. Fogel and F. G. Melson (eds), *Origins of Nurturance*. Hillsdale, New Jersey: Erlbaum.

Goldstein, J., Freud, A. and Solnit, A. J. 1973: *Beyond the Best Interests of the Child*. New York: Free Press.

Grosof, M. S. and Sardy, H. 1985: *A Research Primer for the Social and Behavioral Sciences*. Orlando: Academic Press.

Hardyment, C. 1983: *Dream Babies: child care from Locke to Spock*. London: Jonathan Cape.

Harvey, P. G. 1984: Lead and children's health: recent research and future questions. *Journal of Child Psychology and Psychiatry*, 25, 517–22.

Hess, R. D. 1970: Social class and ethnic influences on socialization. In P. H. Mussen (ed.), *Carmichael's Manual of Child Psychology*, Vol. II, 3rd ed. New York: Wiley.

Hetherington, E. M. 1987: Family relations six years after divorce. In K. Pasley and M. Ihinger-Tollman (eds), *Remarriage and Stepparenting Today: current research and theory*. New York: Guilford.

Hetherington, E. M. 1988: Parents, children and siblings: six years after divorce. In R. A. Hinde and J. Stevenson-Hinde (eds), *Relationships within families: mutual influences*. Oxford: Clarendon Press.

Hodges, J. and Tizard, B. 1989: IQ and behavioural adjustment of ex-institutional adollscents. *Journal of Child Psychology and Psychiatry*, 30, 53–76.

Kerlinger, F. N. 1986: *Foundations of Behavioral Research*, 3rd edn. New York: Holt, Rinehart and Winston.

Kessen, W. 1965: *The Child*. New York: Wiley.

Koluchova, J. 1976: Severe deprivation in twins: a case study. In A. M. Clarke, and A. D. B. Clarke (eds), *Early Experience: myth and evidence*: London: Open Books.

Lamb, M. E. (ed.) 1982: *Non-Traditional Families: parenting and child development*. Hillsdale, New Jersey: Erlbaum.

McCartney, K. 1984: Effect of quality of daycare environment on children's language development. *Developmental Psychology*, 20 244–60.

McFarlane, A. C., Policansky, S. K. and Irwin, C. 1987: A longitudinal study of the psychological morbidity in children due to a natural disaster. *Psychological Medicine*, 17, 727–38.

Minushin, P. 1985: Families and individual development: provocations from the field of family therapy. *Child Development*, 56, 289–302.

Mitchell, A. 1985: *Children in the Middle*. London: Tavistock.

Phillips, D. McCartney, K. and Scarr, S. 1987: Child care quality and children's social development. *Developmental Psychology*, 23, 537–43.

Quinton, D. and Rutter, M. 1988: *Parental Breakdown: the making and breaking of intergenerational links*. Aldershot: Gower.

Rothbart, M. K. and Goldsmith, H. H. 1985: Three approaches to the study of infant temperament. *Developmental Review*, 5, 237–60.

Rutter, M. L. 1979: Maternal deprivation, 1972–1978: new findings, new concepts, new approaches. *Child Development*, 50, 283–305.

Rutter, M. L. 1981: *Maternal Deprivation Reassessed*, 2nd edn. Harmondsworth: Penguin.

Rutter, M. L. 1989: Pathways from childhood to adult life. *Journal of Child Psychology and Psychiatry*, 30, 23–52.

Rutter, M. L. and Madge, N. 1976: *Cycles of Disadvantage: a review of research*. London: Heinemann.

Sameroff, A. J. and Chandler, M. J. 1975: Reproductive risk and the continuum of caretaking casualty. In F. D. Horowitz, M. Hetherington, S. Scarr-Salapatek, and G. Siegel (eds), *Review of Child Development Research*, Vol. 4. Chicago: University of Chicago Press.

Schaffer, H. R. 1977: *Mothering*. London: Fontana; Cambridge, Mass.: Harvard University Press.

Schaffer, H. R. 1984: *The Child's Entry into a Social World*. London: Academic Press.

Schaffer, H. R. and Collis, G. M. 1986: Parental responsiveness and child behaviour. In W. Sluckin and M. Herbert (eds), *Parental Behaviour in Animals and Humans*. Oxford: Blackwell.

Schaffer, H. R. and Emerson, P. E. 1964: Patterns of response to physical contact in early human development. *Journal of Child Psychology and Psychiatry*, 5, 1–13.

Shepherd, D. M. and Barraclough, B. M. 1976: The aftermath of parental suicide for children. *British Journal of Psychiatry*, 129, 267–76.

Starr, R. H. Jr. 1988: Pre- and perinatal risk and physical abuse. *Journal of Reproductive and Infant Psychology*, 6, 125–38.

Tangney, J. P. 1988: Aspects of the family and children's television viewing content preferences. *Child Development*, 59, 1070–79.

Thomas, A. and Chess, S. 1984: Genesis and evolution of behavioural disorders: from infancy to early adult life. *American Journal of Psychiatry*, 141, 1–9.

Tizard, B. 1977: *Adoption: a second chance*. London: Open Books.

Wald, M. 1976: Legal policies affecting children: a lawyer's request for aid. *Child Development*, 47, 1–5.

Weisner, T. S. and Gallimore, R. 1977: My brother's keeper: child and sibling caretaking. *Current Anthropology*, 18, 169–90.

West, M. O. and Prinz, R. J. 1987: Parental alcoholism and childhood psychopathology. *Psychological Bulletin*, 102, 204–18.

Name index

Subject index